European Pottery & Porcelain

FOLK ART IN AMERICA
Painting and Sculpture
Edited by Jack T. Ericson

EARLY AMERICAN SILVER AND ITS MAKERS
Edited by Jane Bentley

European Pottery & Porcelain

EDITED BY PAUL J. ATTERBURY

A Main Street Press Book
Published by Mayflower Books, Inc., USA
New York City

Articles included in this volume are printed as they appeared in the following issues of *The Magazine Antiques:*

Part I: European Folk Pottery, October, 1933; German Stoneware, November, 1932; Italian Maiolica, June, 1947; Five Centuries of Faenza Majolica, June, 1963; Introduction to Dutch Blue and White, September, 1962; Old French Faïence, April, 1947; Strasbourg Faïence, December, 1958; The Lively Forms of Brussels Faïence, March, 1957; Maastricht Pottery, Part I, March, 1931; Maastricht Pottery, Part II, April, 1931.

Part II: Meissen Porcelain, April, 1946; Adding to a Meissen Collection, April, 1966; German Porcelain Factories Other than Meissen and Vienna, May, 1954; A Note on Frankenthal, November, 1952; Some Oriental Aspects of European Ceramic Decoration, Part II, July, 1969.

Part III. Soft-paste Biscuit of Vincennes-Sèvres, January, 1956; The Useful Wares of Vincennes and Sèvres, January, 1959; Some Important Sèvres Porcelain and Its Painters, September, 1960; French Soft-paste Snuff-boxes at Limoges, May, 1961; Chantilly Porcelain in the Last Half of the Eighteenth Century, January, 1961; Jacob Petit, Maker of Porcelain, February, 1937.

Part IV. Early Vienna Porcelain, May, 1955; Christoph and Johann von Jünger, Enamel Manufacturers in Vienna, October, 1959; The Porcelain of Naples, February, 1969; Capodimonte and Buen Retiro Porcelain, May, 1946; The Porcelain of Tournai, October, 1953; Porcelaine de Nyon, May, 1931; The Marieberg Porcelain Factory, February, 1948; Imperial Russian Porcelain, January, 1933; Vista Alegre, April, 1965.

Library of Congress Catalog Card Number 79-87673
ISBN 8317-3056-O

Produced by The Main Street Press
42 Main Street
Clinton, New Jersey 08809

Published by Mayflower Books, USA
575 Lexington Avenue
New York City 10022

Contents

Introduction

The origins of decorative pottery in Europe are surprisingly universal. Many common themes and styles can be found which appeared simultaneously in countries widely separated both physically and socially. At first this may seem curious, but a number of factors help to explain it.

During the period of Roman domination, the European continent was relatively stable both politically and economically. The building of the Roman system of communications that linked Europe from end to end enabled the styles and forms of Roman pottery to be spread very rapidly. As a result English, French, German, and Spanish potters all produced wares that were essentially Roman. The forms and styles of these wares became so well established that they were able to survive the centuries of invasion and counter invasion that followed the collapse of the Roman Empire. Only in areas profoundly affected by other civilizations, as for example in Spain during the period of Moorish domination, were there any radical changes.

During the Middle Ages the maps of Europe were constantly redrawn, but despite this the styles and techniques of many industries remained constant. The guilds, and the rigid appenticeship system that was in operation throughout Europe, ensured that change was only gradual; at the same time, the universality of style and technique was also maintained by the continuous and free-flowing traffic of skilled workmen from one center of production to another, a traffic that paid little attention to national boundaries. This freedom of movement was, of course, made easier by the international power of the Church which was, after all, the main patron for many areas of industrial and artistic production.

The essentially domestic nature of pottery helped to make it one of the most unadventurous, and thus unchanging, of the medieval industries. The functional requirements of pottery are fairly basic, and thus have always been relatively easy to satisfy. Decoration on pottery has always been on a par with icing on a cake; although attractive and sensually satisfying, it serves no real purpose. As a result the decoration of pottery has always been, from its earliest days, a largely derivative activity, dependent entirely upon the styles and forms created in more significant areas of artistic activity. The fundamental lack of originality that characterizes ceramic design and decoration is, however, a feature of considerable value for the historian in that it presents a mirror of the current styles and tastes of any period.

The unity of European styles in pottery was also affected by a common search for technical improvement; in fact, the history of pottery making in Europe from the Middle Ages to the 19th century can be described as a series of technical advances that determined the nature of style and decoration. Through this period, potters in all countries were united by their common search for better clays, glazes, and firing techniques which would enable them to make more permanent, durable, and better finished wares. The essential requirements of a pot, namely that it should be relatively impervious to heat, water, and accidental damage, and that its shape should conform to its function, were made more possible century by century as technology advanced. That they should be cheap and simple to manufacture was also important.

During the medieval period basic domestic earthenwares were produced in vast quantities by potters throughout Europe. These wares, made entirely to satisfy local requirements, were simply decorated with scratched or carved patterns, with limited, lead-based glazes, or with patterns in slip, or liquid clay, raised in relief. Occasionally primitive modeling was used to ornament a basic form, as with the many face mugs made throughout Europe. This simple, universal form with its element of caricature was, of course, a continuation of a well-established classical tradition. Similarly the basic slipwares, as the objects with raised clay decoration were called, were produced in identical styles and forms throughout Europe. These simple styles were also relatively dateless, and so survived unchanged in many rural areas until the late 19th century. However, their coarseness of manufacture, and crude decoration made them increasingly unsatisfactory in a market that demanded greater sophistication.

The period of Islamic influence in Spain introduced new techniques and styles to Europe. The development of opaque white tin-based glazes effectively concealed the basic red earthenwares, and so gave the decorators and painters a wholly new freedom. Rich colors and reflective lusters were painted on to the absorbent and glossy white surface in the dynamic patterns and forms associated with Islam. From

Spain the styles and techniques spread to Italy where the formal geometry of Islam was absorbed and adapted by the pictorial conventions of the Renaissance.

By the 17th century the technology of tin-glazing had spread throughout Europe. Potters in France, Holland, Germany, Scandinavia, and Britain had adopted the decorative traditions of the Middle East and Southern Europe to suit their own styles and tastes. Most significant among these was a style of decoration based loosely upon Chinese motifs. The white surface provided by the tin-glaze technique was suitable for painted decoration in cobalt blue, and so, for the first time, European potters were able to imitate the styles of Chinese porcelain of the Ming period, rare and precious objects which had been coming into Europe since the Middle Ages via the Arab trade routes. With the expansion of international trade during the 17th century, this trickle had become a flood, and every potter in Europe was attempting to copy the style and quality of these Chinese wares. Blue-painted tin-glaze earthenwares, of the type associated with Delft in Holland, were a passable imitation of the Chinese wares in visual terms. However, the thickly-glazed, crude, and low-fired earthenwares of Europe were no real match for Chinese porcelain, particularly in terms of durability and quality of both manufacture and design.

From this point, the potters of Europe had only one goal, namely the reproduction in Europe of a ceramic material as fine as Chinese porcelain. This goal was purchased assiduously throughout the late 17th and most of the 18th centuries, and the pursuit was made even keener by the constant and ever-increasing imports of oriental porcelain into Europe by such trading firms as the Dutch East Indies Company. It took some time for European potters to realize that the secret of oriental porcelain was found in the actual materials used in its manufacture, and so they expended considerable time and effort in trying to reproduce it by imitation. They refined and improved the basic earthenwares and turned the crude red earthenware into a fine white creamware. At the same time, the high-fired stoneware that had been made in Germany since the Middle Ages was developed to a point where it could reproduce many of the qualities of porcelain. The ultimate goal of whiteness and transparency, however, remained defiantly out of reach.

Inevitably, the search for the secret of porcelain became an almost mystical quest. Throughout Europe, the court alchemists and chemists of a hundred princes were threatened, cajoled, and promised wealth beyond imagination to encourage them in their search for the magic material. Vast sums of money were invested in the quest, simply because the rewards were likely to be so high. The first king, queen, or prince to reproduce the material correctly would enjoy not only an enhanced reputation throughout Europe, but would also benefit enormously from the wealth that the discovery would release. Many came near to success. The Medici princes, for example, produced some rare examples of porcelain, but could not control it sufficiently to make it consistently.

After many failures, however, success was finally achieved at Meissen. Despite desperate attempts to hold on to the secret, the technique spread rapidly from Meissen to other centers in Germany and Austria, and so by the middle of the 18th century porcelain was being manufactured throughout Europe. Even in countries as remote as Portugal, Sweden, Russia, and Switzerland the material was in relatively large scale production. For many years, however, the output of the European porcelain makers was not sufficient to threaten the continuing oriental dominance of the market. They could compete neither on cost nor on quality, and so it was inevitable that the styles and decorating of oriental porcelain should continue to influence all the European potters. It was not until the end of the 18th century that the porcelain of Europe was able to compete on equal terms with the oriental, and by then, in any case, the export trade with China and Japan had virtually ceased. Even then, the purely European styles influenced by contemporary art movements such as Neo-Classicism could never really undermine the established oriental designs. Nor could the European factories ever really compete on grounds of cost, for many of them were heavily subsidized by royal patronage.

One of the indirect results of this was that the pattern of stylistic conformity established during the Middle Ages was able to continue in later centuries. Tin-glazed earthenware, creamware, and porcelain itself was manufactured with extraordinary consistency throughout Europe, and so the decorative styles associated with each material were generally universal and little affected by national differences.

I European Earthenware and Stoneware

Although the porcelains made in Europe since the early 18th century deserve thorough study and examination, it is important not to overlook other ceramic materials. Until the 18th century, earthenware and stoneware were dominant in Europe and so were highly developed both technically and artistically. The articles included in this chapter have been selected to show the patterns of stylistic and technical development that took place in Europe between the Middle Ages and the 19th century.

The medieval tradition of lively, colorful, and primitive modeling in basic earthenware survived into the 18th century and beyond. This tradition was also particularly universal and was hardly affected by national or regional differences. Thus the "peasant" pottery of Eastern Europe has close affinities with that of Britain or Spain. Common forms, some based on Roman models, and common decorative details give these wares a popular appeal that has made them virtually dateless. It is hardly surprising, therefore, that these wares have appealed so strongly to craft potters in the 20th century. At first sight, many of these traditions seem to have affected equally the stoneware potters of Germany. It is possible to establish quite specific stylistic links, for example, between the decorative details of early Siegburg stonewares and the slipwares of Wrotham in Southern England.

The fine quality of the stoneware material, however, was also used to express the highly complex decorative details that the German potters of Raeren, Cologne and other centers had absorbed from the Renaissance. These wares represent the transition from primitive to sophisticated in European ceramics and thus pave the way for the porcelains that were to follow.

Much of the decoration used by German stoneware potters was drawn from Italy, where the decorative traditions of the Renaissance were fully explored by the maiolica potters. Italian maiolica is an interesting mixture of Western and Eastern decorative detail, for the painters and decorators drew their inspiration equally from the Islamic and the Classical worlds. The story of Italian maiolica really represents the conflict between these two worlds and the eventual dominance of the Western pictorial tradition. Maiolica was produced at many centers of production, including Florence, Gubbio, Castel Durante, and Venice, but the best known is probably Faenza, which of course has continued the tradition up to the present day. This area has given its name to the generic word "faïence," used very freely since the 17th century to describe any kind of tin-glazed earthenware with polychrome decoration. Other articles in this section discuss French faïence, Brussels faïence, and, more specifically, the faïence of Strasbourg. These Western European earthenwares, particularly those from the French centers at Rouen and Nevers, show very strongly the influence of the Mannerist and early Baroque styles of decoration.

Probably the most familiar style of tin-glazed earthenware was that which emerged in Holland. Here, the long-established trade links with the Far East ensured that Chinese and Japanese styles were dominant. The blue-painted styles associated with the center of production at Delft in fact turned the name of the town into a generic title for all tin-glazed manufacture in this style. Thus there are Delftwares from many countries in Europe. At the same time, many Dutch potters drew their shapes from Mannerist metalwork, and so their products represent an interesting mixture of oriental and Western motifs.

Production at Delft has, of course, continued up to the present, and so the decorative traditions associated with Holland are still very much alive. The variety of these is shown by the articles on the Maastricht Pottery, which illustrate both the development of a more refined earthenware material, and also the close links between this pottery and those producing very similar wares in Staffordshire, England. This connection underlines how dangerous it is to see the products of any one country, or even any one pottery, in isolation.

European Folk Pottery

By Laura Lorenson

Illustrations from the Nadelman Museum of Folk and Peasant Arts

Photographs by Mattie Edwards Hewitt

Fig. 1 — ITALIAN POTTERY
Jars: blue floral motives on white tin enamel.
Casket: blue, with touches of green, on white tin enamel. Mask feet

FOLK pottery, in common with the other folk arts, is rooted in native culture. It reveals a people's manners and customs, and sometimes even its origin. The sturdy, substantial pottery shapes, devised to meet particular needs, have the unconscious dignity of appropriateness. Their ornament is usually simple, gay, and well balanced.

Perhaps it is the unsophisticated, primitive character of folk pottery that has delayed its appreciation by conventional collectors. Mr. and Mrs. Elie Nadelman are not to be registered in that category. That is why the Nadelman Museum of Folk and Peasant Arts, in Riverdale, New York, is unique among American private collections. The section devoted to pottery, alone, represents years spent in scouring Europe for representative examples. Now it comprehends a well-balanced selection adequately illustrating the peasant products of most of the European countries.

In studying the folk pottery of the various nations represented, covering mainly the seventeenth, eighteenth, and early nineteenth centuries, we are impressed by the evidences of an international kinship among strongly marked national characteristics, but even more by the variety achieved within the limited technical resources of the peasant potters. It was Rodin who remarked that only that is ugly which lacks character, an indirect way of saying that character is the essence of beauty. He who accepts this dictum cannot fail to perceive in the strength and honesty of modeling and the appropriateness and originality of decoration of folk pottery a beauty that lack of superficial finish fails to obscure. The potter, were he peasant or village craftsman, unconsciously bared his creative soul in his handiwork.

The decorative effec-

tiveness of pottery was recognized even by those who were slow to accept the ware for ordinary use. Open shelves filled with colorful pieces, used only on festal occasions, and cherished by succeeding generations of a tradition-loving people, played an important part in the interior adornment of provincial European homes. The use of ornamental tile was, also, almost universal. Articles of clay, made for special occasions such as baptisms, weddings, and birthdays — aptly termed "bespoke" — and for the use of guilds, have a personal character, independent of time or place. All the skill and resources at the command of the artisan were lavished on this type of ware. The application of dates and inscriptions was apparently more typical of the northern than of the southern European countries.

A far-flung vein of homely humor frequently found outlet in folk pottery. Conscious humor was expressed in puzzle jugs, used extensively at guild festivals, and unconscious humor crept unbidden into quaint inscriptions and representations of people and animals. The following inscription on an English puzzle jug, dated *1732*, is illuminating:

> "Gentlemen now try your skill
> ill hold you Sixpence if you will
> that you dont drink unless you spill."

Generation after generation of village potters, each adding his mite to the lore passed from father to son, have left no clear pathway of progress in technique. Similar processes were employed in widely separated places, sometimes simultaneously, sometimes centuries apart. Coarse clay, varying from buff to brown in color, was the basic material.

Lead glazes colored with metallic oxides gained a firm foothold, at least as far south as France, in the

Fig. 2 — SPANISH POTTERY
Plate: painted with yellow, brown, and green leaves on slip coating.
Jug: sgraffito design in yellow slip on brown body.
Animal figurine: in yellow slip touched up with brown.
Madonna statuette: mottled glaze

late Renaissance, either alone or in connection with relief ornament. Later these glazes were overshadowed, though never entirely eclipsed, by tin-enameled ware and its humbler relative, slip-coated pottery, which were then at the height of their glory in Italy and Spain. The slip-coated ware — variously decorated with liquid clay, known as "slip," tinted with metallic pigments — was perhaps the most universally popular of the folk pottery.

The peasant potters whose rude kilns were scattered over the countryside surrounding the famous potteries of Italy and Spain during the Renaissance, and long thereafter, in spite of similar materials and technique in both countries, endowed their ware with clearly differentiating local traits. *Sgraffito* pottery — that is, pottery whose decoration is accomplished by incising the pattern in the clay or its slip coating — as well as tin-enameled and slip-coated ware painted with metallic pigments were common to both countries. The painter's meagre palette was composed mainly of blue, green, yellow, and manganese brown and purple.

The Spanish potter's predilection for leaves, flowers, and geometrical designs betrays Moorish influence. He, however, combined these motives with landscapes, religious symbols, and animals and birds of a more or less fantastic character. An English traveler in Spain during the latter part of the eighteenth century, according to Chaffers, described Manises, near Valencia, as a

Fig. 3 — SPANISH POTTERY
Jug: pale manganese-purple ground painted in brown and green.
Lion candlesticks: splashed with green, brown, and cream

pretty village composed of four streets, whose inhabitants were mostly potters making a fine, copper-colored faïence, ornamented with gilding. This ware the people of the locality employed for ornamental and domestic purposes. The small potteries near Talavera turned out a sturdy, unlustred ware, often adorned with landscape backgrounds for scenes of vigorous action. The keynote in the pungent color scheme is usually struck by a bright green derived from copper coins. A collector tells of finding in a secluded community, not far from Talavera, where straw was the only fuel, some large Talavera dishes which a housewife had transformed into a kind of fireless cooker. In the morning she would fill her ancient plates with stew, and then bury them in straw to keep hot against the midday luncheon hour.

Italian pottery betrays the mingled influences of classic art, of the native scene surrounding the potteries, and of the odd mixture of piety and fantasy with which the peasants of southern Europe were imbued. A love of rich, vibrant color was a common heritage. The color note, within the scope of a limited palette, is often distinctive. An unusual hue, once obtained, was perpetuated. Unfortunately, the early potters found red, which usually grows brighter and more prevalent in peasant surroundings the farther south we travel in Italy, a difficult color to achieve. Art was instinctive in the Italian peasant potter, and his modeling, no matter

Fig. 4 (centre) — DUTCH POTTERY (*eighteenth century*)
  Buff earthenware, roof finial with dashes of yellow slip covered with a golden-brown lead glaze. Interesting to compare with a much earlier English jug illustrated in Rhead's *Staffordshire Pots and Potters*, p. 71

Fig. 5 (below) — ENGLISH POTTERY
  Plate: design in light slip on a dark ground, dated *1764.*

Puzzle jug: inscription in light slip on a dark ground, dated *1732.*
Low dish: four compartments covered inside with light slip and outside with brown slip dotted with light.
Hen and brood of chickens bank: covered with dark brown glaze.
Jar: with inscription *The po bee member Whom to give aim,* dated *1610.*
Jug: applied clay medallions on ground in two shades of brown.
Plate: crab design in light slip

Fig. 6 — GERMAN POTTERY
Corner stove tile and small model of earthenware stove: relief designs; covered with green glaze.
Plate: slip coating painted in colored clay and metallic pigments.
Earthenware group: decorated in slip and glaze; sacred monogram.
Earthenware bottle: in pineapple form; green and brown glaze

how humble the vessel, is satisfactory to the eye.

Delft ware, the production of which was centred about Delft, Holland, was, no doubt, influenced by the tin-enameled pottery of southern Europe, and by the porcelains of the Orient. Designs with Dutch landscapes, peasants, and domestic animals were used in conjunction with Oriental motives. Figurines of domestic animals were particularly appealing. The early blue and white ware was later varied by polychrome designs. Much of the Holland ware in the small potteries must have been intended to appeal to simple folk for decorative purposes, since wood and pewter were used in humble Dutch homes for tableware. Yet another use of clay is

DETAIL OF FIGURE 6

also suggested by the lead-glazed busts of coarse buff earthenware used as roof finials.

Slipware is probably the most representative of English pottery. Its charm lies in the clever use which the potters made of clay and glaze. English folk pottery includes picturesque plates and chargers, rotund jugs, friendly tygs and posset pots supplied with enough handles for several drinkers. Many bear dates and quaint inscriptions.

Various types of slipware were made in England, but trailed or dropped slip decoration, of which the Thomas Toft dishes afford outstanding illustration, appears to have been the most popular. Light designs were contrasted against darker grounds

Fig. 7 — TRANSYLVANIAN POTTERY *(early nineteenth century)*
Designs scratched in the clay body and outlined over the dark blue surface coating with white slip

Fig. 8 — SWISS POTTERY
Plate: brown glazed surface touched up in green; decorated in white slip. Dated *1795*.
Ink well: green glaze; with sacred monogram.
Covered jar: brown ground decorated in green, yellow, and white slip, with relief ornaments and scrolled clay straps.
Fountain: green glaze; with figures in relief. Dated *1654*

and *vice versa.* Manganese was used freely to darken clay and glaze. Patterns varied from simple dots, which were none the less attractive for their tendency to amalgamate in firing, to zigzag lines, inscriptions, flowers — among which the tulip was prominent — and attempts at portraiture. The lead-glaze coating often gave the light slip a yellow tint and turned the red of the body to a rich brown.

Colored lead glazes played an important part on German pottery and stove tiles. Copper green was used extensively; but blue, brown, yellow, and manganese violet are also found. Early glazed pottery, known as "Hafner ware," frequently displayed figures in high relief, and even in the round, in niches. The white used to indicate flesh, according to Emil Hannover, was produced with tin; blue was often made opaque with an admixture of tin.

Tin-enameled and slip-coated pottery also found favor in Germany. The slip-coated ware was painted both in colored clay and metallic pigments. The tulip, said to have been introduced into Germany in the latter part of the sixteenth century, played an important part in the decoration. The oak leaf, used as a space filler, was the badge under which the German peasants fought for their faith and rights. Surviving small models and individual tiles give an idea of the monumental, glazed-earthenware stoves that occupied the centre of the main room of a German home. The stoves were frequently two-tiered, the upper part serving at night as a base for a bed. Green was a favorite color; Biblical, mythological, and historical subjects, in relief, were typical decorations.

The central European countries, with their complex mixture of races, are, or were, rich in folk art. It has been said of some of them that they decorated everything they touched

from the cradle to the grave, and we can well believe it. Their pottery was influenced by Germany and Italy; but each race stamped its ware with its own traditions. A great variety of central European pottery and stove tiles is simply but effectively decorated with colored glazes, either alone or in conjunction with *sgraffito* or relief ornament, in one color or a combination of hues. Painted ornament on tin-enameled or slip-coated ware is luxuriant. The large dishes, plates, and two-handled jugs afforded the potter opportunity to express racial conceptions with a poetic exuberance and freedom of brushwork that is charming. The stove tiles are also a treasure house of designs. Gaily colored trailed and dropped slip was also used on slip-coated ware.

Pottery was made in nearly all parts of Switzerland. Slipware and ware covered with colored glazes, in which green plays an important part, are prominent. The color combinations are often daring. The Swiss were particularly lavish in their use of colored clay on both slip and glazed grounds. Orange, brown, blue, green, and yellow are frequently combined. The shapes show considerable originality. The small fountains, usually with twisted handles and flat backs open at the top, are unique. Covered bowls and tureens with finials built up with straps of clay are likewise characteristic. Also to be found are small churns, some of them decorated in light slip.

All the different types of European folk pottery meet and mingle in France. Here we encounter glazed ware, trailed and dropped slipware, *sgraffito* pottery, and slip-coated or tin-enameled ware painted with metallic pigments. Originality was shown in the combination of colored glazes. Among these, a manganese brown and violet spotted glaze is a unique contribution of French inventiveness.

Fig. 9 — FRENCH POTTERY
Fountain (right): covered with mottled glaze; seventeenth century.
Centre fountain: with a bust of Napoleon, covered with dark brown glaze and decorated in light slip; nineteenth century.
Fountain (left): decorated with colored slip and glaze; eighteenth century

Fig. 1 — ORNAMENT BY THEODOR DE BRY (*1528–1598*)
De Bry, born in Liège, died in Frankfort, was one of the best known engravers and illustrators of his day

German Stoneware

By MARION THRING

CONCENTRATION upon the history of Europe's two centuries of searching for a means of making porcelain similar to that imported from the Orient has done much to distract attention from another branch of the ceramic industry that — quite unrelated to experiments with porcelain — was developing in a small corner of Europe. Yet the substance of the vessels manufactured in this less celebrated industry was very nearly related to the precious Chinese porcelain. To be sure, it still retained the opaqueness of common pottery, and was thus unlike the porcelain whose clear translucence had caught the fancy of kings and their courts; but, in common with the latter ware, it was fired at a temperature so high as to

vitrify the body, that is, to fuse the clay to a density sufficient to render it impervious to liquids, even without a coating of glaze. Such ware is known as *stoneware*.

The makers of the earliest European porcelain were usually content, in their enthusiasm for the Orient, to imitate the forms and decorations as well as the material of the Chinese wares. They spared no effort to produce beautiful ornaments.

The appeal of the European stoneware, developed in the Rhineland to meet the daily requirements of the people, is of an entirely different character. The body is relatively coarse, the forms often roughly thrown, the color very much what it happened to be. But a vitality and robustness belonging to

Fig. 2 — GERMAN STONEWARE JUG (*fifteenth century*)
From Siegburg, near Cologne. Evidently formed on a wheel, foot then crimped with thumb or fingers. Encircling bands broken into crude beading with a sharp stick. Medallions, apparently representing the kingly visitants of the Nativity, made by pressing soft clay into molds and applying the resultant reliefs, like stamps, to the surface of the vessel.
The handles are roughly rolled strips of the clay.
Formerly in the Oppenheim collection

Fig. 4 — GERMAN STONEWARE JUG (*second half, sixteenth century*)
By Anno Knütgen of Siegburg. Evidently deriving from the type of Figure 2, but showing far superior care in workmanship and greater sophistication of form. Note the well-turned foot and the fact that the handles, like the delicate medallion, have been pressed into a mold. The impressed decoration was accomplished with wood or metal dies perhaps similar to those employed by book binders.
From the Felix collection

Fig. 3 — GERMAN JUG (*early sixteenth century*)
Still essentially Gothic in character, with the characteristic crimped foot and with pierced medallions suggesting the traceried rose window of a cathedral.
From the Schlossmuseum, Berlin

Fig. 5 — GERMAN STONEWARE EWER (*1591*) By Christian Knütgen of Siegburg. White clay (pipe clay), nobly formed and with its elaborate relief decoration executed with singular delicacy and finesse. Here the Gothic influence has yielded completely to that of the Renaissance. To a considerable extent, the relief ornaments employed by the potters were, like those of workers in metal, based on contemporary engravings. (See *Fig. 1*.) *From the Kunstgewerbemuseum, Cologne*

Fig. 6 — GERMAN STONEWARE JUG (*1597*) Light-brown, salt-glazed. From Raeren. The frieze, a peasants' dance, is after a design by the German engraver Beham (see *Fig. 7*). Detail of the dancers is shown below. *From the Pennsylvania Museum of Art*

things born of the needs of a full-blooded people are evident. We can follow the development of a people through the development of its craft, from the simple and somewhat crude vessels of the late Gothic period to the vigorous but elegant designs achieved by the famous modelers in stoneware of the Renaissance. The molded pictorial ornaments with which these vessels were adorned reveal the costumes of successive generations, their amusements, their religious aspirations, and their conceptions of humor. Probably no other German craft of the Renaissance has left so vivid a record of the popular spirit as has Rhenish stoneware.

Concerning the first discovery of this useful ware nothing is known. Other types of hard pottery were certainly made in countries other than Germany during the mediæval and early Renaissance days, but none of them was moisture-proof. For instance, the Cistercian monks in England produced jugs whose fine-textured clay permitted very delicate potting; but without the protection of a lead glaze these vessels were porous. The invention of stoneware proper — unglazed save for the gloss acquired from vapors of salt thrown to the kilns during the firing — must be credited to the potters of the Rhineland.

Suitable clay for the manufacture of stoneware does not everywhere exist. The fact that ample supplies occurred in the Rhine valley made this district the centre of the industry. Even as early as the 1300's, Siegburg, a community near the

Fig. 7 — PEASANT DANCE BY HANS SEBALD BEHAM (*1546*)
Beham (*1500-1550*) was born in Nuremburg, whence he removed to Frankfort, where he died.
He is notable for his engravings on both wood and copper

city of Cologne, is said to have been making stoneware. In the first half of the next century, guilds were formed to regulate the manner in which the craft should be conducted. (See *Pottery and Porcelain*, by Emil Hannover.)

The chief characteristic of Siegburg ware is its white body, for which the fine clay of the locality is solely responsible. No tinting of the surface of a vessel was needed to disguise or obscure discolored patches due to mineral impurities in the fabric. Early examples from this centre are entirely Gothic in design: for example, the so-called *Ringelkrug* of the fifteenth century (*Fig. 2*), and the funnel-necked beaker jug with open-work tracery (*Fig. 3*). Both pieces have the crimped foot, shaped by pressing the clay with the fingers, frequently found in early vessels. Von Falke calls attention to the fact that, as late as the end of the sixteenth century, the distinguished potter Anno Knütgen was still employing forms derived from these almost primitive types (*Fig. 4*). He adds that this mediæval touch may be regarded as an important characteristic of the work that issued from Knütgen's shops. The fact that this potter held important office in the Duchy of Julich-Cleve-Berg accounts for the frequency with which the ducal coat of arms appears on his vessels. Christian Knütgen, of the same family, produced some of the finest and most finished stoneware vessels in the style of the late Renaissance. Here we have a well-developed feeling for line and form combined with

17

Fig. 8 — WHITE STONEWARE "SCHNELLE" (c. 1585)
By Hans Hilgers of Siegburg. Relief panels pressed in separate molds and then assembled. The scenes depicted are Biblical.
From the Pennsylvania Museum of Art

an ingenious distribution of refined ornament (see *Figure 5*).

Until the end of the sixteenth century, the ornaments on stoneware were formed by pressing the clay in hollow molds called *matrices*. The vessels to be decorated had previously been thrown on the wheel and dried. Ornaments from the matrices were then applied to the vessels by means of wet clay called *slip*. At a later date designs were incised in the moist clay, or impressed with wooden stamps.

Fig. 9 — GERMAN STONEWARE JUG (1609)
By Jan Baldems of Raeren. Known as a "peace jug." Showing increasing elaboration of decorative details. Brownish hue due to some form of iron compound mixed with the salt that produced the glaze

The master potters in all districts used contemporary woodcuts and engravings as designs for their relief ornaments. Christian Knütgen found the style of Theodor de Bry (*Fig. 1*) especially suitable for the friezes around his vessels. Hans Hilgers and other molders often sought their inspiration in the work of Virgil Solis.

An interesting example of the productions of this Hans Hilgers in the Pennsylvania Museum collections is a tall, slender beer

Fig. 11 — BLUE AND GRAY STONEWARE JUG (1598)
From Westerwald, but adopting the colors introduced by Emens. Note the continued use of the arcaded frieze.
Figs. 9 and 11 from the Pennsylvania Museum of Art

Fig. 10 — STONEWARE JUG (1587)
By Jan Emens of Raeren. The influence of design in silver is here very apparent, particularly in the cut-card work below the frieze and just above the foot, and in the fluting of the body. This gray and blue stoneware is colder and less gracious in tone than the earlier brown ware, but from the period of its first production it established a method even yet in vogue among German manufacturers of stoneware. The scenes illustrate the story of Joseph.
From the Kunstgewerbemuseum, Cologne

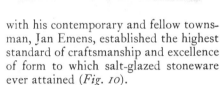

mug known as a *Schnelle*, with characteristic relief decorations in three contiguous panels (*Fig. 8*). The first of these illustrates scenes from the Old Testament with Latin inscriptions: the top, Moses receiving the Commandments; below, the healing of the Children of Israel by the brazen serpent, the Temptation, and a representation of death; finally, as the main figure, a prophet. The second panel shows the Tree of Life with the inscription HOMO. Here likewise occurs the monogram HH with which Hilgers signed his work. The third panel portrays scenes from the New Testament. A noteworthy feature of this *Schnelle* is the decided Byzantine influence in the decoration. The elongated figures, the folds of drapery, the type of head in the John the Baptist of the third panel, the formal trees, and the headgear of the prophet speak strongly of Oriental influence. Hans Hilgers was a follower of Anno Knütgen, and his signed work ranges from 1569 to 1595.

Some of the jugs from Raeren have an entertaining frieze called the *Bauerntanz* (peasants dance), from designs by Hans Sebald Beham (*Fig. 6*). One of these, in the Pennsylvania Museum, bears the inscription:

Gerhat du must daper blasen
So danssen di Buren als weren si rasen
Fry vf spricht Bastor
Ich verdans dy Kap mit den Kor.

[Gerhardt, thou must blow lustily
So the peasants may dance as though they were mad.
Faith, says the pastor,
I will dance away my cap with my cassock.]

A historically interesting flagon, also of Raeren workmanship and likewise in the Pennsylvania Museum, is a so-called *peace jug*, signed by Jan Baldems and dated *1609*, the year of the peace treaty between Spain and the Netherlands (*Fig. 9*). The frieze consists of arches framing effigies of kings and nobles. Above the figures are their names, and below, their coats of arms. The third niche, which is occupied by a Roman emperor, also carried the word *Pais*, from which the jugs have derived their name. Jan Baldems was the son of Baldem Mennicken, who,

with his contemporary and fellow townsman, Jan Emens, established the highest standard of craftsmanship and excellence of form to which salt-glazed stoneware ever attained (*Fig. 10*).

The majority of Raeren vessels are characterized by a brilliant salt glaze varying from red brown to a pale, dusky yellow. The color was produced by the heat of the kiln acting on the oxide of iron contained in the clay, the depth of tone depending on the proportion of the impurity. The gray body of the ware frequently shows through the slightly mottled effect of the glaze. After 1580 Jan Emens introduced the so-called *Blauwerk*, in which he employed a light gray body with reliefs emphasized by applications of cobalt blue. This method was extensively copied by the later stoneware manufacturers in the Westerwald (*Fig. 11*), and set the style for the majority of stoneware pieces produced during the seventeenth and early eighteenth centuries. During this late period, Grenzhausen became the centre of stoneware production, and profited greatly by becoming a haven for refugee potters from Siegburg and Raeren who settled there toward the end of the sixteenth century.

Some of the earliest Rhenish stoneware is ascribed to Cologne and the neighboring town of Frechen. It is in Cologne that the so-called *Bellarmines* or graybeard jugs are thought to have originated. Widely copied by most manufacturers, these grotesque jugs enjoyed a long popularity, though in the later examples the once well-modeled, curly-bearded head became a merely stylized, grimacing mask (*Figs. 12 and 13*).

The manufacture of stoneware in Germany was not confined exclusively to the Rhine country. At Kreussen, near Bayreuth in Bavaria, and in Saxony, the industry was likewise carried on; but its highly colored products were quite unlike the sober Rhenish vessels — and they exercised a far less widespread influence. From Grenzhausen, Cologne, and Raeren, stoneware was exported and was imitated by the English potter John Dwight. It was carried into New England and New York by English and Dutch emigrants, and into Pennsylvania by the German settlers who responded to the siren call of William Penn. But, though the method persisted and still persists, its application all too swiftly degenerated into a crass utilitarianism.

ITALIAN MAIOLICA DISH

(*Faenza, c. 1510*)

Victoria and Albert Museum

ITALIAN

MAIOLICA

BY

W. B. HONEY

*All illustrations from
the Victoria and Albert Museum*

FIG. 1—DISH (*Florentine, c. 1450*). Painted in green and purple. Diameter, 18½ inches.

THE MAIOLICA OF ITALY, that is to say, the Italian painted tin-glazed ware of the fifteenth and sixteenth centuries and later, has now for nearly a century been the most highly prized kind of European pottery. Appreciation was undiscriminating at first, and the collectors of the nineteenth century competed as eagerly for the accomplished but essentially derivative pictorial plates of Francesco Xanto, for example, as for the beautifully fresh and vital work of the earlier part of the sixteenth century and the still finer and more powerful primitives of the *quattrocento*. The sensuous fascination of the golden and ruby lusters added by Maestro Giorgio at Gubbio was apt to blind collectors to some in-

different drawing. In recent years, however, much study of the artists who painted the ware has brought a clearer understanding of the various sorts of excellence shown in successive phases by this splendidly decorative pottery.

Maiolica has been well described as the pottery of humanism. It was a product of the Italian Renaissance and shared the impulse that produced the better-known Italian arts of painting and sculpture. Its themes reflected the classical literatures that occupied the minds of scholars in the revival of learning, and its occasions revealed the same concern with individual self-expression and outward display.

But this art was also the development of a virile potter's craft. Its resources were those of the clays and earthy pigments proper to that craft. Though eventually breaking away from utilitarian purposes the Italian potter was for long primarily concerned to create for use, by the manipulation of clay, a range of vessels of noble form, to which he added as if with a gesture of mastery such simple decoration, plastic or painted or in the finish of handles and spouts, as came naturally to the shape in hand. This sound potter's tradition lies behind all subsequent achievement in the art. Development came with the perfecting of a palette of ceramic colors of unsurpassed richness. Lacking only certain rose-purples and reds, the color of maiolica is dominated by a resonant chord of blue, green, and orange. With these resources the Italian potter went on to enhance with ever greater extravagance the vessels he had originally made for use alone. Chief among the classes of ware so embellished were the various forms of drug vase made to equip the pharmacies, monastic and public, which at that time were places of social resort like the drugstores of present-day America; these vied with one another in splendidly furnishing their establishments with decorated ves-

FIG. 2—DRUG JAR OR ALBARELLO (*Florentine, c. 1460*). Painted in blue and purple in Valencian style. Height, 9½ inches.

FIG. 3—DRUG JAR or "OAK LEAF JAR" (*Florentine, c. 1450*). Painted in *impasto* blue. Height 8¼ inches.

sels to hold drugs, syrups, and confections. A stage was finally reached when a purely decorative or pictorial intention supervened, when the painting became the sole reason for the existence of the ware. The "picture plate," for display on sideboard or dresser, became the logical but absurd conclusion of this development. This desertion of utility is perhaps not surprising, since the potters were working in a period of the highest achievement in the art of painting, and is indeed not entirely without justification, since pottery colors have qualities of tone possessed by no others and are virtually imperishable. Certain qualities of touch and handling called for in ceramic painting give it, moreover, a decision and directness that may be lacking in other media. But the decline of the potter into a mere decorator foreshadowed a decadence in his art, which had produced the most satisfying results when still tied to a practical task. In the period of greatest achievement, however, covered by approximately a century from about 1440 onwards, Italian pottery reached a level of excellence which has seldom been surpassed in the whole history of the art.

Maiolica has thus a double importance — for its place in the history of European culture, and as one of the supreme achievements of European ceramic art — and is on these accounts worthy of detailed study. The collection in the Victoria and Albert Museum, from which the illustrations to this article have been taken, is by general consent the finest in existence; it is larger and more comprehensive than any other and includes also a greater number of masterpieces. Established as a leading collection with the purchases made by Sir Charles Robinson in the 1850's, it was most notably enriched in 1910 by the bequest of George Salting, who had acquired nearly three hundred pieces, all of the highest qual-

ity. In 1940, in the first year of the World War, a full catalogue of that collection was completed after long preparation by Bernard Rackham, but passed almost unnoticed in the turmoil of the time.

The austere primitives of the art date from the middle decades of the fifteenth century. They lack the splendor of color which was soon to become so wonderful, but are unsurpassed for strength of drawing (*Fig. 1*). Here is to be traced the oriental source of much of the early decoration. The potters were at first inspired by the painted wares of Syria and the Near East and especially by the Hispano-Moresque ware of Valencia in Spain. These last reached Italy by way of Majorca and from the name of the latter was derived the term *maiolica*, used originally for the imported wares alone. Painting in green and purple followed a widespread Mediterranean fashion; painting in blue only was probably inspired from Spain but is to be traced to the Syrian wares and ultimately to Chinese blue-and-white porcelain, which already in early Ming times was widely exported. In the painting in blue and purple the latter color was obviously used at first as a substitute for the luster color on the Valencian wares. The characteristic form of waisted drug-jar known as the *albarello* (*Fig. 2*), was also derived through Spain from Syria. Most of these types were made with greatest distinction in Tuscany, and among them the Florentine "oak-leaf jars" (*Fig. 3*), with their rugged drawing and heaped-up sonorous dark blue color, stand as the most original of these Italian primitives. The Tuscan forms were at all times admirable, the jugs in particular being simple yet monumental in outline (*Fig. 4*).

With an improvement in the quality of the tin-glazed surface and the addition of new colors a new harmony became possible, and the wares of Tuscany were soon rivaled by those of Faenza, which often surpassed them in beauty of glaze and

FIG. 4—JUG (*Florentine, c. 1475*). Painted in blue, purple, and yellow. Height, 15 inches.

FIG. 5—DISH (*probably Florentine, c. 1475*). Painted in dark blue, purple, green, and buff. Diameter, 16¼ inches.

FIG. 6—DISH (*Faenza, c. 1485*). Painted in colors, with the arms of Mathias Corvinus, King of Hungary. Diameter, 18½ inches.

FIG. 7—JAR (*Florentine, c. 1470*). Painted chiefly in blue, purple, yellow, and green. Height, 12½ inches.

technical perfection. In the latter part of the fifteenth century new subjects were introduced, in the Renaissance style, strongly recalling in their naive beauty and directness the early Florentine engravings (*Figs. 4 and 5*). Conspicuous among the new motifs, alike on Tuscan and Faentine wares, is the strongly coiled foliage, still Gothic in character, seen on many pieces dating from the last two decades of the fifteenth century (*Figs. 5 and 7*). Some of the finest pieces are panels showing the art already practiced for its own sake, regardless of the requirements of use, while the growing fashion for portraits and armorial dishes (*Fig. 6*) seems to speak of the passion for self-assertion and display characteristic of the Renaissance in some of its aspects. The wares of this period are in general distinguished by strength of drawing and austerely beautiful color, now dominated by dark blue, deep green and manganese purple, and a full-toned orange sparingly used.

With the turn of the century a larger palette was developed and Renaissance motifs (*Figs. 8-12*) began to predominate. Maiolica became an art of superb luminous color, with tones of orange and yellow playing a greater part than before. The Faenza greens and blues, including a blue-stained glaze known as *berettino* (*Fig. 10*), may be contrasted with the favorite orange, green, and yellow of the wares of Deruta and Siena. The influence of Chinese porcelain was strong enough for painting in blue alone to be popular, especially at Venice with its Eastern trade (*Fig. 13*). Luster pigments giving ruby, golden, and bluish mother-of-pearl reflections were sometimes added with charming effect at Deruta and Gubbio (*Fig. 11*). The actual painting was of the greatest refinement, by masters whose works show enough individual character for them to be identified and assembled. The master Giovanni Maria was not only an admirable craftsman and colorist but helped to create some of the most characteristic decorative styles of the time (*Fig. 9*). The painter known as the Master of the Resurrection Panel had an even more skillful hand, and the great dish painted with the scene of Christ among the Doctors is one of the finest of all maiolica paintings (*see Frontispiece*).

FIG. 8—PLATE (*Faenza c. 1510*). Painted by the master *CI*. Diameter, 11½ inches.

FIG. 9—PLATE (*Castel Durante, c. 1500*). Painted in colors by Giovanni Maria. Diameter, 10¼ inches.

Among several artists at the Medici workshop at Caffaggiolo near Florence the painter of "the Vulcan Dish" (*Fig. 12*) shows the most sensitive hand and the most distinguished sense of color. But the Siena "Maestro Benedetto," a painter at Faenza signing *CI* (*Fig. 8*), and several others were hardly less gifted. The great Caffaggiolo jugs sustain the Tuscan tradition in their nobility of form, though almost equaled by those of Faenza (*Fig. 10*).

The establishment of the purely pictorial or *istoriato* style was chiefly due to an artist originally of Castel Durante, named Nicola Pellipario. His earlier work (*Fig. 14*), with its prevailing blue and green tones lightened occasionally with touches of a beautiful purple, marks the highest level reached in the now independent art of the maiolica-painter. His drawing at all times shows an unsurpassed sensitiveness and rhythmic vitality. In his later work, after he had moved to Urbino, his color lost some of its charm, and its brownish orange tone became fixed as a mannerism in the work of his followers. Nicola, too, was the most distinguished painter of the amatory portrait dishes which were a characteristic production of the Castel Durante factory. He had several close imitators, including the famous Francesco Xanto Avelli, who not infrequently signed their painting on the back of dish or plate.

Soon after the middle of the sixteenth century a reaction against the "all-over" pictorial style, which is particularly associated with Urbino though adopted also elsewhere, brought into fashion a new and slighter kind of decoration, with arabesques of fantastic figures and imitation cameos, in the manner of the frescoes painted in ancient Roman style by Raphael and his assistants in the Loggie of the Vatican. This style, too, originated at Urbino. Finally came a vogue for almost plain wares in which the beautiful white tin-glaze was displayed by contrast with painting of the most summary kind in blue and yellow only.

In the seventeenth and eighteenth centuries Chinese por-

FIG. 10—JUG (*Faenza, c. 1539*). Painted in color on a light blue (*berettino*) ground. Height, 15 inches.

24

FIG. 11—PLATE (*Gubbio, c. 1525*). Painted in colors and in golden and ruby luster. Diameter, 10¼ inches.

FIG. 12—DISH (*Caffaggiolo, c. 1520*). Painted in colors. Diameter, 15½ inches.

celain had become more popular than ever, and blue monochrome painting came into favor again, while Genoa and the trading cities of the Ligurian coast became, with those of the Venetian territory, the most important centers of manufacture. Scenes in the style of the contemporary Italian theater, landscapes with fantastic ruins and trees, and views of classi-

cal architecture reflect the fashions of the time. The pictorial style was revived at Castelli in the Abruzzi, but in a low-toned palette. In all this later work a certain exuberance and extravagant baroque fancy hardly compensate for the loss of the splendor or color and masculine drawing which distinguished the wares of the fifteenth and sixteenth centuries.

FIG. 13—DISH (*Venice, dated 1543*). Painted in blue and opaque white. Diameter, 9¼ inches.

FIG. 14—PLATE (*Castel Durante, c. 1519*). Painted in colors by Nicola Pellipario. Diameter, 10¾ inches.

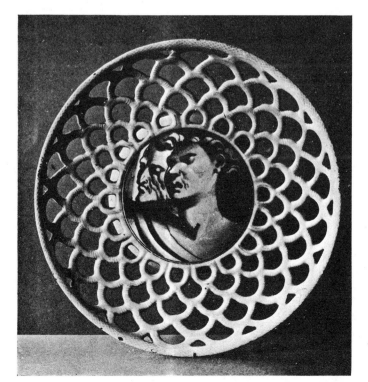

Five centuries of Faenza majolica

BY GIUSEPPE LIVERANI, *Director, International Museum of Ceramics, Faenza*

IN EVERY PART OF ITALY there is evidence of the work of potters but the centers which can boast of uninterrupted activity from Roman times are few. Faenza, at the foot of the Apennines, with close links to Ravenna, is one of the most important. Good geographical position, in the heart of the Romagna, easy communication by land and sea, and a copious supply of excellent clay favored the development here of a distinctive ceramic production which has not been interrupted in eight hundred years. Vitality, creative imagination, and thorough appreciation of the technical possibilities of the material, characterize the ceramics of Faenza.

The earliest record of a potter working in Faenza is a document of 1142 in which a jar maker asked permission to enlarge his workshop; the implication is that his business was thriving by this date. From the thirteenth century through the seventeenth, there is continuing evidence of flourishing potteries producing majolica, or terra-cotta ware covered with an opaque or translucent glaze. According to Carlo Grigioni, more than 270 potters were living in Faenza during the first forty years of the sixteenth century. He suggests that the total number of those who made their living partly or wholly from the majolica industry probably exceeded one thousand, if apprentices, shopboys and assistants, middlemen and retailers are included. At this time the population of Faenza was nine thousand.

Workshops of the period were those of Francesco Torelli, the Pirotti brothers, the Manara brothers, the Bergantini family, the Mezzarisa, the Orcellari, the Fagioli, the Gulmanelli, and later the Dalle Palle, Virgillotto Calamelli, Leonardo Bettisi (Don Pino), Fabio Marchetti, the Mazzanti, and the Tonducci, which became Cavina Grossi and finally the property of the family of Count Ferniani, who managed the workshop until the early twentieth century.

During the Middle Ages Faenza, like other Italian centers, produced earthenware covered with dark green or yellowish brown glaze, typical of Roman art and known throughout Europe and the East. After the eleventh century, however, it developed a characteristic

Fig. 1. Jugs decorated in brown and green. Faenza, fourteenth century.

Fig. 2. Plate with heraldic lion, leaves, and berries; manganese brown outline, dark blue-black and green design in relief. Faenza, 1460.

Fig. 3. Plate with
polychrome grotesques
on dark ground.
Faenza, 1508.
Estense Gallery, Modena;
Alinari photograph.

white glaze—an excellent ground for decoration, which at that time consisted almost entirely of a brown outline filled in with green or, rarely, cobalt blue.

This majolica was produced in the workshops of central and northern Italy in such centers as Orvieto and Siena, as well as Faenza. Unlike the brighter wares of southern Italy, especially of Apulia, it was much like the pottery produced at the same time in southern France, Spain, North Africa, Greece, and the Low Countries. Over one hundred recently discovered jugs, made for a fourteenth-century monastery, are typical (Fig. 1). Similar jugs are seen in a fourteenth-century fresco in the refectory of the Abbey of Pomposa. The decoration usually consisted of naturalistic twigs and leaves, animals, and coats of arms, strapwork bands, and geometrical designs. The designs were strongly outlined on the clear ground and filled in with green or cobalt blue, or were reserved in the light color of the glaze on a ground of brown cross-hatching against wide parallel bands.

Decoration became much richer and more varied in

the fifteenth century, and a striking inky blue-black so thickly applied that it stands out in relief (Fig. 2) became popular. At this time a superior white glaze, hard, thick, and of a brilliant white, was developed. It was the perfect ground for the Italo-Moresque designs, derived from the pottery of the Moors and colored in gray blue, lime yellow, pale green, and purple. Motifs consisted of palms and other leaves outlined as background for the central theme, which was usually a human or animal figure or a religious symbol.

The so-called Gothic-floral patterns developed from the Italo-Moresque were the richest and most popular of the fifteenth century. Designs, as the name suggests, were drawn from flowers and leaves stylized in the Gothic fashion, with figures, busts, crests, and religious badges often framed in a panel (Fig. 3). The colors of the Italo-Moresque—green, blue, yellow, and purple—acquired greater warmth through the substitution of orange for lime yellow. This was the typical palette of the *stile severo* used in the decoration of bowls, dishes, jugs, and

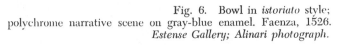

Fig. 4. *Color plate, facing page.*
Pillbox with lid decorated with Persian palmette motif.
Faenza, late fifteenth century.

Fig. 5. Pair of plates with
blue decoration *alla porcellana.*
Faenza, late fifteenth or early sixteenth century.

Fig. 6. Bowl in *istoriato* style;
polychrome narrative scene on gray-blue enamel. Faenza, 1526.
Estense Gallery; Alinari photograph.

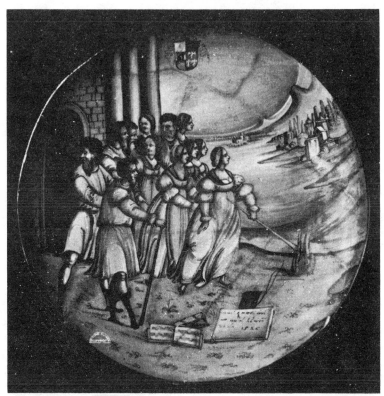

*Except as noted, all illustrations are from
the International Museum of Ceramics;
photographs by Borchi.*

Fig. 7. Molded bowl, or *crespina,*
decorated in polychrome;
a quartieri (paneled) border.
Faenza, c. 1540.
*Civic Museum, Arezzo;
Alinari photograph.*

28

Fig. 8. *Color plate, facing page.*
Crespina in *compendiario* style;
maiden holding a spear. Faenza, 1550-1560.

Fig. 9. Octagonal plate
with floral decoration in polychrome enamel.
Faenza, c. 1780.

apothecary jars, whose greater refinement in both shape and ornamentation suggests a knowledge of Chinese porcelain.

During this period the most popular motifs were the peacock feather, the pomegranate or Persian palmette, and those called *alla porcellana*. The peacock feather, used most often between 1460 and 1490, derived its richness from repetition of the usual colors on a small field. The Persian palmette, which reflected the growing influence of the Near East, had endless variations (Fig. 4 in color). At the end of the fifteenth century the wares *alla porcellana*, inspired by the decoration of rare Chinese porcelain, introduced a monochrome decoration in dark blue that was further developed in the sixteenth (Fig. 5).

Early in the sixteenth century the potters turned from Gothic and Oriental themes to the lively new art that the Renaissance architects, painters, and sculptors had introduced. The *istoriato* style which the ceramic decorators developed was a narrative representation of figures and scenes from the past, suggested by Italian and German prints and paintings of the period. The palette became richer and more varied to do justice to the figures and landscapes pictured. The white glaze acquired a light gray-blue tint—the *berettino* (blue-stained enamel ground) on which the artist painted in polychrome and dark blue and white (Fig. 6).

The anonymity of such artists as the monogrammists B. T., P. F., G. I., F. R., the Master of the Death of the Virgin, and the Master of Selene was ended and full names appeared. In the sixteenth century majolica decoration was a triumph of color in every style—the *istoriato* vying with the grotesques, the fruits, and the flowers. New and more elaborate shapes appeared, many inspired by models in bronze, copper, and silver, rich with relief surface ornamentation. Molded fruit dishes or *crespine* (Fig. 7), wine coolers, salt cellars, and ewers were created in which the shape was even more important than the color.

Potters concentrated on perfecting the white glaze, and in some workshops technicians were employed who did nothing but experiment to improve its brilliance and color. A large jug produced in Francesco Mezzarisa's workshop combined the talents of Pietro Zambalini, who had been commissioned in 1540 to perfect the glaze, and artist Antonio Romanino Cimatti, who decorated the bright white glaze with a design executed in blue, yellow, and orange. This was an early example of the now famous *bianchi di Faenza* decorated in the sketchy *compendiario* style, a manner of painting in short strokes derived from a certain style of Greek and Roman painting. It became the fashion later in the century, when emphasis was on a white, velvety glaze usually sparsely decorated with a crest, figure, or wreath of leaves all executed with the freshness of a rapid sketch in blue, light yellow, and orange (Fig. 8 in color). This style was popular all over Italy, and as craftsmen moved to factories in France, Holland, England, Switzerland, Germany,

Hungary, and Bohemia they carried it with them. Kings and princes ordered this much-coveted white ware by the case and prized it as much as silver. Soon the French word *faïence*, from the name of the city, became the accepted name for the ware.

As a center of highly respected workshops and craftsmen Faenza flourished for the next two hundred years. At the end of the seventeenth century, Count Annibale Carlo Ferniani acquired the workshop of Tonducci Cavina and it remained in the family for the next two centuries. Baroque, rococo, and blue ware in imitation of Chinese porcelain followed as the fashions changed. In the late 1700's contemporary English wares influenced the shape and neoclassic design of such pieces as the plate in Figure 9.

The nineteenth century brought a great display of technical virtuosity in oversize vases, relief plaques inspired by Della Robbia, and decoration *a impasto* (with pigments applied so thickly as to stand out in slight relief). About 1870 Achille Farina established the last great school of the century when he brought together a group of skillful painters in fresco and on canvas to work on majolica. Among his pupils, the Minardi brothers of the early twentieth century did much to keep ceramic art flourishing in Faenza.

We are indebted to McGraw-Hill Book Company, Inc., of New York and to Electa Editrice of Milan for the use of two color plates from Professor Liverani's definitive book *Five Centuries of Italian Majolica*, 1960.

Introduction to Dutch blue and white

BY PHELPS WARREN

THE FALL OF THE MING DYNASTY in 1644 and a decline at about the same time in the consumption of domestic Dutch beer are, unlikely as it seems, among the causes cited for the rise of the Dutch pottery industry in the mid-seventeenth century.

Conditions in China during the last two Ming reigns are described by Sir Harry Garner in his *Oriental Blue and White* as "very unsettled, the country being under continuous attacks." He notes "the absence of any record of the Imperial and other potteries after the reign of Wan Li" (1619) and suggests "that either the Imperial potteries closed down or else that they reached a very low ebb indeed. . ." This dearth of supply at its source was reflected in the cargoes of the Dutch East India Company (formed in 1602), which had been bringing Chinese porcelains to a developing north European market for twenty years prior to the Ming collapse.

Coincidentally, the Dutch brewing industry suffered from foreign competition. It was natural, therefore, that idle breweries should be refitted as potteries and that the Dutch potter should try his hand at imitating the refined Chinese product, for which there was an eager market at his door. In time he was to use the blue and white pottery medium for articles wholly European in both shape and decoration.

The late W. B. Honey, in his *European Ceramic Art*, noted two major divisions of Dutch blue and white: blue and white in the Chinese style, and blue and white with Dutch subjects. In the latter category he grouped objects painted with European landscapes, portraits, and decorative compositions in the baroque style, as well as views of towns, series of plates, painted versions of Bible stories, drug and tobacco jars, and the like. Examples of both these groups are illustrated here. The prime period for the output of this diversified material was the century between 1640 and 1740.

In measuring the achievement of the Dutch ceramist, it must be remembered that he was trying to make pottery look like porcelain. "Real porcelain was never made [by the Dutch]," explains the Rijksmuseum handbook

1

2

1 *Left:* Long-necked vase, 13 inches high; a form popular with the Dutch. *Author's collection.* This example of about 1700 is shown with a late twelfth- to early thirteenth-century Persian luster ewer (*right*), raising a question as to which way the "influence" was exerted —by the Near East on the East, or the other way around. The decoration of the vase is in a fine deep strong blue, bringing to mind the term "Muhammedan blue" applied to the Persian ore exported to China for its early blue and white production. *Metropolitan Museum of Art; bequest of William Milne Grinnell.*

2 *Left:* Plaque, 1700-1720; height 9¾ inches. With its European-style frame and Chinese-style picture, this plaque exemplifies the blend of East and West which gives a special charm and interest to Dutch pottery. The inner frame is a strong yellow; olive green was also sometimes used effectively to complement the basic blue and white scheme. Though this plaque is equipped with its own loop for hanging, similar pieces were frequently set permanently into the walls in the manner of tiles. *Right:* Plaque, 1675-1700; height 11½ inches. The affinity of this plaque to a painting in the Rijksmuseum showing a Dutch interior with woman and child, *De Kelderkamer* by Pieter de Hooch (c. 1632-1681), supports the date ascribed. The plaque illustrates one of two main divisions of Dutch blue and white of the third quarter of the seventeenth century, "in the style of the oil painting of the period." But the diapered border pattern was borrowed from fourteenth-century Chinese blue and white. *Author's collection.*

3 *Left:* Faceted cube bottle, c. 1685, 7¾ inches high; bearing the S V E mark of Samuel van Eenhoorn, owner from 1674 to 1685 of the factory *De Griecksche A* (The Greek A). (Van Eenhoorn had received the factory as a wedding present on September 24, 1674.) The birds, perhaps cranes, are shown amid rocks and foliage in the Chinese taste; the seven-character mark on the foot is an invention. *Author's collection. Right:* Hat or wig stand, also a faceted cube, by the same S V E. *Victoria and Albert Museum, crown copyright.*

4 *Left:* Long-necked ribbed octagonal vase, c. 1697; one of a pair standing 16½ inches high. Signed with the initial of Johannes Knotter, who bought the Delft factory *De porceleyne Fles* (The Porcelain Bottle) on February 4, 1697. Previously in the collection of the Dukes of Leinster, the contents of whose County Kildare seat, Carton, were sold at auction in 1925. *Author's collection. Right:* Covered vase, c. 1680, 26 inches high. Also ribbed and octagonal; initialed AL or A V L. *Colonial Williamsburg.* Such pieces are decorated with flowers composed of tiny dots, known to collectors as "parsley," which appear to be a Dutch invention and are perhaps without precedent in the Chinese porcelain the Dutch craftsmen were imitating.

5 Pair of casters, c. 1763; height 9 inches. Signed with the initials AK and attributed to Albertus Kiehl, who took over *De witte Starre* (The White Star) factory in Delft in 1763. These are among the latest objects illustrated. In shape they are rococo, but their painted scenes, perilously close to the repetitious and sentimental decoration of nineteenth-century souvenirs, foreshadow the deterioration in design which followed Delft's golden period (1640-1740). The form is certainly extremely rare; a single example in the Philadelphia Museum of Art is the only other instance known. *Author's collection.*

3

4

5

6 *Left:* Jar, height 9¾ inches. A small capital D on the base of this piece indicates that it may have been produced by Jan Theunis Dextra at *De Grieksche A* factory between 1759 and 1765. However, since the jar carries a second, larger mark of two interlocking V's, which is recorded as an "old pottery" mark, it may well date from about 1700. *Author's collection. Right:* Details in the painting of this Chinese vase (K'ang Hsi, 1662-1723) which are repeated in the Dutch jar give support to the earlier attribution for the Dutch pot; its exceptionally lustrous glaze and its strong rich blue on a fine white ground further suggest the earlier date. *Metropolitan Museum of Art; gift of Mary Sinclair Burkham.*

7 *Left:* Ewer, c. 1671. This 10-inch-high ewer carries the mark AK attributed (in this case) to Albrecht de Keiser, who was master from 1642 of the Delft factory *De porceleyn Schotel* (The Porcelain Dish) and who died in 1671. *Author's collection.* It has a most interesting form: to its inverted pear-shape body, flattened on two sides, have been added a base, a neck and spout, and an elegant twisted handle which links it to the Hampton Court ewer (*right*), one of a number of pieces made about 1690 to the order of King William III and Queen Mary, and attributed to Daniel Marot; 3 feet, 10 inches high over all. *Collection of Queen Elizabeth II (Hampton Court); copyright reserved by the Ministry of Works.* A very similar twisted serpentine handle shown by Garner in *Oriental Blue and White* is dated Yung-chêng, 1732-1734.

8 *Tulipière* of extreme rarity, probably unique in this country; other examples are at Hampton Court and Chatsworth in England. One of a pair attributed to Adriaenus Kocks (w. 1687-1701) or to Albrecht de Keiser (w. 1642, d. 1671), two masters with the same initials who were working at approximately the same time. Over-all height, 52½ inches. There do not seem to be any contemporary illustrations of a *tulipière* in use; apparently the flower stems were set into the protruding nozzles. *Colonial Williamsburg.* Another example of the obelisk form is shown in a smaller version on the cover.

9 Gourd bottle, one of a pair with initials of Lambertus Cleffius, master in 1667 of *De metale Pot* (the brewery of *De Ham,* which was converted into a pottery in 1639); c. 1667; height 9½ inches. The gourd shape (sometimes referred to erroneously as double gourd) is known in Chinese blue and white from the fourteenth century. Dutch versions were popular in both blue and white and polychrome. The delicately drawn and colored decoration of this piece exemplifies the craftsmanship of the best Delft period. *Author's collection.*

10 *Left:* Plate in star shape, c. 1700; diameter 13½ inches. The dragon motif, the "auspicious object" symbol, and the flower panels make this plate, attributed to Adriaenus Kocks, interestingly Chinese in character. *Author's collection.* But more important is the plate's eight-pointed star form, relating it to Islam. *Right:* An earlier use of the star shape occurs in this thirteenth-century Persian tile wall decoration. *Metropolitan Museum of Art; gift of Horace Havemeyer.*

Another association for the eight-pointed star, a later one but most interesting, is the Dutch Indonesian *rijsttafelstel,* a star-shaped serving plate with eight dishes for accompanying condiments fitted into its perimeter. There is such a service in the collection of the Stedelijk Museum, the Prinsenhof, Delft.

8

9

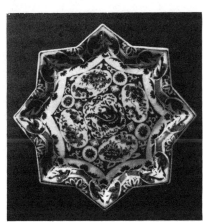

10

Delfts Aardewerk, "because the potters lacked the necessary fine kaolin" for bonding the white tin glaze to the brittle earthenware core. However, the mid-seventeenth-century Dutch potters called their wares "porceleyne," to distinguish them from the coarse earlier pottery which was still being produced.

The town of Delft had no monopoly on the manufacture of blue and white, although the universal use of its name suggests that it may have had one. Arnhem, Haarlem, Makkum, Rotterdam, were also important pottery manufacturing towns. And just as Delft had no monopoly of blue and white production among the towns, the Netherlands had no such monopoly among countries. Factories in Germany, France, England, Ireland, and Scotland subsequently joined the Netherlands in meeting the demand for articles in this coloring. Nevertheless, so great was the Dutch, and particularly the Delft, influence in this field that the word delftware (with a small letter d) is today commonly used for tin-glazed pottery in general. (It is said that in Ireland today the humble people refer to their dishes as "delf": ". . . after supper, wash the delf.")

Marks seldom are found on Dutch blue and white plates and are absent from a large proportion of other objects. However, when dates, portraits of historical personages, and references to notable events are included in the decoration, these help in the dating of unmarked pieces. On the other hand, marked pieces, which one would expect to be easier to attribute than unmarked ones, may be in fact more difficult. Signature calligraphy was seldom uniform; marks perhaps legibly painted in the first place were obscured in the glazing and firing; marks of leading makers were forged; in several instances the same initials were used as signatures by different potters. Finally, pieces come to hand with legible marks which are as yet unassigned to either an individual potter or a particular factory.

Photographs of objects in the author's collection are by Taylor and Dull.

OLD FRENCH FAIENCE

By ARTHUR LANE

W E TEND TO REGARD the eighteenth century in European ceramics as the Age of Porcelain; but beneath all the glitter and show of this luxurious fashion a much more momentous thing was happening. On the one hand Josiah Wedgwood and his competitors were inaugurating the age of useful, white-bodied earthenware in which we still live; and on the other, the age of white-glazed, painted earthenware, which had lasted since the beginning of the fifteenth century, was drawing to its final close. The "Hispano-Moresque" luster wares, the Renaissance "maiolica" of Italy, the delftware of Holland, and the "faience" of France and Germany, represent successive generations of a great family that became virtually extinct about 1800. All were technically similar; their material was a soft-fired buff or pinkish earthenware, with a fine white glaze made opaque by the incorporation of tin-oxide. Originally practiced by the Islamic potters of Mesopotamia in the ninth century, this "tinglaze" technique spread via North Africa and Moslem Spain to reach Italy in the fifteenth century. It offered the first satisfactory medium for painting on pottery known to modern Europe.

Emigrant potters from Italy started making Italian-style maiolica in the Low Countries about 1500. There the industry grew and reached maturity in the factories of Delft, nearly two hundred years later. Italian potters also settled in France, but found it harder to popularize their fashions. The Frenchmen Masseot Abaquesne of Rouen and Sigalon of Nîmes made Italian-looking tiles and drug jars that are now extremely rare; but their factories hardly survived the founders. At Lyons and Nevers, where there were important Italian colonies, there was made maiolica with figure subjects hardly to be distinguished from the contemporary wares of Urbino in Italy. Nevers alone successfully continued manufacture into the seventeenth century, and not till about 1650 did the Nevers potters shake off the subservience to Italian fashions implied by the word "faience" (derived from the French name for the famous Italian pottery-town of Faenza).

Figure 1 shows a great Nevers dish of about 1650, whose subject, the *Rape of Europa,* is derived from an engraving after the French master Simon Vouet *(1590-1649).* The weaker drawing, softer color, and wide ornamental border unmistakably distinguish it from the Italian maiolica with figure subjects. Chinese porcelain must have been well known at Nevers, for landscapes with Chinese figures were often painted there in blue with purple outlines. Such pieces are often hard to distinguish from the imitations of Chinese porcelain made at Delft. But the shapes borrowed from Chinese vases were given more billowy outlines to suit the European baroque taste, as in Figure 2. Here the tin glaze has been stained a rich dark blue, and the painting is in white, orange, and pale yellow — the so-called *bleu persan* palette that is perhaps the most distinctive of all the Nevers fashions.

Potters from Nevers must have helped in establishing the other French factories that grew up during the seventeenth century. The greatest of these was at Rouen, founded in 1647. Its early productions were no doubt plain white or simply-painted wares that have failed to survive. But from about 1670 to 1720 great quantities of ware were painted in the "blue-and-white" coloring made fashionable by Chinese porcelain; sometimes with details picked out in a sticky-looking brownish red pigment peculiar to Rouen. The radiating patterns *(Fig. 3)* give an extremely rich effect, but tend to become monotonous. Louis XIV's long wars so exhausted the French treasury that in 1709 the courtiers were encouraged by royal example to send their silver plate to the Mint for melting down. As a result the demand for table services in faience greatly increased, and many Rouen pieces bear the heraldic arms of the families for whom they were made. From about

FIG. 1 — DISH from Nevers factory *(c. 1650-1670).* Diameter 21½ inches.

FIG. 2 — NEVERS VASE *(c. 1650-1680).* Height 9 inches.

FIG. 3—ROUEN PITCHER with radiating patterns. *(c. 1700-1710).* Height 9¾ inches.

FIG. 4—SAINT JEAN DU DESERT DISH (c. 1680-1709). Diameter 22½ inches.

FIG. 5 — MOUSTIERS PLATTER (c. 1710-1740). Width 17¼ inches.

1720 on polychrome painting and mock-Chinese or rococo decoration succeeded the blue-and-white *style rayonnant* at Rouen, but the gaudy coloring, clumsy drawing, and coarse greenish-white glaze detract somewhat.

Faience factories were started about 1680 at Saint Jean du Désert near Marseilles, and at Moustiers, a small hill-town sixty miles to the northeast. For a long while both used the fashionable blue-and-white palette, and a closely similar range of designs. Typical of the period 1680-1710 are the huge dishes with hunting scenes in spacious ornamental frames (*Fig. 4*); though the subjects were borrowed from engravings, the painters showed great individual skill in adapting these and in painting the figures. From about 1710-1740 a more delicate kind of ornament was based on the engraving of Jean Berain and other court designers (*Fig. 5*). After 1740 Moustiers and Marseilles, each now boasting a group of faience factories, abandoned the blue-and-white color scheme in favor of polychrome painting with blue, green, orange-yellow, and purple in various shades. And at this point each group developed characteristic local styles. Moustiers went in for exquisite miniature painting, whereby mythological figures, grouped or singly, were shown in little wreathed medallions, with hanging festoons and swags round the border of the vessel (*Fig. 6*). No photograph can do justice to the delicate charm of this style, which appears to have been introduced by Joseph Clerys, a French potter who had previously worked at Alcora in Spain. There is close similarity between Moustiers and Alcora faience, but the latter can

usually be distinguished by its redder clay. Yet a fourth Moustiers style came in about the middle of the eighteenth century, showing small grotesque figures loosely scattered among fantastic plants: they are usually painted in yellow or green monochrome, but sometimes in other colors as well.

At Marseilles, from about 1740 on, Joseph Fauchier's factory was using polychrome colors for painting mythological scenes with rococo borders in a much bolder style. But it was in the second half of the eighteenth century that Marseilles produced the faience for which it is so justly renowned; and by that time it had generally accepted an important modification of technique. Hitherto faience had been painted over the "raw" white glaze before the pot went to be fired. The firing of glaze and colors was completed in a single operation in the high temperature (*grand feu*) kiln. But comparatively few colors could withstand so great a heat. So in the new procedure the pot was first glazed and fired; the painting was added afterwards, in "enamel" colors mixed with ground-up glass; and this painting was then fused onto the hard glaze by a second firing in a special kiln at a much lower temperature (*petit feu*). "Enamel painting" had been current in porcelain factories, both in France and Germany, for many years before it was introduced into the French faience factories. Among

FIG. 6 — MOUSTIERS DISH (c. 1740-1760). Diameter 10 inches.

FIG. 7 — MARSEILLES DISH, Veuve Perrin factory (c. 1760-1770). Diameter 9¾ inches.

its wide range of colors were crimson, violet, pink, and black, and leaf gilding.

It is not easy to distinguish between the work of the different Marseilles manufacturers, but the capable widow Perrin seems to have dominated her competitors for nearly half a century (she used the monogram *VP,* for *Veuve Perrin,* as her factory mark). Several of the faiencemakers also attempted to make porcelain, so that the miniature-like delicacy of painting required for porcelain is likewise apparent on faience decorated at these factories. Another influence contributing to the excellence of Marseilles faience painting was the local Academy of Painting and Sculpture (founded in 1753) where some manufacturers sent their apprentices to learn. Foremost among the designs on Marseilles faience are the naturalistic flower paintings, whose apparently random disposition over the surface is in fact carefully studied and extremely subtle in its meandering rhythms *(Fig. 7)*. Still-life subjects of fish were painted with keen appreciation — Marseilles has long been famous for this line of cookery *(Fig. 8)*. And there were also picturesque harbor scenes, suggested by the paintings of Claude Joseph Vernet; Dutch farmyard subjects in the manner of Teniers; and of course the inevitable *chinoiseries.* One color scheme for such paintings was peculiarly attractive; the subject was drawn in brilliant black, with an overlaid wash of clear emerald-green enamel. The shapes of Marseilles faience include wavy-edged plates and dishes, handles formed like natural twigs, and rococo scrolls in relief. Great quantities were exported both to the Levant and to the French Atlantic islands; it would be interesting to know if any pieces later found their way thence to the United States.

Strasburg, founded in 1721, was the leader in a whole group of faience factories in eastern France. They did not assume a distinct local character till about 1750, when Paul Hannong, then proprietor of Strasburg, introduced the enamel-painting technique already described. The shapes tended to a wild rococo extravagance, with relief scroll and shellwork, and naturalistic surprises such as tureens in the form of birds, cabbages, or melons. Most prominent of the enamel colors was a rich crimson produced by dissolving gold in *aqua regia* (nitric acid and sal ammoniac) — the "purple of Cassius" named after Andreas Cassius of Leyden, who first discovered it in the mid-seventeenth century. The color could be modified into numerous pink and violet tones. Flower painting might

FIG. 8 — COVERED BOWL from Marseilles *(c. 1770)*. Height 9⅞ inches.

be of great magnificence — for example, the naturalistic *fleurs fines* shown in Figure 9; or it might take the simpler form known as *fleurs des Indes,* which had black outlines filled in with graded washes of color by less skillful painters. *Fleurs des Indes* plates of Strasburg or its imitators in eastern France and Germany are still fairly common: Strasburg pieces can be recognized by the monogram initials of Paul Hannong *(proprietor 1739-1762)* and Joseph Hannong *(1762-1780)* on the back.

The faience of Niderviller in Lorraine *(1754-1789)* may be decorated even more finely than that of Strasburg; but this factory was noted for its exquisite faience figures *(Fig. 10)*.

Enough has been said to show that the leading faience factories in France were in the provinces. There existed in fact a great many more factories than those here mentioned, but these tended to copy the leaders with rather less skill. The court never showed much interest in faience — except when, as in 1709, emergency caused it temporarily to dispense with silver plate. Such encouragement as the court thought fit to extend to the ceramic art was bestowed on porcelain factories — especially that at Vincennes (transferred in 1753 to Sèvres). One faience factory alone was geographically near enough to the French court to follow closely the metropolitan fashions — the factory of Sceaux (1750-1793). Here wares of extremely fine quality were produced, imitating now the porcelain of Sèvres, now the faience of eastern and southern France. It is always tempting to ascribe to Sceaux pieces that do not quite fit in anywhere else; for the fact that the great majority of marks found on French faience give no clue to the factory of origin has left the collector plenty of scope for connoisseurship in the discriminating of styles.

FIG. 9 — STRASBURG DISH, marked *JH (Joseph Hannong, 1762-1780).* Diameter 9⅞ inches.

FIG. 10 — NIDERVILLER FIGURE *(c.1765-1770).* Height 8¼ inches.

All illustrations except Figure 8 are from the Victoria and Albert Museum.

Strasbourg faïence

BY HANS HAUG, Director of the Strasbourg City Museums

THE CERAMIC FACTORY OF STRASBOURG had an existence of only sixty years (1721-1781), which were shared in three equal parts by three successive generations of one family. Its first products, characteristic of the Louis XIV period, were modeled on the faïence of Rouen and Moustiers. Later it drew inspiration from China, by way of the soft-paste porcelain of Chantilly. And finally the influence of Meissen led it to the glorious period when its celebrated wares in their turn spread Strasbourg's influence all over Europe.

In 1709 Charles François Hannong, a maker of clay pipes who was a native of Maastricht in Holland, had established himself at Strasbourg with the intention of founding a "porcelain" factory. This meant actually a faïence works, for the secret of making porcelain, hitherto unknown in Europe, was not discovered until that very year at Dresden by Johann Friedrich Böttger, who long succeeded in keeping it.

Hannong's attempts remained fruitless up to the time when he became associated with Johann Heinrich Wachenfeldt, a faïence painter from the Ansbach factory who arrived in Strasbourg in 1719. The combined efforts of the two ceramists resulted two years later in the factory's first successes: table services and other pieces of every kind, decorated in the manner of Rouen with blue strapwork and lambrequins. In 1723, Wachenfeldt retired from the firm and founded the Durlach factory on the other side of the Rhine. The Strasbourg works, in the meantime, prospered: a subsidiary was founded in 1724 at Haguenau, in the wooded region north of Strasbourg, where clay deposits had long been used in the making of pottery.

In 1732 Charles François Hannong entrusted the direction of the two factories to his two sons, Paul-Antoine and Balthasar; in 1739 he died. Paul Hannong, soon the sole head of the two establishments, is the great man of Strasbourg faïence history. To him are due all the innovations, all the improvements, which, about the middle of the century, made the faïence of Strasbourg celebrated.

First of all, about 1740, he enriched the palette of the lambrequin decoration, adding to the blue two different greens, a yellow, a manganese violet, and finally an iron red—though this last was brownish and poorly assimilated by the glaze. The same colors served later, between 1744 and 1748, for new decorative formulas: the border disappeared in favor of floral motifs inspired by the Far East, and sometimes also of chinoiseries—dancing or hunting scenes placed in more or less Chinese landscapes. At the same time the first figures and other modeled forms appeared, but these still had a utilitarian purpose: candlesticks, cruet stands, and potpourri jars; also jam pots, sweetmeat dishes, and tureens in the form of fruits and vegetables painted in natural colors. The modelers of these pieces were Johann Wilhelm Lanz, who developed into a sculptor of great talent, and Jean-Jacques Louis, whom we find again later at the factories of Sceaux and Orléans.

Strasbourg faïence centerpiece and "pyramid" with lambrequin decoration in blue; Charles François Hannong, c. 1730. *Illustrations from the Musée des Arts Décoratifs, Strasbourg.*

Strasbourg faïence round platter with scrolled edge and *fleurs des Indes* decoration in "high-temperature" colors; Paul Hannong, c. 1745.

The influence of Rouen was succeeded by that of the soft paste of Chantilly, which extended to forms as well as decorations.

From the technical point of view, it may be said that no sooner had Paul Hannong added to the blue the so-called "high-temperature" colors (manganese green, purple, and brown, and iron yellows and reds) than he turned from this method to the use of the muffle kiln. That is, the decoration was no longer painted on the unbaked glaze and fired at the same time as the latter; "enamel" colors were painted on the fired glaze and then given an additional firing, a procedure permitting the much more extensive gamut of colors developed in the years 1748 and 1749. From then on the Strasbourg palette was dominated by a purple derived from gold.

This success was due to a new crew of workers who came, directly or indirectly, from the Meissen porcelain works. Paul Hannong knew how to attract and retain painters and chemists—then called arcanists (masters of the secret of porcelain)—and their presence resulted also in the successful production of true hard-paste porcelain, the first made in France.

In 1748 the painter Christian Wilhelm von Löwenfinck arrived; he was a renegade first from Meissen, then from Höchst, where he had worked in the pottery founded and directed by his elder brother, the celebrated Adam Friedrich von Löwenfinck. The latter, also abandoning Höchst, appeared at Strasbourg in May 1749 accompanied by his young wife, Séraphie Schick, who specialized in painting landscape and figures. A flower painter, Johann-Gottlieb Roth (or Rothe), came with them, as did the painter and chemist Ringler, who was probably responsible for the successful completion, in 1750 or 1751,

of the porcelain research long pursued in the Strasbourg pottery.

From this time on the variety of forms was very great: table services including baroque or rocaille pieces; fountains, cases for wall clocks, tureens of different shapes; receptacles in the form of farmyard fowl, boars' heads, cabbages and lettuces, all painted in natural colors; platters and plates holding *trompe l'oeil* vegetables, salads, and fruits. Finally there were whole sets of figures and figure groups—hunters, shepherds and shepherdesses, chinoiseries, *singeries*, the four seasons, the continents, crafts and trades—rivaling those which, following Meissen's lead, the German factories were then bringing into vogue.

During the same years, 1750-1755, occurred what we may call the first porcelain episode. From the last quarter of the seventeenth century on, France had been producing soft-paste porcelains in the factories that had sprung up one after another at Rouen, St. Cloud, Chantilly, Mennecy, and elsewhere, and finally at Vincennes (after 1755 the royal manufactory at Sèvres) under the protection of the king and Madame de Pompadour. The great fault of soft paste, an artificial porcelain difficult and costly to produce, was its fragility—the price paid

Strasbourg faïence covered dish in form of turkey painted in natural enamel colors, modeled by Lanz; Paul Hannong, c. 1755.

Strasbourg faïence platter with blue border and *fleurs fines* in polychrome enamel colors; from the service of the Cardinals de Rohan at Saverne; Paul Hannong, c. 1760.

Strasbourg faïence soup tureen with relief decoration picked out in gold, and "fine flowers" in polychrome; Joseph Hannong, c. 1770.

for the extraordinary charm of this ware in which the colors "melt" into the translucent glaze. Paul Hannong, doubtless with the aid of Ringler, had succeeded in 1750 or 1751 in producing a very beautiful hard-paste porcelain and the first examples to appear on the market excited an attack from Vincennes, the privileged factory. The lengthy altercations that ensued forced Paul Hannong in 1755 to transfer the new production outside the country. He installed it at Frankenthal under the protection of the Elector Palatine, keeping only the pottery manfacture in Alsace. If we must regret the loss to Strasbourg and to France of this industry, which in the Palatinate was responsible for some of the finest German porcelain, we must also remind ourselves that without the intervention of Vincennes, Hannong would

soon have abandoned the making of faïence. Now it was precisely after 1755 that the latter achieved, especially in floral decoration, its highest degree of elegance and refinement. A year earlier the famous PH mark in blue had been introduced.

However, the group which had come from Germany in 1748 and 1749 had been dispersed; of the Löwenfincks, the younger had died at the age of thirty-three, in 1753; the elder, at forty the following year. Ringler and Roth left at about the same time for other destinations, and the Strasbourger Lanz, modeler of all the plastic productions, was sent to the new Frankenthal factory. The only one left was the widow of Adam Friedrich von Löwenfinck, who, at barely twenty-five, took over the direction of Haguenau on the death of her husband and for a short time (1761) directed the two establishments. Among the native Strasbourg personnel, two young brothers, François-Antoine and François-Michel Anstett, were lured away by the neighboring factory of Niderviller, which had just been founded by the Baron de Beyerlé.

In spite of these difficulties, the factory found markets all over Europe—and imitators as well, in Lorraine, at Marseilles, and even at Rouen. Through personal contacts the Strasbourg style was carried into Sceaux right in the Ile de France, into Switzerland, north Germany, and Sweden; entire services were furnished for princely French and German houses.

The death of Paul Hannong in 1760 temporarily jeopardized the progress of the two establishments. His eldest son, Charles, had died the preceding year at Frankenthal, where he was in charge. The second son, Joseph, had replaced him, and their restless younger brother, Pierre-Antoine, to whom his co-heirs had entrusted the direction of Strasbourg, declared himself unable to stay there. From 1760 on Joseph Hannong, who had sold the Frankenthal factory to his protector, the Elector Charles Theodor, took the two Alsatian establishments in hand. He was a modern industrialist in every sense of the word. A concept of labor relations that even guaranteed the security of the worker's family, a school of design and a porcelain research laboratory, a printed price list keyed to figures beneath his monogram on the underside of the pieces—all these he introduced in the middle of the eighteenth century with an astonishing modernism.

The quality of his faïence and its decoration of *fleurs fines* equaled that achieved under Paul Hannong. Production became even more regular, and its elegance, while becoming more and more French, still kept the traditional Alsatian characteristic of closeness to nature. Along with "fine flowers" and chinoiseries, which were to be copied by many a pottery of Lorraine, Hannong continued to produce more modest services with their floral decoration outlined in black; and he introduced —sign of the approach of classicism—tablewares ornamented only with gold bands.

But the demon of porcelain returned to haunt the last of the Strasbourg potters. In 1768 the monopoly of Sèvres began to be less effective, and the first deposits of kaolin were discovered in France at St. Yrieix in Limousin. In that year Joseph Hannong resumed production of porcelain and three years later put his new product on the market. 1771 is the date when Sèvres and several small Paris factories, thanks to the kaolin of St. Yrieix, likewise succeeded in producing hard-paste porcelain.

And yet, the royal manufactory succeeded once more in circumventing the competition of Strasbourg: Alsace was now classed as a foreign province, and porcelain imported from it into the kingdom was subject to so heavy a duty that sale became impossible. Hannong, awaiting relief from these duties and vainly appealing to the highest authorities, had to borrow considerable sums, first from the Cardinal Constantin de Rohan,

bishop-prince of Strasbourg, then, without the cardinal's knowledge, from his treasurer. De Rohan's death in 1779 brought to light in the episcopal accounts a deficit of nearly half a million pounds; Hannong and the treasurer were arrested and spent a year in prison. On his liberation Hannong could not put his factory back into operation, for the personnel had sought employment elsewhere. Bankruptcy was inevitable.

Those who, since 1769, all over Europe had profited from the teachings of the Strasbourg pottery—Niderviller, Lunéville, the factories of the south of France, of south Germany, of the Baltic—continued for some time to produce floral decoration, but the day of faïence had passed. Porcelain, and even more the English creamware, whose influence was spreading over the whole Continent, had killed it. At the beginning of the nineteenth century the faïence factories which still operated, particularly in the east of France, no longer enjoyed a fashionable clientèle.

It goes without saying that the Strasbourg Museum of Decorative Arts, installed in the magnificent eighteenth-century palace of the Cardinals de Rohan, possesses the most complete public collection of Strasbourg faïence and porcelain. But the rich variety of material from other factories and other lands shown by this museum is equally important to any estimate of the international influences felt and exerted by the celebrated factory directed through sixty years by three generations of the Hannong family.

Strasbourg faïence oval platter with "fine flowers" decoration in polychrome, c. 1761-1762, bearing the very rare BL mark used during the interim direction of Séraphie de Becke-Löwenfinck.

Flora. Large figure in Strasbourg porcelain, modeled by Lanz—the first piece of hard-paste porcelain made in France; Paul Hannong, c. 1751.

BY KITTY RUEFF

The lively forms of Brussels faïence

UNLIKE BRUSSELS TAPESTRIES, Brussels lace, Brussels sculpture, and Brussels silver, which are known and admired in all parts of the globe, Brussels faïence is comparatively unknown; even students and collectors of faïence of the period often ignore it. Yet from the beginning of the eighteenth century through the first quarter of the nineteenth, the potters of Brussels produced some outstandingly fine pieces—beautifully modeled, full of strength and individuality, in a range of strong, lively colors closely copying those of nature.

Only a few pieces of Brussels faïence are marked with identifying inscriptions (there are no known factory marks), most of the artists are unknown, and the pieces themselves sometimes resemble the products of Rouen, Sinceny, Nevers, and Delft; but it can be distinguished by the glaze—rich, oily, and magnificent—and the lovely colors, quite different from those of French or German potters. The blue most used is a mottled version of the *bleu-de-roi;* the yellow typical of Brussels verges on a mustard; greens range from emerald to copper green. Aubergine, in shades from very light to almost black, is frequently encountered.

There were faïence factories in Brussels as early as the middle of the seventeenth century, but the first of any significance was founded in 1705 by a Belgian named Corneille Mombaers and a Hollander, Thierry (Dierick) Witsemburg. Some of their monochrome pieces (one is illustrated) show great skill, but the factory was a financial failure. The first successful Brussels faïence factory was that of Philippe Mombaers, son of Corneille. Philippe's earliest known work is the signed and dated checkerboard shown here, done in 1709. After that he spent a number of years in France and Italy, studying the manufacture of faïence to such good effect that his own factory, started in 1724, was highly successful.

Beginning with the production of utilitarian pieces, Mombaers soon progressed to the wares which today are outstanding in any collection of Brussels faïence: plates, vases, *cachepots*, baskets, mugs, complete table services, ornamental busts and figures, fountains for washing the hands, and—most sought-after today— tureens, always in three parts (tray, tureen, and cover), in the form of extremely lifelike animals, birds, fruit, and vegetables. The light-yellow clay used for these came from quarries near Tournai and is similar to that used at Delft and at most northern French factories. A type of decoration characteristic of the Mombaers factory but later copied by Artoisenet is the so-called butterfly design, in which the artist scattered a variety of charmingly painted butterflies over the piece; edges were often scalloped, and the glaze was a rich coppergreen.

Philippe Mombaers married Jeanne van den Driessche, a member of a well-to-do family. The marriage of their only daughter to Jacques Artoisenet resulted in great unhappiness for Mombaers: his son-in-law opened a rival factory under the protection of the Empress Marie Thérèse, where, with the help of some of Mombaers' best workmen, he copied many of the older man's finest pieces. Grieved as well by the early death of his daughter, Mombaers did not survive long. His widow continued the factory, taking two grandsons into the business and finally uniting the Mombaers and Artoisenet enterprises. Many of the fine pieces they produced are indistinguishable from the Mombaers originals.

Toward the end of the eighteenth century a number of other factories were started which lasted into the nineteenth; Ghobert and Van Bellinghen were two of the more successful. Their wares were not so artistic or so finely modeled as those of Mombaers, but they had a number of good years in which they made such decorative pieces as the famous pewter-lidded mugs, often in the rich Brussels blue or aubergine with polychrome decoration. However, when English *faïence fine* (especially Wedgwood's creamware) began to be imported in large quantities, all the Brussels factories were forced one after the other to close their doors.

Polychrome statuettes representing a young couple, the boy carrying a water container and the girl, a cheese. Very similar to early Delft in coloring and glaze, but a shade more crudely potted and with the glaze sometimes running characteristically into the color. *Collection of Marcel Rueff.*

Plate in monochrome depicting St. Michael, patron saint of Brussels; dated 1705 and initialed WB (Witsemburg) and MB (Mombaers) for the founders of Brussels' first important faïence factory, Corneille Mombaers and Dierick Witsemburg. *Except as noted, illustrations are by courtesy of the Musée Communal, Brussels.*

One of a set of four figures in white representing the arts, beautifully modeled after those at the foot of the seventeenth-century tomb of Archbishop Triest in the Church of St. Bavon, Ghent. Figures of this type are known to have been produced at the factory of Philippe Artoisenet. *Collection of the Countess de Kerchove de Denterghem.*

Checkerboard in blue and white, inscribed *Philippus Mombaers tot* [in or at] *Bruxelles 1709.* In 1709 Philippe, son of Corneille, was sixteen years old. *Musées Royaux, Brussels.*

Philippe Mombaers made a number of bird cages. This one, in white, has a figure in yellow and green on the door. *Musées Royaux.*

The infant Bacchus sitting on a barrel covered with vines and grapes in relief, supported by four dolphin heads. White ground, decorated in manganese purple, blue, and green. Such pieces are among the most original of Philippe Mombaers' production. *Musées Royaux.*

Box in the form of a bunch of asparagus, in natural colors. Such boxes were often used as containers for butter. *Musées Royaux.*

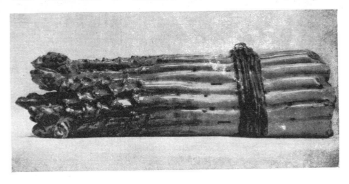

The type of decoration on this polychrome font and basin is reminiscent of Sinceny. In spite of its size this example does not look at all heavy. *Musées Royaux.*

Brussels faïence rarely bears a mark, but this soup tureen with polychrome floral decoration and artichoke finial has an identifying inscription: *Brussel le 15 Nouvamber 1746 / P. Mombaers.*

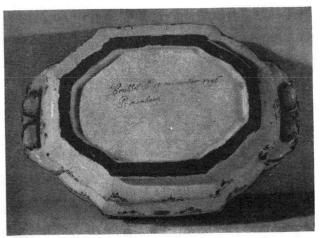

Many artichokes were produced; this one is exceptional for its truly masterly execution. *Musées Royaux.*

One of the many *trompe l'oeil* pieces: nuts and red-cheeked apples on a white plate. *Musées Royaux.*

Egg-shape pumpkin tureen in a rich copper green, with stalks and leaves in relief in shades of green and yellow. *Rueff collection.*

Tureen in the shape of a cabbage; bird finial.

An example of Mombaers' most original type of decoration, this tureen with copper-green décor has flowers, insects, and butter-flies in polychrome on the stand. *Collecion of Marcel Rueff.*

Rabbit tureen in strong colors,
decorated with
stems and flowers in relief;
morning-glory finial.

Large (twenty-six inches) fish,
decorated *au naturel* in ivory, pale
blue, and lilac. The eyes are
in two different shades of brown.

One of many tureens in the form
of ducks sitting on nests; duck in
blue, white, and brown; yellow
nest filled with green grass.

Tureens in the form of a pair of pigeons,
decorated in pale shades of yellow and blue.
Collection of Henri Delattre.

Three little frogs in green
with black markings, yellow feet.

Maastricht Pottery

By Ferrand W. Hudig

Part I

Note. For the suggestion that led Antiques to request the preparation of the following article, acknowledgment is due to Harry S. Koopman of Boston. Mr. Koopman has frequently called the Editor's attention to the similarity in fabric and decoration between the mid-nineteenth-century ware of Staffordshire and contemporary articles bearing the mark of a firm of potters in Maastricht, Holland. His gift of a Maastricht saucer, here reproduced, made possible a closer study of the Dutch product, and served to emphasize the liability to confusion between unmarked Continental and English specimens. Antiques feels particularly fortunate in having persuaded Doctor Hudig of the University of Amsterdam to discuss the subject of Maastricht ware. Doctor Hudig is an authority on ceramics and has written extensively on the pottery of Holland. — *The Editor.*

Fig. 1 — Maastricht Saucer: "Gleaner" Pattern
Printed in purplish brown and elaborated with gold. Brilliant, hard, blue-white glaze, now much crackled. This saucer suggested the study of Maastricht ware. Below is shown the mark.
From the Harry S. Koopman collection

UNTIL lately little attention has been paid, in the Low Countries, to the pottery made during the nineteenth century. Since, however, on several occasions visitors to this country have expressed an interest in the work of the Maastricht potters, I have willingly complied with the Editor's request to collect some data about this industry. At first this appeared an easy matter, in view of the fact that only a generation ago Maastricht pottery was to be found in dining room and kitchen, and even in bedrooms of every Netherlandish household. In reality, the task has proved more difficult than I anticipated. Since 1900, taste has changed, or rather, has developed rapidly after a period of indifference. Dissatisfied with the late and inartistic products of the previous era, people have been glad to replace them with modern and more attractive ware. Curiously enough, a similar phenomenon occurred a century earlier during the decline of the Delft potteries. In the nineteenth century, just as at the close of the eighteenth, it was England that drove the Netherlandish manufacturers out of their place in the sun. It is desirable, therefore, to present a short review of these earlier events in order better to explain the history of the Maastricht pottery.

Delft earthenware, in all its beauty of brilliancy and color, had the fault of brittleness. Hence it was not well adapted to everyday use. Moreover it could not satisfactorily resist the action of acids and salts. The German salt-glazed stoneware and the English crouch ware, on the other hand, lacked an agreeable coloring. When, however, in the middle of the eighteenth century, the porcelain manufacturers of Worcester and the potteries of Staffordshire began making new kinds of porcelain and earthenware, which, besides fulfilling artistic needs, offered the additional advantages of convenience and durability, the Netherlandish public readily neglected the products of its own industry in favor of the English goods.

Meanwhile, English manufacturers spared no amount of effort to introduce their wares into the country whose ceramic preëminence had recently been recognized throughout all Europe. The first evidence of the English invasion of the Holland market appears in the journal of Leeuwarden of the year 1753, where a merchant announces for sale "all sorts of English porcelain according to the new fashion." From this document we learn, further, that the new wares had been sold at Amsterdam even before that date. Already, in 1756, Sadler and Green of Liverpool had patented their invention for making prints on pottery, and, in 1760, Josiah Wedgwood began making creamware, which, shortly after, was decorated according to Sadler and Green's method. We may properly assume that examples of these novelties were to be found among "all sorts of fine English and other porcelain," which a Rotterdam shopkeeper, who called himself "Merchant in English Porcelain and Pottery," offered for sale in an announcement of 1765. In the same year, an Englishman proudly declared that "in all Netherlands houses nowadays the old Delft services are replaced by Staffordshire pottery." In fact, I have found "English tea services" mentioned in the inventories of the inhabitants even of Delft as early as 1764. Wedgwood and

Bentley had their own representative in Amsterdam in 1777, and kept him traveling all over the country. Other English works also made pottery meant especially for the Holland market. [It would appear that some of them exported blank ware to the Low Countries, where suitable decoration was applied. See Antiques, Vol. XVI, p. 272.—*Ed.*]

Some of the Delft potters, as the demand for their products decreased, endeavored to imitate their English rivals. Even the famous workshop *'t Moriaenshooft*, where, at the end of the seventeenth century, the Hoppesteyns had made the most beautiful delft, gave up its old methods and steered a new course. The renowned workshop *De Roos* did likewise. The difference in the methods followed by the old potters of Delft and those of Staffordshire may be defined as follows: the old Delft potters employed a mixture of clays that, after the first baking, became rough and yellowish gray. Articles thus made were then entirely covered with a thick coating of tin glaze. On this coating the decoration was painted by hand, and subsequently covered with a second glaze of lead, which, becoming transparent in the firing, gave the work its final brilliant appearance. The blend of clays

48

used by the English potters yielded, after the first baking, a smooth yellowish or white surface. Painting or printing could be done on this surface without preliminary coating, and a single layer of lead glaze, applied after decoration, was sufficient to impart the required brilliancy. Thus, instead of tin glaze and lead glaze combined, the English potters used only one finishing lead glaze.

The manner in which the Delft potters adopted the English materials and the English form of decoration, and how they began doing so, are not yet fully understood, and little we know of their first attempts. Their simplest course was to copy the appearance of the competitive ware without changing their own methods at all. An effort in this direction may be seen in a plate from the collection of Mr. van Tijen (*Fig. 4*), which seems to be closely related to the "willow" pattern first exploited by Thomas Turner of Caughley, and subsequently the most popular decoration of English ceramics in general. [Its more immediate inspiration may be the so-called Leeds creamware decorated in blue. — *Ed.*]

Another trial in the same direction was made by the well-known Delft workshop *De 3 vergulde Astonne*, when they imitated in ordinary delftware the form and yellow color of the English cream-colored wickerwork, trying to surpass their model by adding a decoration of flowers painted in blue, orange, and red (*Fig. 2*). Nevertheless, during this period, several attempts were made to find the secret of the new English mixture.

It is probable that another plate in the collection of Mr. van Tijen (*Fig. 5*) is also of Netherlandish origin. Its material is similar to that of the English pottery, though coarser; the decoration, however, is more akin to that of delft. A peculiarity of this piece is its yellow painted rim, often found on the later delft plates to prevent damage, though on the hard English ware it was not needed. The plate of Figure 4 has a similar rim, in brown.

A plate of hard earthenware made in the English fashion and decorated in colors with the picture of a maker of brooms and with a little song, dated *1784*, and signed *Arend de Haak*, formerly in the collection of John Loudon, is now in the Ryksmuseum to which this collection has been presented. (See Havard's catalogue of the Loudon collection, 1877, No. 503.)

The secret of English decoration with transfer-printing was not so soon discovered in Holland. Still there seems to have been one potter in Delft who understood it. No documentary evidence has yet been found relating to his workshop, but in the

Fig. 2 — YELLOW DELFT EARTHENWARE (*late eighteenth century?*)
Decoration essentially Netherlandish, but pierced basket rim in imitation of Wedgwood designs. Mark: *3 Astonne*.
From the Ryksmuseum, Amsterdam

museums of Amsterdam and Delft are pieces of hard earthenware made according to the English method, two of which have impressed in the clay the name JAN DERKS, DELFT and the other JAN DIRKS, DELFT. The Amsterdam pieces are dishes of yellow material with a perforated border, imitating wickerwork in the way introduced by Wedgwood, and thus akin to the fruit dish shown in Figure 2. They are, however, of real, hard earthenware. The piece in the museum at Delft (*Fig. 6*) is a plate of pale, cream-colored ware with a design printed on it in two shades of blue. It is very similar to some of Wedgwood's products, and the ware is so perfect and so much like that of genuine English make as to suggest that Jan Derks, instead of being a potter, was, in reality, a merchant who imported his goods from England with his name already impressed upon it.

In the meantime the ceramic industry of Delft, which had once been so flourishing, was dying. Only a few Delft potters maintained themselves into the nineteenth century. Among these a single new firm, Sanderson and Bellaert, has to be mentioned. In the year 1808, they are qualified as "manufacturers of the so-called English earthenware," and probably Sanderson, who no doubt was an Englishman, brought some knowledge from over the sea. On what grounds, however, Havard ascribed to them most of the plates commemorating William V, Prince of Orange, and his wife, Princess Frederica of Prussia, I cannot say. At any rate, these plates must have originated before 1795, and the majority of them certainly were made in

Fig. 3 (*above*) ENGLISH CREAMWARE PLATE (*late eighteenth century*)
Decorated in blue, this type of ware and the English "willow" pattern apparently suggested the plate at the left

Fig. 4 (*left*) — DELFT EARTHENWARE PLATE (*late eighteenth century*)
An attempt to imitate contemporary English creamware.
From the van Tijen collection

Fig. 5 — HARD DELFT EARTHENWARE PLATE (*late eighteenth century*)
Material similar to that used by English potters, but coarser.
The decoration is Netherlandish.
From the van Tijen collection

England. (On this point see Havard, *Histoire de la Faïence de Delft*, 1875, p. 135, and ANTIQUES as previously noted.)

Of all these manufacturers, Captain H. A. Piccardt showed the greatest perseverance in accepting new ideas. In the year 1800, he assumed management of the Delft works *De Porceleyne Fles*, the only one of the old Delft potteries that has survived and is still working. Piccardt imported workmen from England and adopted the new methods. His products are well known; for he signed them with his full name. He did not use the best English models, but imitated the crude yellow ware, decorated in harsh enamels, of the Herculaneum Pottery at Liverpool. The plate reproduced here (*Fig. 7*) is marked PICCARDT DELFT impressed in the clay. It shows a wedding scene painted in violet, green, blue, and brown, and belongs to a series representing the Roman Catholic Sacraments. Other examples, as the set of vases in the Municipal Museum of The Hague, do not encourage a higher estimate of the æsthetic value of Piccardt's products. We receive a dismal impression of the general level of the ceramic industry in Holland at this time, on hearing that at the exhibition of national industry held at Haarlem, in the year 1825, Piccardt's work was mentioned with distinction. A small collection of his products is still preserved by the present owners of his workshop,

the *Porceleyne Fles*. After the death of Piccardt the making of English-type pottery was continued by his daughters, during whose régime, according to information kindly communicated by the managers of the factory, transfer-printing was practiced; but no examples of it are known to me.

In 1876 Joost Thooft bought these works, and gave them a new start by trying to return to the old Delft way of working. After he had accomplished some excellent work in this direction, the English method was again adopted. Recently a series of new inventions has been developed in this workshop; but here is not the place for their consideration.

Piccardt's undertaking, however, was not the only one of its kind in the nineteenth century. In the year 1833, a merchant of Maastricht, Petrus Regout, erected glassworks in the town, and in the next year began the making of pottery as well. It was rather a daring thing, at the time, to start a new business in that locality. Maastricht stood in the very midst of the trouble existing between the northern and southern provinces of the Low Countries. After the union of these provinces, by the treaty of Vienna in 1815, industry had developed, especially in the southern part of the country, where many raw materials were available. The probability of a separation, eighteen years later, promised excellent opportunities for the exploitation of new industries in the north. But it was not at all certain whether Maastricht would eventually find itself in Holland or in Belgium. However this may be, Regout must have weighed all the chances when he established his pottery works. As a potter, and certainly as a glassworker as well, he followed English methods; and from the very outset he must have been a serious competitor for Piccardt. It is his products that I shall consider next month.

An Editorial Postscript

Overseas discussion between author and editor concerning minor aspects of a contribution is difficult. Even the proper interchange of proofs is fraught with delays. In the present instance it has been impossible. For any discoverable errors in Doctor Hudig's text, therefore, the Editor must accept full blame. He has, in two instances, taken the liberty of introducing a comment of his own, conspicuously guarded by brackets. In this connection, he may be allowed to suggest that the Jan Derks plate discussed by Doctor Hudig and illustrated in Figure 6 possesses interesting characteristics. If printed in two distinct shades of blue, it would seem to represent a fairly late departure from the full cobalt-printing introduced in England in 1787.

Fig. 6 (*above*) — HARD EARTHENWARE PLATE (*nineteenth century*)
Impressed mark of Jan Derks of Delft. Printed in two shades of blue.
From the Ryksmuseum Lambert van Meerten, Delft

Fig. 7 (*right*) — DELFT CREAMWARE PLATE (*c. 1810*)
Mark of Piccardt of Delft.
From the Ryksmuseum, Amsterdam

Fig. 8 — "PLEASURE PARTY" (c. 1835)
Printed in deep blue

Fig. 9 — "WILD ROSE" (c. 1851)
Printed in black; colors applied by hand

Maastricht Pottery

Part II

By Ferrand W. Hudig

WHAT were the first Regout products like? Frequently pottery is found bearing the mark shown in Figure 20, centre, and one might be inclined to assign it to a date soon after the works had begun to operate. But the year given in this mark has nothing to do with the manufacturing date of the piece on which it appears. It seems simply to record the year in which the works were established (why it has been postdated by two years I cannot fathom) and of the pieces I know with this mark none dates earlier than 1870. Any exact information about the products of the first fifteen years I have not yet been able to obtain; but most probably Petrus Regout began in the same way as Piccardt by decoying skilled workmen from potteries in England.

I know one piece that I am inclined to consider as of the first years of the manufactory. It is a saucer in the possession of Mr. van Tijen of Amsterdam. At this point in my narrative I seize the welcome opportunity to express a word of thanks to this gentleman, who has generously allowed me here to reproduce pieces from his extensive collection, culled by him with great perseverance and knowledge. This item (Fig. 8) is made of light, rather soft, cream-colored

Fig. 10 — "WILLOW" (c. 1854)
English type of pattern printed in deep blue

material. The glaze is decidedly cracked, but bears a handsome printed decoration in a deep blue tone. In the centre is represented a merry company of ladies and gentlemen, in the costume of about 1835, making a boat trip through a sumptuous park. The border is decorated with anchors and flowers on a ground of seaweed, with shells on the rim. The mark accompanies the picture. The P R between the points of the garland stands for Petrus Regout, as does the P R impressed in the clay. The management of the works, who kindly supplied me with information, was of the opinion that this decoration was used as late as 1874; but, comparing the material and the make of the piece with those of later periods, I feel quite safe in assigning it to the period of the party represented in its decoration, that is, one of the very first years after the works were established. [The border should be compared with that of William Ridgway's *Catskill Moss* earthenware issued in 1844. See ANTIQUES for September, 1930. — *Ed.*]

That, in the year 1851, the products of the works were on such a level as to compete in the world market is indicated by a prize that was awarded to Petrus

Regout at the International Exhibition of London. The fact has been registered, but the management could not tell me the nature of the prize. We must not exaggerate its importance, however, considering that the Minton works of Stoke-upon-Trent, also a new concern, was distinguished by fourteen prizes at the same exhibition.

The piece here reproduced (*Fig. 9*) must, according to the register of the works, be dated in the year of the exhibition, but it certainly would not have obtained a prize, although it demonstrates the practice of a new technique. An ornament of scrollwork and flowers, characteristic of the time of crinolines, has been printed in black on the cream-colored hard material. The flowers have been painted by hand, in a rough and ready way, with shades of pink, yellow, blue, and green. The mark, printed in English, proves that, in this case again, as in, that of the preceding example, English ware has been imitated. Besides the printed initials P R this piece bears the name in full, PETRUS REGOUT, MAESTRICHT, impressed in the clay.

More interesting is a plate of about 1854 (*Fig. 10*) bearing the mark shown in the same figure. The decoration follows Thomas Turner's well-known "willow" pattern in full detail. Irregularities in the rim point to imperfections in the printing technique of the time, but, in other respects, the thin, light, and hard material, as well as the deep blue color of the decoration, has been entirely successful. The mark clearly exhibits an endeavor to pass off the product as of English make. The ware itself, however, has nothing in common with the ironstone china patented in 1813 by Miles Mason and made out of a mixture of

Fig. 11 — "RUTH AND BOAZ" (c. 1854)
Printed in blue

ground iron slag, quartz, Cornwall stone, and feldspar. But imitations of this body, made from other ingredients, were produced also by English manufacturers. On the particular plate in question, the inconspicuous initials identify the maker; yet plates are to be found with exactly the same pattern and mark but without the initials.

An illustrated catalogue issued by Petrus Regout, and dating from 1854, is extant. It is mentioned in Solon's *Ceramic Literature* (1910), but I have unfortunately not been able to obtain access to a copy. Likewise dating from 1854 is the plate portraying *Ruth and Boaz* (*Fig. 11*). This romantic and theatrical representation well befits the period of the Second Empire, and the border agrees in its principal details with that of the saucer of Figure 9. In this case, however, the execution of the design has been carried out with greater care. The ground is white, and the design is in strong blues of various shades.

Completely divergent are other sets and services made about 1861, which bear classic themes executed in a romantic style on a pure white ground — for instance, Hebe and Bacchus (*Fig. 17*). The material is a heavy and hard earthenware, which approaches ironstone china. The pattern is printed in dark purple-blue, but the material was not apt for decorating and the blue coloring has spread under the glaze, and, even on the back, has given a blue tinge to the glaze. Belonging to the same species are sets decorated with large flowers and leaves, and others with a Chinese landscape. The title of the Hebe and Bacchus plate is *Mythology*, and the mark, the arms of Maastricht (the same as in

Fig. 12 — "AMAZONE" (c. 1862)
Printed in carmine

Fig. 13 — RED CROSS (c. 1871)
Printed in colors

Fig. 14 — "Plough" (*c. 1874*)
Printed in blue

Fig. 15, — Plate Printed in Violet
on Cream Ground
Manufactured by N. A. Bosch,
Maastricht (*c. 1855*)

Fig. 16 — Transfer Print
"Packhorse" (*c. 1869*)

Design dates from 1851, but
mark places teapot later

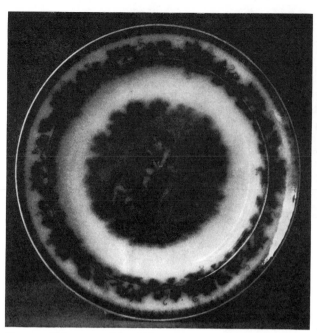

Fig. 17 — "MYTHOLOGY" (*c. 1861*)
Printed in a dark purplish blue, which has spread under the glaze,
and has given the plate a bluish tinge even on the back

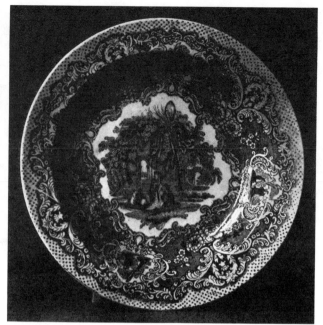

Fig. 18 — "SYRIAN"
Manufactured by N. A. Bosch, Maastricht (*c. 1851*)
Printed in blue

Figure 12). The name P. REGOUT appears also in a mark devised as a strap with buckle. It is worthy of note that a similar strap with buckle was used as a mark on English earthenware as early as 1830. Regout continued this device for some time.

Next to the services printed in blue, those in red and in violet are numerous. The service to which belongs the specimen illustrated in Figure 12 dates, according to the makers, from 1862. The color is a crude carmine. The print pattern shows a tendency to deterioration in finesse, and has been engraved in a monotonous manner, with infinitesimal lines and dots. The mark consists of the arms of Maastricht.

The transfer print with which the teapot of Figure 16 is decorated, known under the title of *Packhorse*, was used as early as 1851. But, though the material here is still a cream-colored, light earthenware, the mark, consisting of a knot and a crown (*cf. Fig. 14*), apparently copied from the English mark used about 1870 by the Crown Staffordshire Porcelain Company of Fenton, makes me date the teapot toward the end of the 1860's. The year 1851, occurring in this mark, has nothing to do with the actual date of the piece, but refers to the prize medal won at the London Exhibition.

About 1870 important changes were introduced both in the components of the ware and in the method of its decoration. It was in this period that the eighteenth-century hard English earthenware was superseded by a heavier, more luminous, and whiter material, which had not the fault of absorbing the colors, as was the case with the ware of which

Fig. 19 — CARTOON PLATE PRINTED IN BLACK
Manufactured by Société Céramique, Maastricht (*c. 1890*)

an example is shown in Figure 17. The bowl illustrated (*Fig. 14*), with a ploughman and milkmaid in blue printing, exemplifies the new and better composition. It bears the same crown mark as the above-mentioned teapot, with the indication, *Prize Medal 1851*. The pattern title *Plough* is added. It must be dated 1874.

Until about 1870, Regout's decorations had been printed in one color only, whether blue, black, red, or violet. If multicolored decoration was wanted, the printing was done in black and the colors were applied by hand. On a piece that, on historical grounds, may be dated with great certainty, we find a new method brought into practice. It is a plate (*Fig. 13*) showing a scene connected with the Franco-Prussian War of 1870–1871. The printed mark embodies a red cross. An F is impressed in the clay. On this piece not only the black delineation but also the various colors have been printed. Some of these colors have been executed in dots, others in strokes, others in crossed strokes, and others, again, solid. Thus, by superimposing various colors one upon another, intermediate shades have been obtained. The method produced a pleasing result, but it must have been rather expensive, and was therefore soon replaced by another new invention. The latter had originated about the same time with a German printer of Leipzig: the *Metachromatypia* or *Dekalkomania*. By means of lithography, different colors are printed on a soluble paper, which, being moistened and laid on the object, can easily be rubbed away leaving the colors behind. We find the process employed on services showing scenes of Chinese

Fig. 20 — SOME LATE MAASTRICHT MARKS

romance and imitating Chinese porcelain of the Yung-chêng and the Ch'ien-lung periods. Some of these bear the aforementioned mark *Anno 1836* (*Fig. 20, centre*).

The change in marks that now occurs is the result of a reorganization of the firm, which, in 1879, became a private limited liability company with the name *Petrus Regout & Co.* In 1883, the Sphinx mark (*Fig. 20*) was brought into use.

The toilet jug shown in Figure 21, printed in pale blue on a white ground, bears this mark with the title *Orient*. It may be dated about 1883, although its figure of a crusader on horseback was adopted as a decorative motive as early as 1859. This piece as well as that of Figure 16 shows how the Second Empire somewhat clumsy rococo shapes were long maintained.

The Merchandise Marks Act, introduced in England in 1887, contained a clause that was particularly directed against the method of imitative marking, which the firm of Regout had been in the habit of employing. By this clause, the importation into Great Britain of goods bearing marks in the English language was prohibited unless the name of the country of origin was distinctly added thereto. Thenceforward, Regout's mark was changed to that shown in Figure 20, second mark from left.

In 1899 the firm's organization was further changed into that of a public limited company under the name of *N. V. Kristal-, Glas- en Aardewerkfabrieken De Sfinx, v.h. Petrus Regout & Cie.* But the previous mark was maintained until 1929, when, in consequence

Fig. 21 — "ORIENT" (*c. 1883*)
From the collection of Miss H. Hudig

of the new Netherlands law on limited companies, it was changed to that shown second from the right, Figure 20.

It must be borne in mind, however, that, before this date, old marks may have been used for a long time following changes in the firm, since a mark, once applied to a certain type of article, cannot conveniently be altered. The collector may, therefore, be warned that neither marks nor decorations form an absolutely reliable guide in determining dates. Only the combination of these characteristics may lead to a safe decision.

To avoid confusion, it is imperative, in concluding these notes about the Regout factory and its products, to make some mention, likewise, of two other factories operating in Maastricht, which, to some extent, produced similar ware.

In 1850, according to particulars kindly supplied by the archivist J. Blonden, pottery works were established at Wijk

near Maastricht by N. A. Bosch. This factory was, however, closed down in 1866. During its short term of existence it accomplished excellent work. N. A. Bosch followed P. Regout's example in making ware after the English style. The plate shown in Figure 18 illustrates the elaborate designs employed. A scene from a harem, in light blue, is presented in a frame consisting of other scenes set among carefully composed ornaments on a pseudo-powder-blue ground.

It bears the mark   N. A. BOSCH.
                    SYRIAN

The material is light but somewhat rough to the touch.

The design for the second plate here illustrated (*Fig. 15*), to judge by the dress, dates from about 1855. With particular care, the engraving has been printed in violet on the cream-colored ground. The material is light; the glaze somewhat crackled. The mark is in the Netherlands language. Next to it the impress N. A. BOSCH, MAASTRICHT appears.

A third earthenware factory was established, about 1845, at Maastricht. Until 1859, it belonged to Messrs. W. N. Clermont and Ch. Chainaye. Then it was taken over by the private company, G. Lambert & Cie. In 1863 a limited liability company was established to carry on the business under the title *Société Céramique*. For its mark, an English shape was again chosen (*Fig. 20, extreme right*). It resembles the form used by Adams of Tunstall from 1804 until 1840, and the various marks adopted in 1833 by Copeland and Garrett of Stoke-upon-Trent. After 1887 the words MADE IN HOLLAND were added to the mark.

The product must have been similar to that of the two other factories. According to the statement of the management, the first work was produced by hand on the potter's wheel, printed in a single color, and, on occasion, colored by hand. Later on, mechanical motive power was introduced for the potter's wheel and decoration was applied by the *Dekalkomania* method. At the end of the nineteenth century, casting into molds was begun, and painting by means of paint squirts and stencils. Then the factory produced gaily colored peasant earthenware, which, for a time, was popular for country dwellings. Here is shown a plate (*Fig. 19*), black printed, belonging to a series of caricatures put on the market about 1890.

I am convinced of the incompleteness of these notes, but as a first attempt to delve in a hitherto untouched domain of research they may serve as a guide for further investigation.

II German Porcelain

Although there were early and rather limited experiments in other countries prior to the 18th century, it is common knowledge that European porcelain was first developed commercially at Meissen in Germany in 1710. The story of Böttger is well known, but it is a common error to assume that all Meissen products followed the styles laid down by Böttger and others during the first years of the factory's existence. In fact, Meissen styles are very varied and show a mixture of both Western and Eastern influences. The articles on Meissen reveal an extraordinarily wide range of styles, drawing extensively from Chinese, Japanese, European Baroque, metalwork, naturalist, and even contemporary faïence sources. They also show that within 20 years of its founding, the Meissen factory had developed the full range of its versatility, despite the total novelty of the porcelain material itself. The technical skill of Böttger, combined with the artistry of Herold or Kändler, ensured that the Meissen factory was able to achieve levels of artistic and technical excellence that have never really been bettered. Subsequent makers or decorators of porcelain have merely had to feel satisfied if they could attain the same level.

It would be both incorrect and unjust, however, to see Meissen as a unique achievement. The knowledge, the skills, the styles and the artists themselves spread rapidly from Meissen to other factories, encouraged by the extravagant offers made by rival courts and princes. Nymphenburg, Höchst, Furstenberg, Ludwigsburg, Frankenthal, and Berlin, among others, have all added something distinctive to the development of European porcelain. That, like Meissen itself, many of these factories have managed to survive until today has given added interest to the story. However, it is curious that, almost without exception, they produced wares during their early years that have never really been matched. The figures modeled at Nymphenburg by F.A. Bustelli are, for example, quite without equal within the field of figure modeling in ceramics. There is, in fact, always the danger that the fame of Meissen will overshadow other German factories and therefore make it impossible to assess their products with any degree of dispassion. Frankenthal is a good example of this process. The products show the same quality and the same interesting mixture of Eastern and Western decorative elements as those made at Meissen, and yet they are rarely considered in the same league. Such a judgement is, of course, both misleading and harmful, for all these factories show in their early products both high quality and a range of decorative detail that has never been bettered.

It is perhaps dangerous, however, to see the story of German porcelain as the story of a series of quite separate factories. First, the factories themselves were closely interrelated on both technical and artistic levels, and second, they were all involved equally in the expression of contemporary trends in style and decoration. To see any one factory, or even any one artist in isolation, therefore, is to misunderstand the broad pattern of artistic development during the 18th century. All the porcelain makers and decorators were totally dependent upon the styles that surrounded them, and it is therefore more relevant to study the history of a style rather than the story of a particular factory or individual. The last article in this section makes this point particularly and shows that styles can not only cross factory walls, but also national boundaries; they should therefore be seen as part of a far wider European movement and not be forced into the narrow straight jacket imposed by the limitations of porcelain manufacture and decoration.

MEISSEN
PORCELAIN

By W. B. HONEY

All illustrations, except Figure 9, are in the collections of the Victoria and Albert Museum.

FIG. 1 — TEAPOT (*c. 1715*). Böttger's red stoneware, with polished decoration.

IT IS NOT AT ALL UNUSUAL to hear the porcelain of Meissen spoken of as if it were all pretty much alike, guaranteed, so to speak, by the famous crossed-swords mark. Yet the great Saxon factory has existed for more than two hundred years — from 1710 until the present day. Many fashions have come and gone during that time, not all of them favorable to the art of porcelain, while the fortunes of the factory have varied from the greatest prosperity to a miserable following of other factories' styles and a wholesale revival of its own. It will be worth while, therefore, to define the period of the factory's best work and to describe some of its greatest artistic achievements, distinguishing them from the superficially similar work done later, both in the Meissen factory itself and elsewhere.

The great period belongs wholly to that time in the eighteenth century when porcelain was the subject of excited admiration in Europe. It was then hardly thought of as pottery at all, but as a semi-precious substance of mysterious origin. Porcelain

FIG. 2 — CUP AND SAUCER (*c. 1715-1720*). Böttger's white porcelain, applied decoration.

had been newly brought from China in quantity by the Dutch East India Company in the seventeenth century and before long was being widely imitated in Europe. But only superficial imitations in delftware and soft paste had been made before the early years of the eighteenth century, when Johann Friedrich Böttger made his great discovery.

Böttger was an alchemist working at Dresden in the service of Augustus the Strong, Elector of Saxony and King of Poland, and with his fellow-worker Ehrenfried Walther von Tschirnhausen, about 1708-1709 hit upon the right principle and materials for making a true hard-paste porcelain of Chinese type. As a result the great factory was founded at Meissen in 1710. Just before Böttger's death in 1719, runaway workmen managed to start two small rival concerns (at Vienna and Venice), but from this time onward the Meissen secret was so well guarded that there was no serious rival factory for nearly forty years after the invention. Meissen kept its technical and creative lead in the world of German, and indeed all European, porcelain until the disaster of the Seven Years' War *(1756-1763)*.

Saxony was then overrun by Frederick the Great and his Prussians, and the Meissen premises were occupied. The European leadership passed to the French national factory at Sèvres, while Frederick's new Berlin factory aspired to supremacy in Germany. But it was in each case a barren lead, for porcelain by the last quarter of the eighteenth century had lost much of its novelty and glamor.

The world-wide neo-classical fashions of the late eighteenth century called for a new medium. This was found eventually in the unglazed jasper, basalt, and other stonewares made by Josiah Wedgwood in England, and at Sèvres and elsewhere in biscuit porcelain, which renounced the special charm of the porcelain

FIG. 3 — TRAY (*1725-1730*). With Japanese (Kakiemon) decoration.

FIG. 4 — PART OF TEA SERVICE (c. 1730-1735). Painted by A. F. von Löwenfinck.

material in a vain imitation of marble. The neo-classical was in fact distinctly unfavorable to porcelain; its antique seriousness and symmetry were at war with the frivolity and "modern fancies" of the essentially rococo porcelain.

The period of supreme achievement at Meissen thus dates from 1710 to 1756. It covers the periods of the late baroque with its often hard symmetry, and of the lighter asymmetrical rococo. The Seven Years' War was a blank for the factory, apart from the work done for Frederick, and from 1763 on it was either breathlessly trying, but without much success, to catch up with the French fashions, or lifelessly repeating its former successes. It sank to nothing in the time of the Napoleonic Wars, being occupied again by the invaders. An attempted revival in the later nineteenth century brought some prosperity again.

FIG. 5 — VASE (c. 1725). Marked A R.

But it was a dubious success; for thèn were made the copies of eighteenth-century models which the inexperienced collector of today often mistakes for old.

To describe even a tenth of the wares produced in the great time is plainly impossible within the limits of an article. All that can be done here is to indicate within the framework of a broad classification the general characters in coloring, design, and figure modeling of the outstanding types.

Earliest of all are the wares of the period named after the inventor himself, from the foundation of the factory in 1710 until his death in 1719. Böttger as an alchemist had sought to make porcelain by way of artificial semi-precious stones, and the first result of his research was an intensely hard red stoneware resembling porphyry and jasper. It was in fact so hard that it could be cut and polished on the lapidary's or glass-engraver's wheel (Fig. 1). Böttger's stoneware is indeed one of the most thrilling of all ceramic materials.

Böttger's white porcelain is of a smoky-toned or creamy color; the unfired paste was evidently exceptionally plastic, and could be finely wrought into characteristic applied decoration (Fig. 2). Silver shapes were favored as befitting so precious a substance. Böttger porcelain is usually found plain white, and the painting if any is in imperfect enamels, obviously experimental and excitingly primitive.

Next comes the period of greatest achievement of the first Meissen manager of genius — the color-chemist and painter-designer Johann Gregor Herold. This corresponds with the last ten years or so (1720-1733) of the reign of Augustus the Strong, founder of the factory. The porcelain at first was, as before, faintly smoky or creamy in tone, but before long was

FIG. 6 (center, below) — TEAPOT (c. 1730-1735). From a tea service painted in red monochrome and gold by C. F. Herold.

FIG. 7 (below) — SNUFFBOXES. Left, painted by C. F. Herold (c. 1735); right, dates from about 1760.

FIG. 8 *(right)* — FIGURE *(c. 1733)*. Probably modeled by Gottlob Kirchner.

made a brilliant, glittering, pure white. The period saw Herold's invention of his famous fantastic *chinoiseries,* or pseudo-Chinese scenes, usually framed in profuse scrollwork in red, gold, and luster *(Fig. 18)*, as well as many adaptations actually from Chinese (early *famille rose*), Japanese *(Kakiemon)* *(Fig. 3)*, and other Oriental wares. Developed from the Kakiemon type was the exceedingly beautiful work of Adam Friedrich von Löwenfinck *(Fig. 4)*, who was perhaps the most gifted of all porcelain painters. Gift tankards, often mounted in Augsburg silver, received some of the finest painting, which was occasionally by Herold's own hand *(Fig. 18)*. It was the period above all of the great vases *(Fig. 5)* made for the king and marked with his initials *A R* in monogram (for *Augustus Rex*). About 1730 appeared the first of the famous Meissen harbor scenes, at first "Chinese," then European, painted notably by the manager's own kinsman, Christian Friedrich Herold *(Figs. 6 and 7)*. Superb colored grounds — yellow, red, green, and turquoise or "sea green" — were mastered as early as 1727. The typical coloring of the period was full-toned and inclined to be hard, in the baroque manner. Powerful red, yellow, blue, and black were dominant for twenty years or more. Red and black monochrome painting, with lavish gilding, and a sonorous discord of

FIG. 9 *(right)* — "CALLOT" FIGURE *(c. 1720-1725)*. Made after a Dutch print. Painted later at Augsburg. *From the collection of Otto Blohm.*

FIG. 10 *(below)* — GROUP OF LOVERS *(c. 1740)*. From a model by J. J. Kaendler.

red and rose purple were typical colors of the baroque.

Figure modeling in the 1720's and 1730's was relatively unimportant, but included, on the one hand, some small, often grotesque, models in the style of carved ivories *(Fig. 9)*; and on the other the life-size figures of animals and birds made as a sort of *tour de force* to the order of Augustus the Strong for the furnishing of his Japanese Palace. These last were the work of the sculptor Gottlob Kirchner, who was at the factory between 1727 and 1733, and of J. J. Kaendler (1731 onward), who eventually created the typical Meissen figure. The Japanese Palace animals are seldom found in the antique trade, but the smaller models attributable to Kirchner *(Fig. 8)*, including some fountains and basins and elaborate clocks, are among the most-sought-after rarities.

The next period, from 1733, might well be named after Kaendler, though Herold was still active, but it was above all the taste of the director, Count Heinrich von Brühl, minister of Augustus III, which largely determined the styles adopted. The factory turned more and more to figure modeling. At first inclining to the monumental, the figures eventually took the form of table decorations, for display in series, such as allegories, folk types, satirical groups, and characters from the Italian Comedy *(Fig. 11 and Cover)*. These were modeled with superb vigor by Kaendler and his assistants J. F. Eberlein and Peter Reinicke, whose work is scarcely distinguishable. This was the period of the famous crinoline figures and groups *(Fig. 12)*. The coloring was dominated by the usual strong red, yellow, and black of the baroque, changing to softer tones of mauve, green, and pale yellow with the coming of the rococo style toward 1750.

The modeling in the earlier style was powerfully rhythmical, at times even heavy and almost brutal in sentiment, with a kind of "ugly" beauty which is

FIG. 12 *(below)* — "CRINOLINE" FIGURE *(c. 1744)*. From a model by J. J. Kaendler.

FIG. 11 *(below)* — SATIRICAL GROUP *(c. 1755)*. From a model by J. J. Kaendler.

Fig. 13 (*far left*) — Jug (*1740-1745*). Painted with *deutsche Blumen*.

Fig. 14 (*left*) — Dish (*c. 1740*). Painted with pastoral scene.

this, of course, lies outside the scope of this article.

The collector's task is therefore to distinguish the productions of the greatest period, lying between 1710 and 1756. First, as to marks. Until 1723 no factory mark was added to the porcelain, but the table wares of the early 1720's sometimes show an unexplained nick near the foot ring known in Germany as the *Dallwitzer Nagel*, after a collector of that name who first called attention to the feature. The marks added to the ware from 1723 on give some help, but need to be interpreted with caution. The first of these, *KPM* (Königliche Porzellan Manufaktur) dates from a year or two about 1723-1724, as does an imitation Chinese mark resembling the snake-entwined staff of Mercury. Both marks are comparatively rare. Then the famous crossed swords, from the arms of Saxony, were introduced and have remained the regular factory mark from 1724 to the present day. A dot

very characteristic. In the rococo style, toward 1750 and later, a lighter movement prevailed, and scrolled bases (*Fig. 11*) replaced the earlier pedestals and simple mounds. A new modeler in the rococo period was Friedrich Elias Meyer, whose slender elegant figures are distinct from those of his master Kaendler.

In this period Kaendler also introduced on table wares the low-relief borders in the style of silver, which set a universal fashion that is still current, while for Count Brühl he created the famous swan service, as well as others, with elaborately modeled decoration.

The painting on vases and table wares included a novelty in naturalistic "botanical" flowers (called "deutsche Blumen" to distinguish them from the earlier Oriental flowers), at first painted with a clean precision (*Fig. 13*), which later softened and eventually lapsed into mannerism and insignificance. At the same time a new influence came from the stock of French prints sent to the factory about this time by Brühl's librarian. This was shown in the painting of Watteau subjects and pastoral scenes (*Fig. 14*), as well as in fantastic rococo scrollwork (*Fig. 15*).

During the Seven Years' War the notable work done for Frederick chiefly comprised snuffboxes (*Fig. 7, right*), for which he had a well-known passion, and huge services ordered for his generals and friends (*Fig. 16*).

After the War, pictorial painting inspired by Sèvres and neo-classical sentiment in the French manner marked the so-called "Academic Period" (*1763-1794*), when the Saxon court painter and leader of the Dresden Academy C. W. E. Dietrich was adviser to the factory, and the same tendency was continued under the management of Count Marcolini (*1744-1814*). Though some good and accomplished work was done in both periods and later, the inspiration and vitality of the earlier time had obviously departed. Excellent work has been done at Meissen in recent years, especially in figure modeling, but

Fig. 15 (*above*) — Tableware (*c. 1740-1750*). Decorated with fantastic scrollwork.

Fig. 16 (*below*) — Pieces from a service made for General Möllendorff to the order of Frederick the Great (*c. 1761*).

between the hilts indicates a date in the "academic Period" for the manufacture of the ware (but much defective ware made earlier was decorated in that period, when the factory needed funds). A star between or below the hilts indicates the "Marcolini Period"; but a star sometimes appeared in the mark on the early and usually unimportant blue-painted porcelain of the 1720's. Between 1814 and 1924 the plain crossed swords were used again. Since 1924 a dot has been added between the points. The most famous of all the marks of the great period, and one most outrageously abused by forgers, is the *Augustus Rex* monogram already mentioned; it usually indicates a date between 1725 and 1730, but was occasionally used later. Besides these marks, there are often, on early wares, gold letters and numerals of uncertain significance, and incised and impressed mold numbers which began to be regularly used not earlier than 1763, when an inventory was made.

But the mark on the ware (since it is in underglaze blue) can only give the date of making of the actual porcelain, which may have been decorated much later. This was often the case indeed with the painting done outside the factory. This *Hausmalerei,* as it is called, is of great interest but is too big a subject to be dealt with here. One much-disputed class alone must be mentioned, with decoration often in gilding only, of *chinoiseries* distinct from Herold's *(Fig. 17)*. This was formerly mistaken for factory work but is now known to have been done in Augsburg about 1725-1735 on porcelain dating from the 1720's. These Augsburg-decorated pieces sometimes bear pale red "luster" marks, usually initial letters. The *Hausmaler* using Meissen porcelain were as a rule unable to secure any but outmoded and defective ware, and even that was obtained only surreptitiously. Eventually (about 1760) to protect itself against loss of repute due to incompetent decorators, the factory began to "cancel" the mark on defective ware sold "in the white," by one or more cuts made on the glass-engraver's wheel. Such a canceled mark indicates that the piece was not decorated at the Meissen factory itself.

Other marks are sometimes mistaken for the Meissen swords. Some of these are eighteenth-century marks of other factories, intentionally written to resemble that of their famous rival. Such are the crossed swords and three dots of Weesp, the crossed L's of Limbach, the crossed hay-forks of Rudolstadt, and the crossed torches of the Paris factory of La Courtille. The *W* of Wallendorf and even the *C V* of Kloster Veilsdorf were sometimes made to resemble the swords. In modern times various devices of crossed swords or strokes occur alone, or with *D*, or *H*, or *T* (for Carl Thimve of Potschappel near Dresden), or *S* on French forgeries. Marks with the word *Dresden* or a crowned *D* are of course never Meissen marks but are quite often those of modern decorators, such as Wolfsohn. As already mentioned, the *A R* mark occurs absurdly on modern cups and saucers with colored grounds in panels alternat-

ing with "Watteau scenes" and the like.

But far more important for the collector is a knowledge of period peculiarities and a sense of style. These can only be acquired by familiarity with genuine specimens. A few points of detail may, however, be useful. First of all, it must be insisted that the type of decoration or the date of the model does not necessarily indicate the period in which a given specimen was made; it may be made from the original molds at any later time. Some aspect of color or style will, however, generally be found to give away its later date. As to color, the characteristic strong red, yellow, blue, and black of the baroque style, and the paler colors of the rococo have been mentioned already. The soft browns and pinks and pale and bright blues of the period after 1760 may also be noted. All are distinguishable from the pale, sickly pink and pale blue and yellowish green pervading the figures of the nineteenth-century revival of eighteenth-century models. The form of base also varies with the period. The nineteenth- and twentieth-century revivals are commonly on circular or oval pedestals with classical ovolo and other patterns on the edges. The applied flowers are more elaborate, and naturalistic and frilly lace-work has sometimes been added.

None of these criteria can, however, be regarded as infallible "rules of thumb," and a specimen may be right in almost all the respects mentioned and yet be a forgery. Greater reliance must be placed on a sense of the right sort of vitality in modeling and painting. This is hard to define, but as an illustration I give here *(Fig. 19)* for comparison with the masterpiece shown in Figure 18, a passage of decoration believed to be the work of one of the most skillful of modern forgers — one who studied very closely in the Dresden Royal Collection. Excellent and true in color though the painting is, there is a lax and flaccid quality in the brushwork, an insincerity it may almost be called, as well as a certain modern sentiment and grace, which must accuse it at once in the eyes of the discerning.

FIG. 17 *(above)* — CUP AND SAUCER *(c. 1720)*. Decorated at Augsburg about 1730-1735, in *chinoiseries* distinct from Herold's.

FIG. 18 *(left)* — TANKARD. Mounted in Augsburg silver. Perhaps painted by J. G. Herold, about 1725.

FIG. 19 *(below)* — MODERN PAINTING in imitation of Herold's *chinoiseries.*

BY ILSE BISCHOFF

Adding to a Meissen collection

WHEN I BEGAN collecting German eighteenth-century porcelain I coveted every piece I saw in a shopwindow. I had no standards of perfection. I was delighted if I could spot an example from the eighteenth century and not slip into the nineteenth. So at the start my collection represented a wide range of objects, factories, and periods.

Eventually my taste changed and my preference narrowed to the work of Meissen, Höchst, and Nymphenburg. But it was predominantly Meissen that I sought, for three reasons: It was the first European hard paste; more pieces were available; and the ware was beautiful, varied, and rich in figures and dishes. Except in rare instances I did not want examples that were made after 1745, the beginning of the decline of Meissen. For Nymphenburg and Höchst I could set a later date, as the height of their achievements was reached after 1750.

It was fortunate for the quality of the collection that prices suddenly became staggering and I could no longer afford to buy in quantity. I had to be satisfied with one or two good pieces a year instead of a dozen. I tried to heed the advice of the dealer who told me every piece I bought must supersede the last in quality or rarity, that a small excellent collection was preferable to a larger one of lower standards.

There are many ways of forming a collection. One is to rely on a dealer in whom one has implicit faith and follow his advice exclusively. Another is to buy at auction—though the hysteria which is apt to overcome one may raise the price of a desired object. By far the greatest fun is to prowl in shops both here and abroad and occasionally find an unexpected treasure. My collection has become international, not only in the sense that it is of German porcelain with a smattering of English and French pieces, but also in that it has been acquired all the way from the boot of Italy across France and Germany to Bond Street. Each piece purchased in a foreign country has the delight of a memory—of a flight of stairs to a dark little shop, of a companion who shared my enthusiasm, of a dealer who was wise, and a distant city.

In ANTIQUES for June 1953 (p. 512) I told of the beginnings of my collection and illustrated some of my initial prizes. In the thirteen years since then I have acquired only a dozen pieces, but they are eminently satisfactory.

The earliest (Fig. 1) is a white Böttger tankard with raised flowers and silver-gilt cover and base rim, made, I believe, about 1723. It found its way into my hands from a small shop in Lucerne and I remember my excitement as I carried off my treasure in a downpour which completely obliterated the lake.

The Meissen cockatoo by J. J. Kändler (Fig. 2) was made about 1734, during the great modeler's period of large-bird production. When it appeared in the Viennese market an American dealer flew to Austria and personally conducted it to New York. The bird is extraordinary; he measures just under fourteen inches high and is beautiful in form and color. His body is white; head feathers are

Fig. 1. White Böttger tankard with raised flowers, silver-gilt cover and base rim; Meissen, c. 1723. *All illustrations are from the author's collection.*

Fig. 2. Meissen cockatoo by J. J. Kändler, c. 1734.

Fig. 3. Meissen figure of Pantaloon by Kändler, c. 1741.

Fig. 4. Pair of incense burners in the form of Chinese figures, Meissen, modeled by J. F. Eberlein, c. 1735.

purple, red, and turquoise, while his tail and back feathers gleam with the additional brilliance of blue, green, and yellow. His head is cocked, his beak open, his eyes pop as if he has just sighted his prey and is about to pounce on it; his vicious claws clutch the trunk of a tree gaily decorated with mushrooms and flowers. In the Rijksmuseum in Amsterdam there is a similar cockatoo, though painted in different brilliant colors, and I have been told there is another example in the Hermitage in Leningrad.

To the Meissen figures I added a rare Kändler Pantaloon (Fig. 3) of about 1741, a model more often seen in a group than singly. He stoops, with hands hidden in back beneath his cloak. His breeches and blouse are deep orange, his pointed slippers yellow.

The Chinese figures (Fig. 4) modeled for Meissen by J. F. Eberlein in 1735 are incense burners. Their garments are painted in a fine allover pattern of burnt orange; sleeves and necklines are edged with purple, sashes are yellow, the cocky hats are black. The woman beams at her pet orange, yellow, and green parrot while her mustachioed partner tempts a grimacing monkey with a morsel of food. The mouths of all the figures are open to permit the escape of incense. There is a pair of figures from the same models in the Irwin Untermyer collection (Hackenbroch, Figure 25) but with entirely different coloring from that of my pair; they differ too in that the cushion on which the man is seated does not have tassels and the parrot is perched at a different angle. Such minor variations in similar figures provide one of the delights of collecting.

One of my most enchanting acquisitions is *The Impetuous Lover* (Fig. 5) by Franz Anton Bustelli, made for Nymphenburg between the years 1754 and 1763. It consists of a young man kneeling before a half-reclining young woman who protests the passionate eagerness of her lover while Amor takes active part by perching on his back and pulling his hair. She wears a white dress with a yellow scarf carelessly tossed over one shoulder. Her colors are a perfect foil for the lavender of the youth's

stume. Both figures are modeled with Bustelli's cus-
mary excellence and elegance in the faces, hands, and
e rococo twist of the bodies. There is an example of
e same group in the Bavarian National Museum in
unich, with slight variation in the tree trunk and differ-
ces in the painted colors.

To the tableware in my collection I have added a silver-
pped Meissen tankard (Fig. 6) painted by Adam Fried-
ch von Löwenfinck, about 1735. The scene consists of
hinese figures beside a wine barrel; one is drinking,
other fills his cup from a very sophisticated golden
igot, still another strums a musical instrument. The
mposition is flanked by brilliant Indian flowers. The
lors are rich, as always in Löwenfinck's work, ranging
om an intense forest green to deep orange, blue, purple,
d yellow, with the usual outlining of folds and figures
delicate gold.

Four covered bowls with saucers (Figs. 7-10) cover the
an of years from 1725 to 1735 and show great differ-
ces in both shape and decoration. The Germans call a
all tureen of this kind *Wochenschüssel* because it was
ed to serve the first soup to the mother of a newborn
by. Some are plain, others are elaborately decorated.
Figure 7, the earliest, is meticulously painted with
inoiserie figures at play and at work; the colors are
urple, blue, red, and gold, with touches of the light
een so often found in early Meissen. Figure 8, of about
28, is painted in blue, turquoise, red, and yellow
eightened with gold. The decoration consists chiefly
Indian flowers; the diapering of the border on plate
d bowl was inspired either by the Chinese or possibly
y Du Paquier of Vienna. A bright-eyed squirrel, crouch-
g, forms the handle of the cover. Figure 9, more bul-
ous and less delicate, is nevertheless a handsome ex-
mple and dates from about 1730. Harbor scenes are
rongly painted on the saucer and on the bowl; on the
ver peasants move lazily along the edge of a river, and
ldiers rest and converse. The cartouches framing these
enes are purple and gold, as fine as lace. Figure 10,

my latest acquisition, resembles several examples in the
Bavarian National Museum which have ornate gilded
patterns with figures and were evidently intended for
mothers in patrician and wealthy families. Extraordinary
in quality and color, it dates between about 1730 and
1735; the fine painting of flowers and the sinister black
birds in the brilliant foliage may have been painted by
Johann Ehrenfried Stadler, or perhaps more likely by
Löwenfinck.

Figures 7 and 9 were bought *in absentia* at an auction
in Munich, to which I had not dared go after an inspection because of my habit of overbidding myself, while
Figure 8 brings back the memory of a shop in the Fau-
bourg St. Honoré which was rich in porcelains of many
nations. I found Figure 10 on my latest trip to Europe.

As I was idling along Madison Avenue one day a slim-
necked bottle (Fig. 11) in a glass case in the interior of
a shop caught my eye. To my delight I found that it
was early Meissen identified by a Johanneum mark,
N 338 W, indicating that it came from the royal porcelain
collection at Dresden. It is white, sparsely decorated with
small flowers and insects in the Kakiemon manner; on one

Fig. 5. *The Impetuous Lover,*
Nymphenburg figure group by Franz Anton Bustelli,
1754-1763. Ex coll. *Von Pannwitz.*

Fig. 6. Meissen silver-mounted tankard
with painted decoration
by A. F. von Löwenfinck, c. 1735.

Fig. 7. Meissen covered bowl with saucer, c. 1725.

Fig. 8. Meissen covered bowl with saucer, c. 1728.

Fig. 9. Meissen covered bowl with saucer, c. 1730.

Fig. 10. Meissen covered bowl with saucer, c. 1730-1735.

side of the round body a Japanese man huddles his arms in his sleeves, and on the other a playful tiger, with gold mane and gold on his twisted tail, spews golden fire from his mouth.

The painting on Figure 12, attributed to F. J. Ferner, probably dates from the late 1740's, but the bowl itself with underglaze blue and gold decoration is of a much earlier time and was probably sold outside the Meissen factory because its shape is imperfect. The unusual colors of the painting—burnt orange, brown, and green—suggest Ferner's work. The idyllic scene on the inside of the bowl shows a man strumming an instrument while his lady seems about to break into a dance; between them are trees, a sheep, a dog, and in the background rises a castle with a turret. The charm of the piece warrants its presence among earlier examples of Meissen.

While I no longer collect in quantity, I still hope and expect to add a fine piece from time to time, at a price within my reach. The porcelain lover can take heart, go to shops and auctions, and know that good examples appear and reappear in a flourishing and changing market.

Fig. 11. Meissen bottle with Johanneum mark, c. 1730-1735.

Fig. 12. Meissen bowl with underglaze blue, early 1720's; overglaze painted decoration attributed to F. J. Ferner, late 1740's.

German porcelain factorie

Columbine,
Italian Comedy figure
by F. A. Bustelli,
Nymphenburg (c. 1760).
Schlossmuseum, Berlin.

Coffeepot,
Nymphenburg (c. 1765).
*Museum für Kunst
und Gewerbe, Hamburg.*

MANY OF TODAY'S COLLECTORS are showing increased interest in a number of German porcelain factories which competed successfully with Meissen and Vienna in the second half of the eighteenth century. Individually and collectively these factories made outstanding contributions to the porcelain art, and their products are apt to be more available, less expensive, and in some respects more interesting than those of the two great factories which have so long dominated the field.

The first of these later factories was established, with royal patronage, at Höchst in 1746. Its brief period of greatness was from 1767 to 1779, when the modeling of the young sculptor Johann Peter Melchior won popular acclaim. Melchior's figures and groups are warm, animated, and often sentimental. They include religious subjects, children, pastoral and harvest scenes, and mythological characters supported on grassy mounds or moss-covered rock bases. The early figures were painted primarily in light pink and blue with spotted and striped patterns, while the later products were decorated in darker colors. Like the other old factories Höchst made attractive tableware and other useful articles, but they

May, 1954

were overshadowed by Melchior's figures. After fifty years of operation the factory closed in 1796.

The Nymphenburg factory, famous for the figures and groups modeled by Franz Anton Bustelli between 1754 and 1763, was founded near Munich in 1747 under the protection of the Bavarian Elector Maximilian III. Bustelli's best-known works include characters from the Italian Comedy, coquettish ladies in crinoline and native costume, gay gentlemen, busts of leading personalities, children, and groups of peasants and Asiatic peoples—all supported in the most delicate and graceful manner on characteristically flat thin bases. The useful porcelain of the early period of Nymphenburg (1755-1763) is of admirably fine quality, but it was so outshone by the fantastic figures of Bustelli that it never received the recognition it deserved. It includes a great variety of tableware and services, snuffboxes, and other household items, sensitively decorated in rococo style with ornamental flowers, fruits, birds, figures, and landscapes predominating. The factory is still operating in the Nymphenburg Palace grounds of Munich, and is one of modern Germany's outstanding enterprises.

The accompanying chart showing the principal factory marks was prepared with the assistance of German ceramics experts and collectors, and represents the most prominent existing German porcelain marks. Generally speaking, porcelain pieces of eighteenth-century German factories are characteristically marked in blue under the glaze. The marks may vary somewhat in size and shape within a single factory, since they were hand drawn. The old factories exercised caution in preserving their distinguishing marks along with their artistic reputations, but experienced collectors realize that there are many forgeries and imitations. They also realize that identification rests not only on the mark but also on the paste, glaze, form, and decoration.

The Frightened Children, by J. P. Melchior, Höchst (c. 1770). *Museum für Kunsthandwerk, Frankfurt.*

Potpourri vase, Fürstenberg (c. 1760).
Schlossmuseum, Berlin.

Above. Dish painted after Johann
Esajas Nilson's *Peacetime Gladness*,
Frankenthal (c. 1765). *Museum für
Kunst und Gewerbe, Hamburg.*

Left. Plate with landscape decoration
and osier relief border,
Ludwigsburg (c. 1770).
Author's collection.

Masked teapot in rococo design,
Ansbach (c. 1765).
Adolf Bayer, Ansbach.

Tea service for two, Berlin, KPM (c. 1770). *Thiers collection; photograph courtesy of the Louvre Museum, Paris.*

Karl I, Duke of Brunswick, who was envious of the other royal porcelain factories, founded one at Fürstenberg in 1747 mainly to satisfy his own vanity. Johann Simon Feilner (1753-1768) is the best known of the Fürstenberg modelers, but his productions do not compare with those of Meissen's Kändler, Nymphenburg's Bustelli, or Höchst's Melchior. Fürstenberg is known for its vases and useful porcelain in the neoclassic style, produced between 1760 and 1790. The factory passed into private hands in the middle of the nineteenth century and is still operating.

From 1751 to 1757 a cloth manufacturer named Wegely operated a factory in Berlin with the support of the Prussian king, Frederick the Great. He was unsuccessful, and another factory was opened here by Johann Ernst Gotzkowsky in 1761. King Frederick's chief ambition was to make Berlin porcelain equal to or better than Meissen, so when Gotzkowsky too ran into financial difficulties, in 1763, Frederick bought the factory and continued it as a royal enterprise under the name of Berlin or KPM (*Königliche Porzellan Manufaktur*). Although Frederick was able to force artists from Meissen and other factories to work for him, he never achieved the superlative, and the art of his factory declined after his death in 1786. The figures modeled by the brothers Friedrich Elias and Wilhelm Christian Meyer (1766-1783) are interesting and attractive, but Berlin's fame is associated with its useful wares, especially its dinner services. The factory has operated continuously to date, but since the destruction of the Berlin plant during the war its principal production has been carried on in Selb, Bavaria—the center of Germany's present-day porcelain industry.

The Frankenthal factory was established in the town of that name near Mannheim in 1755 by Paul Anton Hannong with the permission of Elector Karl Theodor, who bought the enterprise in 1762. The factory, which closed in 1799, is best known for figures and groups modeled by Johann Wilhelm Lanz (1755-1761), Johann Friedrich Lück (1758-1764), and Karl Gottlieb Lück (1756-1775). Since the factory operated during the best of the rococo period, most of its pieces, both figures and useful wares, were excellently modeled and decorated, and the best items are eagerly sought by collectors.

Ludwigsburg, the last of the eight major German factories, had no real excuse for existence except to increase the magnificence of Karl Eugen, the luxury-loving Duke of Württemberg. It was founded in 1756. Although this factory's general production does not compare with that of Meissen, Nymphenburg, Frankenthal, or Höchst, miscellaneous items designed by Gottlieb Friedrich Riedel (1759-1779) and the figures of Johann Christian Wilhelm Beyer (1761-1767) are interesting and attractive. Ludwigsburg also produced a variety of tablewares and ornamental items in rococo style during its early years; elaborately decorated teapots, vases, urns, and three-legged coffeepots are typical, as are the *rocaille* ornaments in relief and the white osier (basket-weave) patterns characteristic of this charming period. Quality and production declined after the death of the duke in 1793, and the factory closed in 1824.

As the factories of Höchst and Frankenthal closed before 1800, and Ludwigsburg soon thereafter, original items from these establishments are of course antiques. However, old models of these factories, as well as of Vienna and some of the other enterprises (particularly

Group of musicians under a trellis,
Fulda (c. 1770).
Schlossmuseum, Berlin.

Meissen) which are still operating, are frequently copied and similarly marked by modern factories. With experience it is not difficult to distinguish the comparatively poor copies from the original masterpieces.

In addition to the factories discussed above at least twenty minor factories were established in German provinces during the last half of the eighteenth century. These include Ansbach (1758-1860), Kelsterbach (1761-1802), Ottweiler (1763-1775), Fulda (1765-1790), Kassel (1766-1788), and Gutenbrunn (1767-1775). Ansbach is particularly well known for its fine useful wares, and some of the figures Fulda produced during its brief operation are among those most sought after today. Most of the minor factories, like the major ones, bear the names of the cities in which they were established, and many of the marks are symbolic of home cities or royal patrons.

As a whole, the porcelain produced by the early German factories is colorful, extravagant, animated, and of considerable variety; but there are noticeable differences in the style, paste, form, and decoration of the products of the various enterprises. In some European countries life was concentrated around one court, but in Germany during the eighteenth century many small courts competed strenuously as centers of culture. This explains the great variety of porcelain produced—a variety great enough to attract and interest practically all collectors.

Allegorical group, *The Three Fates*, referring to the death of the infant son of Elector Carl Theodor, modeled by Konrad Linck (1773). *R. Thornton Wilson collection, Metropolitan Museum of Art.*

Candlestick with two lovers, Joseph-Adam Hannong period *(c. 1760). R. Thornton Wilson collection, Metropolitan Museum of Art.*

A note on Frankenthal

BY JOHN A. TOWNLEY

WHEN ONE THINKS of eighteenth-century German porcelain, one thinks of Meissen, and there the thinking often ends. It is unfortunate that the amazing range and excellence of Meissen's productions so overshadow the other German factories that they are given little or no consideration by American collectors. The beautiful products of Höchst, Berlin, Frankenthal, and Nymphenburg, to name a few, are too frequently relegated to the background.

If by some strange cataclysm the exquisite products of the Meissen factory prior to 1750 were destroyed, and the remembrance of them wiped out of men's minds, I believe we would have a situation in German porcelain analogous to that in English porcelain. We would then have half a dozen great factories vying for preference among collectors, with Meissen only one among several. Meissen's Kändler, then past his baroque prime and forced into an unwilling adherence to the rococo by changing taste, would have to compete on an even basis with Bustelli, the great exponent of rococo figure model-

ing at Nymphenburg, with Konrad Linck and Karl Lück at Frankenthal, Beyer at Ludwigsburg, Melchior at Höchst, the brothers Meyer at Berlin, and many others. And in the tablewares, which to my way of thinking are the more attractive and rewarding collector's items (not to mention considerably less expensive), Meissen would be equally hard pressed to establish a superiority.

It is not my desire to detract from Meissen's pinnacled reputation, for in my estimation the Meissen products of the period 1720-1750 stand as the supreme achievement of European ceramic art. I am merely trying to emphasize that there are other German factories whose productions merit serious consideration by the American collector of ceramics.

Such concentration on Meissen to the exclusion of the other factories is not true in Germany itself. In talking with German dealers and collectors, I concluded that while they are extremely proud and appreciative of Meissen, they are almost equally proud and appreciative of the other eighteenth-century factories. In fact, I got the

74

impression that many Germans feel the products of Frankenthal, for one, surpassed the contemporary products of Meissen.

The history of Frankenthal properly begins with Strasburg. Here in 1709 (the same year in which Böttger discovered the secret of making hard-paste porcelain and started Meissen on its brilliant history), the family Hannong founded a faience manufactory. In 1750 Paul Hannong, then proprietor of the establishment, acquired the secret of hard-paste porcelain from Joseph Jacob Ringler, the wandering arcanist from Vienna, who visited in turn Höchst, Strasburg, Nymphenburg, and Ludwigsburg.

In 1755, when the Vincennes manufactory (later moved to Sèvres) was granted a monopoly on porcelain manufacture in France, Paul Hannong was forced to move the porcelain part of his operation to Germany. He settled in Frankenthal and established a porcelain factory there, under a privilege from Carl Theodor, Elector Palatine, placing the factory under his son Charles-François Paul. The latter was succeeded by another son, Joseph-Adam, who operated the plant from 1759 to 1762.

In 1762 the factory, having fallen into debt, was purchased by Carl Theodor, who installed Adam Bergdoll as manager. Simon Feilner succeeded Bergdoll in 1775. The operation was acquired by the Von Recums in 1795 and ceased in 1799.

During the best period of Frankenthal's production (1755-1775) the porcelain was exceedingly fine in texture, milk-white in color, and beautifully decorated. The finest examples of Frankenthal porcelain will stand comparison with similar items produced at any other factory during the third quarter of the eighteenth century.

Cup and saucer of the Joseph-Adam Hannong period (1759-1762), with the lion and JAH marks, decorated with asymmetrical sprays of flowers in colors. *Author's collection.*

Pieces from a breakfast service (c. 1765-1770), with the C T mark (for the Elector Carl Theodor). Feathery gilt scrollwork frames a variety of country scenes in crimson-purple monochrome, depicting an old mill, a half-timbered mansion, barns, and sailing craft on the river. *Author's collection.*

Teapot and coffeepot dated *1774,* with C T mark. The floral decoration in colors is enhanced by the molding of the porcelain itself. *Author's collection.*

Some Oriental aspects of European ceramic decoration

Part II. Chinoiseries *in gold on German porcelain of the eighteenth century*

BY HANS SYZ, *Honorary fellow, division of ceramics and glass, Smithsonian Institution*

A previous article by Dr. Syz, published in ANTIQUES for May 1969 (p. 670), dealt with the general influence of Far Eastern designs upon the decoration of European ceramics. Here Dr. Syz discusses decorations showing Oriental motifs in gold on the products of German factories of the eighteenth century. A third article, to appear shortly, will cover this same type of decoration on the work of European factories other than the German. References throughout are to the publications of the authorities cited which are listed in the appended bibliography.

WHILE GOLD *chinoiseries* on early Meissen porcelain were produced (mainly at Augsburg) in considerable numbers, and are represented in many museums and collections, this type of decoration is relatively rare on porcelains from other European factories. After I had come across pieces of Frankenthal porcelain in this category, I began to collect examples from other ceramic centers, and in time had assembled a series of specimens that in addition to its aesthetic value demonstrates a variety of techniques employed in bringing about similar decorative effects.

Without having made a thorough study of designs in gold on seventeenth- and eighteenth-century Far Eastern porcelains, I can say at least that this type of decoration was not common in the East but it was occasionally used, as may be seen on a few large Chinese vases of the K'ang Hsi period (1662-1722) at the Victoria and Albert

Museum which show Oriental figural and landscape designs painted in gold on a powder-blue ground.

An especially rich assortment of Oriental gold decorations came to the awareness of the European public through the importation of lacquer work from China and Japan which, together with its European imitations, occupied a prominent place in the extension of the Chinese taste to practically all objects of the decorative arts in Europe. The real vogue for this type of decoration developed after the Portuguese and later the Dutch had established trade relations with the Far East, and imported a great deal of lacquer ware among a variety of other Oriental commodities. In these lacquer techniques Chinese decorations in gold on a black ground were the dominant theme, although other lacquer colors —red, brown, yellow, blue, and green—were also used, often in combination with gilding. The background at times was also in other colors, most frequently red (Holzhausen).

Fig. 1. Silver-mounted box in Mennecy soft-paste porcelain; diameter 3½ inches; c. 1735-1745. Decorated with two Chinese figures in raised and tooled gilding, enriched with green and red translucent enamels and set in a landscape painted on the glaze in polychrome enamels. *Collection of Lion Golodetz.*

Fig. 2. St. Cloud *cachepot* marked St-C/T incised; height 4 1/16 inches; c. 1730-1740. Decorated with raised gilding and green and red enamels in the same design as on the Mennecy box in Fig. 1, probably by the same hand. *Metropolitan Museum of Art.*

In ceramics, lacquer imitations are found in early Meissen stoneware of the Böttger period (1710-1720). Here the red-brown quality of the material, covered by a blackish glaze, provided a background closely akin to black lacquer. The early Meissen stoneware teapot of 1710-1715 (color plate, p. 99) gives an example of this type of ornamentation. The sitting Chinese figure, painted in gold combined with pale red and brown lacquer colors on the blackish brown glaze of the stoneware, suggests in its simplicity that it may have been copied from an Oriental prototype such as might have been found on one of the numerous Far Eastern porcelains in the collection of Augustus the Strong, owner of the Meissen factory. A monkey on the other side of this piece may be one of the first uses of this motif at Meissen. Monkeys and other small animals are frequently found in polychrome *chinoiseries* of about 1725-1735 as well as on Augsburg gold Chinese decorations on Meissen porcelain. Such animals may be seen in the engravings of Stalker and Parker. Although it is doubtful that their book, published in England in 1688, served specifically as inspiration for Oriental designs at Meissen, it was extensively used on the Continent as a guide for the art of lacquering, or "japanning," as well as for other applications of *chinoiserie* motifs. As Menzhausen recently pointed out, different types of lacquer painting occur on black-glazed Böttger stoneware. A style excelling in softly shaded designs and using especially blue and red can be attributed to Martin Schnell, who, employed from 1710 by Augustus the Strong of Saxony as court lacquerer, worked from about 1712 for a few years in the Meissen factory. Our teapot shows another style of decoration which must have been done by a lacquer painter whose name is not known.

That gold Chinese decoration was applied there at this early period is attested also by an entry of April 1710 found in the Meissen archives which gives notice that Böttger sent to Augustus red stoneware objects some of which were "decorated with Indian figures in gilt" (Rückert). It may be added that in German ceramic tradition the term *indianisch* was generally used for Far Eastern designs. Zimmerman (1) presented a variety of Böttger stoneware vessels decorated with these gold designs on black glaze, and more recently Rückert showed an attractive example of gold Chinese decoration heightened by lacquer colors, on an early Meissen stoneware teapot.

Toward the end of the eighteenth century gold *chinoiseries* on a black ground in the manner of lacquer decoration were used by other Continental porcelain factories, notably by Vienna of the Sorgenthal period and by Sèvres. Chinese gold decoration on a black ground is rare on Meissen porcelain, however. Examples of this unusual technique can be seen on a Meissen cup and saucer of the Margarete and Franz Oppenheim collection (Pazaurek, 2) and on two beaker vases of the Irwin Untermyer collection whose gilt painting is of such fine quality that Hackenbroch tends to attribute it to Johann Gregor Höroldt.

On early white Meissen porcelain we find essentially two types of gold decoration with Oriental motifs: a small number is ascribed to Christoph Konrad Hunger and a larger group mainly to craftsmen in Augsburg, which for centuries had been a center of gold- and silversmiths.

C. K. Hunger, a goldsmith and enameler, was a rather restless and unreliable but enterprising adventurer, actively engaged in the establishment of several ceramics factories. The dates of neither his birth nor his death are known, but he seems to have traveled in France and around 1715 appeared in Dresden, whence he was lured to Vienna in 1717 to join Claude Innocent du Paquier in the founding of the porcelain factory there. But he seems to have promised more than he could deliver, and from 1720 to 1724 he was in Venice lending a guiding hand to Francesco Vezzi in the first Italian undertaking that produced hard-paste porcelains. Later he reappeared in Dresden, where in 1727 he was appointed at the Meissen factory as "gold enameler" to succeed Johann Georg Funke. From there he traveled to Sweden, Denmark, and finally to St. Petersburg (1744-1748), where his attempts to produce porcelain led to only slim results terminating in his dismissal (Pazaurek, 1; Walcha; Seitler).

An example of Hunger's decorative technique is shown on a Meissen bowl signed by him and illustrated in color in Pazaurek (1). This bowl, dated about 1715, was probably decorated by Hunger outside the factory, as were a cup and saucer, previously assumed to be Meissen, to whose Oriental provenance Rückert has drawn attention. Hunger's decorative style consists of small Oriental figures, pagodas, flowering trees, birds, and insects applied in gold relief and often embellished by translucent enamels, mostly in red, green, and blue. Details on the raised gilding seem to have been worked in with a rather blunt tool. Other pieces of Meissen or Vienna porcelain with this decoration are, for instance, a teapot and a cup and saucer at the Metropolitan Museum of Art. An especially beautiful cup and saucer of the Vezzi factory at Venice, decorated in raised gold without enamels, has recently been published in color by Stazzi. On French soft-paste porcelain a similar technique was employed with green and red enamels, most often on small boxes, as may be seen at the Musée des Arts Décoratifs in Paris, or here in Figures 1 and 2. One wonders how this may relate to the rumor that Hunger traveled in France at an early age. Did he acquire there the technique he later applied, or was he in some way responsible for originating the French type of raised gilding? In France this is often applied in somewhat bolder strokes than is the case with the gold relief designs in small scale attributed to Hunger. The decoration on the small Mennecy soft-paste box in Figure 1 is practically identical with that on a St. Cloud *cachepot* (Fig. 2), which may indicate not only that they are from the same hand, but also that porcelains from different French factories were decorated with raised gilding at an independent workshop. This supposition appears more plausible than the assumption that an artisan used almost exactly the same design during his successful employment at two different factories.

The other type of gold Chinese painting on early Meissen porcelain relates in its concept and design to the wealth of polychrome *chinoiseries* developed by Höroldt shortly after he had entered the factory in 1720 and was made *Hofmaler* (court painter) in 1723. He not only introduced an entirely new and rich scale of colors, he cre-

Except as noted, illustrations are from the Hans Syz Collection of the Smithsonian Institution.

Fig. 3. Pair of Meissen tea bowls and saucers, in creamy white porcelain of the Böttger period, 1713-1720. Bowls have applied wild roses with stems in gold and the leaves painted in green enamel, and saucers are decorated with silhouetted pseudo-Chinese scenes in gold, with details engraved in dry-point technique. Decoration attributed to Abraham Seuter, goldsmith and *Hausmaler* at Augsburg; 1725-1735. Birds on the inside of tea bowls and baroque lacework with rows of points were frequently used at Augsburg.

ated in his *chinoiseries* a fairy-tale world in which pseudo-Chinese figures in exotic scenes pursue various activities— a genre of ceramic decoration which in its charm, wit, and versatility had no precedent. The freshness of some of the *chinoiseries* in gold comes close to that of those executed by Höroldt and the decorators working under his guidance. It is known that specimens were sent from Meissen to Augsburg goldsmiths and enamelers for decoration as early as 1711, and that this tradition was kept up in ensuing decades. J. G. Keyssler (1729) and Paul von Stetten (1765, 1779) reported that painting and gilding on Meissen porcelain was performed at Augsburg, especially by Bartholomeus Seuter and Johann Aufenwerth (Pazaurek, 1). Thus a question early arose as to whether these gilt Chinese decorations were products of the Meissen factory or were executed by craftsmen specializing in gilt work at Augsburg. For the past forty years many outstanding authorities in the ceramics field have expressed their views on this problem: Zimmermann (2) and Schnorr von Carolsfeld favored the theory that they were of Meissen factory origin, whereas Pazaurek (1), Hofmann, Honey (1, 2) and more recently Ducret (1, 2, 3, 5, 6) have suggested that many of these gilt *chinoiseries* were *Hausmaler* work done at Augsburg. (The term *Hausmaler*, literally "home painter," is used for independent German faïence and porcelain painters who in various ways obtained ceramics in the white, or at times decorated in underglaze blue, over which they applied their enamels and gilt.)

The Augsburg origin of some of these Chinese gilt ornaments was corroborated when Ducret (6) found several signatures of Abraham Seuter on such porcelains which permitted him to attribute to this artisan a fairl characteristic group of gilded decorations (Fig. 3 painted between about 1725 and 1747 (the year of Seuter's death) with considerable originality, humor, and fine sense of composition.

With the emphasis on Abraham Seuter's work that o his older brother Bartholomeus, who has been often men tioned in the literature, recedes somewhat into the back ground. The latter, apparently a rather prominent per sonality, was not only goldsmith and ceramics painter, bu also an engraver, publisher, and dealer, who probably ar ranged for some of the decoration of Meissen porcelain On the basis of a gold-decorated flowerpot in a painting depicting Bartholomeus Seuter shown by Rückert and by Ducret (6), a group of rather simply painted gol *chinoiseries* has now been attributed to him.

Johann Aufenwerth, to whom Pazaurek had attributed a great many Augsburg gilt *chinoiseries*, was later con sidered the originator of only a limited number of these (Honey, 2; Rückert; Ducret, 6). He died in 1728 and a great deal of gold *chinoiserie* painting is of later date. To judge from a few signed pieces, Aufenwerth painted in a style which permits us to distinguish his gilding from that of other Augsburg workers (Pazaurek, 1; Ducret, 6)

A special variety of gold decoration at Augsburg is seen on plates and other vessels, mostly of Chinese porcelain which have been completely covered with gilding and then engraved with Chinese motifs or with hunting scenes after engravings by Johann E. Ridinger published in the 1720's. Most of these specimens apparently were decorated between 1730 and 1735 and practically all are in the Bayerisches Nationalmuseum in Munich (Rückert).

A typical feature of the Augsburg gold technique is the fine engraving of details on the gold-silhouetted figures done with sharply pointed tools. These details achieved by a dry-point technique give life and quality to the decoration. There is a great latitude in the artfulness of these gold engravings which possibly may help in attributing them to specific decorators. For instance, those of Abraham Seuter seem to have been done with greater care and vivacity than the ones Ducret now assigns to his brother, Bartholomeus (Fig. 6, saucer).

Another characteristic of the Augsburg style is the interlacing late baroque scrollwork with sketchy foliage which was used for the framing of the *chinoiseries* and for the base supports upon which they rest. The probable derivation of this *Laub und Bandelwerk* can be seen in the work of Paul Decker and others whose engravings were published in Nuremberg shortly after 1700; in turn, their style was probably influenced by ornaments Jean Bérain (1637-1711) had designed in France at the court of Louis XIV (Reinheckel). Such decorative motifs as strings of dots and of arrowheads, as well as borders of C scrolls, often partly outlined with dots, are considered especially characteristic of Augsburg. However, one has to keep in mind that similar motifs occur also in Meissen factory work—for instance, C scrolls on an early Höroldt cup (Seitler) and arrowheads in underglaze blue on a small cup shown by Rückert.

In examining the details of this gold work, we were assisted in the ceramics division of the Smithsonian Institution by the use of a stereoscopic microscope with a binocular telescope system. With its aid we were able to examine fine nuances of the surface painting, and to observe how the angle of light changes the appearance of engraved lines from glistening gold to darkened traces. As Mields and Lauschke point out, the craftsmen at Meissen used tools of iron or agate for polishing the gold and for engraving designs on the unpolished gilded surface.

Some of these Augsburg gilt designs, as well as polychrome Meissen *chinoiseries,* can be traced to pictures in travel books (for instance, that of Arnold Montanus, 1669) which in part were re-engraved and published in the early eighteenth century by J. C. Weigel in Nuremberg and by Martin Engelbrecht and others in Augsburg. Other travel books which offered inspiration to *chinoiserie* painters were those of Johan Nieuhoff (1665), Athanasius Kircher (1667), D. O. Dapper (1670), and Simon de Vries (1682). An especially valuable discussion of Augsburg engravings after such travel books has been given by Schulz in a number of well-illustrated articles published between 1926 and 1929; and more recently a series of engravings with *chinoiseries* by Petrus Schenk Jr., published in Amsterdam between 1700 and 1705, was made available by Den Blaauwen, who shows that some of these motifs were copied by Meissen decorators (many of them deviating somewhat from the classical Höroldt style) as well as by Dutch *Hausmaler* and Delft faïence painters. Most important, however, for understanding the origin of the *chinoiseries* introduced by Höroldt are the six original etchings executed by him in 1726 (Ducret, 4), and the hundreds of black ink sketches (the *Schulz-Kodex* in the Grassi Museum, Leipzig) which he apparently drew as models for the Meissen decorators. It is characteristic of the artistic genius of Höroldt that he did not follow exactly the engraved prototypes or even his own drawings, but always used them in free and ingenious combinations. Some of the Augsburg *chinoiseries* also follow closely the Höroldt etchings and drawings (Du-

Fig. 4. Meissen porcelain tankard covered on the outside by brown glaze, with gold *chinoiserie* painting deeply engraved in part. Three Oriental figures, the one at the left holding a cartouchelike object with the inscription *Christian Friedrich Hörold Meissen d 8. Apr 1732;* flying dragon, bird, and butterflies. Gold scroll borders. Underglaze-blue crossed swords mark. Height 6 inches. Silver cover with Augsburg master mark EA (Elias Adam). *Metropolitan Museum of Art.*

Fig. 5. Bayreuth bowl in red earthenware with dark brown glaze; height 2⅞ inches; 1730-1740. *Chinoiseries* and scrollwork in gold, with fine details made by a sharp stylus cutting through the gold to the brown glaze after firing.

Fig. 6. Fürstenberg tea bowl, c. 1760. Gold decoration of *chinoiserie* figures in simple style with sparse engraving, on a faint rose ground; the scrollwork is like that on the saucer, which is early Meissen, 1715-1720. The decoration on the saucer, depicting an ostrich hunter, can perhaps be attributed to Bartholomeus Seuter of Augsburg, a brother of Abraham Seuter; 1730-1735.

cret, 6), and one wonders how the Augsburg decorators obtained access to this material. In view of the extensive *chinoiserie* production at Meissen and the long tradition of dealing with Augsburg decorators, it seems likely that at times polychrome *chinoiserie* pieces decorated at Meissen served as prototypes for the Augsburg craftsmen.

Most of the Augsburg gold *chinoiseries* were painted on unmarked, slightly yellowish Böttger porcelain (c. 1712-1724), of which large quantities must have found their way to Augsburg dealers and craftsmen for decoration. But there is gold Chinese decoration also on some early Meissen red stoneware tankards.

Design and gilding on a few Böttger stoneware tankards illustrated in Rückert's catalogue differ from those usually employed by Augsburg decorators. The Chinese figures on these pieces, including the motif of the *Hirschreiter* (the rider on the stag), are not typical of Augsburg, but are found on faïences and on a special type of colored Meissen *chinoiseries* which has been related to the work of Adam Friedrich von Löwenfinck (Wark). On one of the tankards (Rückert) where the gilding has been fired on the unpolished surface, the details are not engraved but are painted on the gold in shades of black and brown—an unusual technique that may not have been employed by Augsburg craftsmen. On the other two tankards the gilding has been deeply engraved so that the brown polished surface shines through—again a procedure which is not common at Augsburg but is usual on the brown-red earthenware pieces of Bayreuth (Fig. 5). The

fact that one of the tankards has a C-scroll border at the base of the *chinoiserie* design is not necessarily proof of an Augsburg provenance because these motifs, as has been pointed out, also occur on Meissen-decorated porcelains. It is thus quite possible that the gilt ornaments on these tankards are of Meissen origin, although some of them may have been done outside the factory. A question may arise as to whether the work of independent decorators at Bayreuth should also be considered in this connection. While *chinoiseries* in gold and silver were frequently applied to brown earthenware made there, the independent decorators in that center of *Hausmaler* activity usually painted in polychrome enamels, and their predominant style does not show any close affinity to that used on the tankards.

As a last example of gold *chinoiseries* on Meissen porcelain, I should like to refer to the tankard in Figure 4, which has three Oriental figures on a dark brown glaze. The one to the left is holding a cartouchelike object with the inscription: *Christian Friedrich Hörold Meissen d 8 Apr 1732*. It is reasonable to assume that this legend refers to the decorator of the piece, but as painters' signatures were in general not permitted at Meissen, the gilding may have been done outside the factory. Hörold (not a relative of J. G. Höroldt), a painter at Meissen from 1725 to 1778 known especially for his harbor scenes, was accused in 1737 of doing *Hausmaler* work (Honey, 1). The gold on this tankard is engraved through to the glaze, which thus appears as a darkly colored design similar in technique to that on two of the stoneware tankards mentioned above. The decoration differs from that done at Augsburg in that the figures give the impression of a more courtly elegance, and their costumes show some Persian or contemporary European influence. In any case, there seems to be no reason to attribute this *chinoiserie* decoration to Augsburg.

Fig. 7. Fürstenberg coffee or chocolate pot; height 6½ inches; c. 1765. Gold *chinoiseries* in Höroldt style on dark brown ground, with details painted on the gold in dark and light brown; reserves framed by gilt scrollwork; shading on scale ornament produced by polishing the gold.

A good example of the gold *chinoiseries* applied to the brown-glazed surface of red earthenware produced at Bayreuth can be seen on the bowl in Figure 5. The Bayreuth factory was famous for the splendid polychrome faïences which it began to produce in the second quarter of the eighteenth century. At the same time the brown, as well as a yellow and more rarely a blue, variety was manufactured. Preferred patterns for the gold and silver designs were coats of arms, monograms, and *chinoiseries*. The Oriental figures are framed by *Laub und Bandelwerk* like that used by many *Hausmaler* of that period (1730-1740). The detail on the figures was done by a dry-point technique, scratching through the relatively soft gold film to the brown glaze, which appears as a dark design somewhat similar to that on a few Meissen tankards mentioned previously.

These brown Bayreuth wares have at times been confused with brown Böttger stoneware. However, the Bayreuth earthenware is only lightly fired and is porous, not vitrified as is the Meissen stoneware. It is lighter in weight and the gold can be rubbed off rather easily. The type of Böttger stoneware which is somewhat like the brown Bayreuth pieces is represented by the Meissen pieces in the color plate opposite page 98.

The Fürstenberg tea bowl in Figure 6 shows a Chinese figural design and scrollwork which in its simplicity and sparse engraving is rather similar to the Augsburg decorated Meissen saucer with which it is "married." As a number of similar Fürstenberg and Augsburg-decorated pairs appeared some time ago on the market in New York, it probably is correct to assume that the Fürstenberg cups were made to replace missing Meissen pieces in an Augsburg *chinoiserie* service painted perhaps thirty years earlier (c. 1730).

Only a few polychrome *chinoiseries* are known to have originated at the Fürstenberg factory, of which a bowl and a cup with saucer are in my collection at the Smithsonian. As far as gold *chinoiseries* are concerned, the only other type that came to my attention is that shown on a coffee or chocolate pot (Fig. 7) which belonged to a service of about 1765 in the Czermak collection. The decoration is unusual in that the gilded Chinese figures in Meissen style are painted on a dark brown ground in quatrefoil reserves framed by gilt scrollwork. Underglaze-blue decoration is visible beneath some of the foliate designs. The detail work on the figures is painted on in light and dark brown enamels, but in some places it is achieved by cutting through the gold to the dark brown ground.

Very fine engraving may be seen on the gold work of a Nymphenburg teapot (c. 1761-1764) on which the *chinoiseries* and the scrollwork imitate Augsburg designs (Fig. 8). The silhouetted figures appear to be covered by a thin layer of gold on which the details are indicated in heavier gilding combined with engraving. A Nymphenburg *solitaire* (tea set on tray for one person) by the same hand is in a private collection at Munich, and there is a large coffeepot with similar *chinoiseries* in the Bayerisches Nationalmuseum. Pieces of this kind were probably painted, or at least designed, by Ambros Herrmandorffer, who was chief painter at Nymphenburg from 1761 to 1764 (Bäuml).

While these Nymphenburg specimens definitely show the influence of Augsburg decoration, this influence is less apparent on a few Frankenthal pieces in my collection, a tea canister (Fig. 9) and two cups and saucers. Here the technique of engraving has reached the peak of refinement, with very vividly modeled figures and garments. By this time (1770-1772) butterflies have replaced the birds which animate earlier *chinoiseries*. There is a sugar bowl probably belonging to the same service in the Victoria and Albert Museum.

On the Höchst tray in Figure 10 the gold *chinoiseries* are no longer painted in silhouette, but are applied with a fine brush to imitate engraving. At first sight the rim decoration might suggest a later date, but according to available information the impressed wheel mark indicates that the tray was made about 1755-1760, and on closer inspection it appears that the framing is probably an adaptation in gold technique of the red rim decorations frequently used on Japanese Kakiemon plates and copied by Bow, Chelsea, and Worcester on pieces with Kakiemon designs (see Chelsea dish, ANTIQUES, May 1969, color plate I; and ANTIQUES, September 1965, p. 337). Meissen also used this type of rim ornament, as is shown on a service in my collection decorated with floral patterns in underglaze blue and purple with gold, made about 1730-1735. At Höchst Oriental decorative designs in colors are quite rare, and no other pieces with gold *chinoiseries* from this factory have come to my notice.

Fig. 8. Nymphenburg teapot with impressed small shield mark; height 3½ inches; c. 1761-1764. *Chinoiseries* painted in a thin layer of gold with details in heavier gold, partly engraved; scrollwork in imitation of Augsburg decoration, with typical C scrolls and dots on upper rim of teapot and cover.

Fig. 9. Frankenthal tea canister with gilt design of a man in Oriental costume with bow and arrow, and on the reverse a woman sitting in a fenced landscape; height 4⅜ inches; 1770-1772. The engraving on the gold is extremely fine.

Fig. 10. Höchst tray, with impressed wheel mark; length 13¼ inches; 1755-1760. Chinese figures in semitropical landscape painted in gilt by brush in the manner of an engraving. The border appears to be an adaptation in gold of similar rim decorations in red found on Japanese Kakiemon plates and on pieces of Bow, Worcester, and Chelsea, as well as Meissen.

See page 83

Left: Meissen octagonal teapot of red-brown Böttger stoneware with blackish brown glaze, decorated in gold, pale red, and brown lacquer colors and showing a seated Chinese on one side and a monkey on the other alternating with panels of flowers; height 4 inches; 1710-1715. The form was designed by court goldsmith J. J. Irminger after a silver teapot.
Right: Meissen coffeepot in red-brown stoneware with blackish brown glaze, decorated with eight alternating panels of foliate and diaper patterns in gold; height 7¾ inches; 1710-1715. The form is in Turkish style. According to Menzhausen, the similar decoration of a coffeepot of the same form in the Staatliche Kunstammlungen in Dresden may be attributed to Martin Schnell, court lacquerer of Augustus the Strong.

BIBLIOGRAPHY

Bäuml, Fritz

"Sieben Nymphenburger Maler des 18. Jahrhunderts," *Keramos;* October 1966.

Den Blaauwen, A. L.

"Keramik mit Chinoiserien nach Stichen von Petrus Schenk, Jun." *Keramos;* January 1966.

Ducret, S.

1) "Augsburger Hausmaler," *Weltkunst,* No. 19; 1949.
2) "Chinoiserien in Gold," *Faenza,* Vol. 39; 1953.
3) "Nochmals Chinoiserien in Gold," *Weltkunst,* No. 2; 1955.
4) "Die Arbeitsmethodem Johann Gregor Höroldts," *Keramik-Freunde der Schweiz,* No. 39; 1957.
5) "Frühmeissner Dekor," *Keramik-Freunde der Schweiz,* No. 50; 1960.
6) "Augsburger Hausmalerei: 1) Augsburger Goldchinesen," *Keramos,* July 1967.

Hackenbroch, Yvonne

Meissen and other Continental Porcelain, Faience and Enamel in the Irwin Untermyer Collection; Cambridge, Mass., 1956.

Hofmann, Friedrich W.

Das Porzellan der Europäischen Manufakturen im XVIII. Jahrhunderts; Berlin, 1932.

Holzhausen, W.

Lackkunst in Europa; Braunschweig, 1959.

Honey, W. B.

1) *Dresden China;* London, 1934.
2) "Zwei deutsche Porzellanprobleme. 1) Augsburger Goldchinesen und Watteaubilder auf frühem Meissner Porzellan," *Pantheon;* December 1938.

Menzhausen, Ingelore

"Die künstlerische Gestaltung des Böttgersteinzeugs und des Böttgerporzellans," *Böttgersteinzeug Böttgerporzellan aus der Dresdener Porzellansammlung;* 1969.

Mields, Martin, and Lauschke, Rudolf
Praxis der Porzellanmalerei; Munich, 1965.

Pazaurek, Gustav E.

1) *Deutsche Fayence und Porzellan-Hausmaler,* 2 vols.; Leipzig, 1925.
2) "Porzellan-Chinoiserien," *Kunstwanderer;* February 1928.

Reinheckel, Günter

"Plastische Dekorationsformen im Meissner Porzellan der 18 Jahrhunderts," *Keramos;* 1968.

Rückert, Rainer

Meissner Porzellan, 1710-1810 (exhibition catalogue); Bayerisches Nationalmuseum, Munich, 1966.

Schnorr von Carolsfeld, Ludwig

Klemperer Collection Catalogue; 1928.

Schulz, Georg Wilhelm

"Augsburger Chinoiserien und ihre Verwendung in der Keramik," *Das Schwäbische Magazin;* 1926, 1928, 1929.

Seitler, Otto

"Konrad Christoph Hunger und Johann Gregorius Höroldt," *Keramik-Freunde der Schweiz,* No. 39; 1957.

Stalker, John, and Parker, George
A Treatise of Japanning and Varnishing; Oxford, 1688. Reprinted, London, 1960. With introduction by H. D. Molesworth.

Stazzi, Francisco
Porcellane della casa eccellentissima Vezzi (1720-1727); Milano, 1967.

Walcha, Otto

"Christoph Conrad Hunger; Ein wandernder Arkanist des 18. Jahrhunderts," *Keramik-Freunde der Schweiz,* No. 41; 1958.

Wark, Ralph

"Adam Friedrich von Löwenfinck einer der bedeutendsten deutschen Porzellan und Fayencemaler des 18. Jahrhunderts—1714-1754," *Keramik-Freunde der Schweiz,* No. 34; 1956.

Zimmermann, Ernst

1) *Die Erfindung und Frühzeit des Meissner Porzellans;* Berlin, 1908.
2) *Meissner Porzellan;* Leipzig, 1926.

III French Porcelain

The early history of porcelain making in France is very similar to that in other countries. It is a story of continual costly experimentation, mostly in vain, with only the extensive royal patronage making it all possible. Perserverance proved worthwhile, however, and at Vincennes, and later at Sèvres, there developed a royal factory that has become synonymous with French porcelain.

The porcelain associated with this factory is quite distinctive, having little in common with its German and Austrian rivals except the broad pursuit of the oriental ideal. The porcelain developed at Vincennes was of the so-called "soft paste" variety, a dense white creamy material that was nearer in composition to opaque white glass than actual oriental porcelain. This material, later produced at many other factories in France, England and elsewhere, had a quite definite quality of its own; however, it was really no more than an imitation of the oriental model which reproduced some of its more obvious features. It was not until later in the century that the French potters were able to emulate their German rivals and produce a true oriental porcelain.

The styles associated with Vincennes were also much softer, which not only suited the material, but perhaps was also a reflection of the current situation in France. Both in shape and decoration the porcelain expresses the flowing curves of the mid-18th century Rococo style. The soft porcelain was ideal for the richness and opulence of this period, for it could be painted with glowing colors, modeled into exuberant shapes, richly gilded, and even incorporated with other exotic materials into pieces of furniture. The style of Vincennes, however, was really characterized by the figures. In many cases modeled by leading sculptors such as Falconet and Pigalle, or adapted from paintings by Boucher, the figures represent an advanced use of the material simply through being linked closely with contemporary art. The other great feature of Vincennes was the development of unglazed, or biscuit, figures. It is commonly believed that the figures were at first left unglazed because the potters could not control their glazes and colors. While there may be some basis in this theory, however, the sheer quality and detail of the models would in any case have justified their remaining unglazed. It is important to remember that the glazes used with soft paste porcelain were thick and soapy and so would always obscure much of the detail of the modeling.

The style of Vincennes was continued after the move to Sèvres; moreover, while the Rococo was still dominant, there was an increasing use of Neo-Classical detail and decoration. This new style, of course, dominated all French porcelain after the Revolution because of the inevitable association of the soft, flowing Rococo style with the monarchy. Although probably the most significant, Vincennes-Sèvres was only one of a number of French porcelain factories. Others were established at Chantilly and in the traditional ceramic production area around Limoges. The articles about these factories serve as reminders that ordinary tablewares and other simple domestic objects made up a large part of 18th-century porcelain production in France.

During the 19th century, many German factories either continued the styles they had established during the 18th or adapted their products to suit the demands of contemporary taste. The changes in France were more dynamic, mainly because of the Revolution. State patronage replaced the monarchy and the Church, and only the avant garde was politically acceptable. Early 19th-century French porcelain, particularly that from the Paris area, was therefore stylistically advanced. At the same time, the makers could not ignore popular taste, and so, when the restored monarchy favored a return to the styles of Rococo, they had no choice but to conform. They also responded to the new influences coming from England, where the development of bone china had supplied the ceramic world with the most effective and cheapest reproduction of oriental porcelain yet known. Jacob Petit, typical among these 19th-century French potters, was able to combine technical and stylish novelty with the legacy of the 18th century in a very effective and realistic manner. He and his contemporaries were able to ensure that France was in a position to contribute as much to the 19th century as his predecessors had to the 18th.

The Gardener's Girl with a Vase, by Suzanne (modeler at Vincennes c. 1755), from a drawing by François Boucher (1703-1770). One of the series known as "Vincennes Children." In 1752 the all-powerful Mme. de Pompadour bought the entire series, ensuring by her interest the success of the venture.

Soft-paste biscuit of Vincennes-Sèvres

BY WILFRED J. SAINSBURY

THE VINCENNES PORCELAIN FACTORY, better known to fame under the name of Sèvres (it moved there in 1756), commenced operations just before 1740. The early years were difficult: mistakes were made, and a great deal of money was lost. By 1750, however, Vincennes was producing in all fields save one porcelain articles which could compare in every way with the best work of the most successful porcelain factory in Europe, that of Meissen. In that one field, the production of colored figures and groups, it lagged far behind. In a world enamored of the shepherds and shepherdesses and stage figures which poured out of the Meissen factory under the great artist Kändler, a factory which did not produce competitive articles could not be considered in the first rank.

In a little booklet entitled *Mémoire Historique* Jean Jacques Bachelier (1724-1805), who occupied a position in the Vincennes factory corresponding to that of a modern executive vice-president, has explained the difficulty: it was so hard to get the colors to run true that the factory seriously considered abandoning figures altogether.

At this stage Bachelier suggested selling the figures uncolored and unglazed, and it was to these products that the name "biscuit" (or "bisque") was given.

The material used for biscuit (and, indeed, for all the porcelain of Vincennes-Sèvres and other French factories during the period) was not the true hard-paste porcelain used in the Far East and at Meissen; it was an artificial "soft paste," or *pâte tendre.* The kaolin or china clay required for true hard paste was not discovered in France until about 1770, and the soft paste every French factory had to use before that date was, from its nature, liable to collapse in the kiln. By about 1750 this difficulty had been largely overcome and, as the illustrations show, the medium had been mastered for biscuit production.

The first Vincennes-Sèvres products in soft-paste biscuit appeared about 1750 and the last about 1775, when hard-paste porcelain replaced it. All the groups and figures discussed here were, therefore, made in the third quarter of the eighteenth century. The number of different models was about three hundred, ranging in size from

Left. *The Girl with the Apron*, by Blondeau from a drawing by Boucher; 1752. One of the most popular of the Vincennes Children. *All photographs by Raymond Fortt.*

Right. *Boy Playing Bagpipes*, by Blondeau from a drawing by Boucher; 1752. Another of the Vincennes Children.

a single three-inch figure to a group of four, five, or even six figures up to fifteen inches in height—though anything over twelve inches is unusual. No other factory, at that time or later, in France or elsewhere, had any substantial production of soft-paste biscuit figures, so that any example is almost certain to have come from Vincennes-Sèvres. I have never seen a good or even a tolerable fake of Vincennes-Sèvres biscuit, probably because the manufacture of soft-paste porcelain is so difficult and because the many undiscriminating buyers of German porcelain offer fakers a more remunerative field.

All that the collector needs, then, is the ability to recognize soft paste—and for that the best course is to live with a piece of soft-paste biscuit and a piece of hard-paste biscuit and allow the characteristics of each to soak into one's consciousness. The former is white, slightly rough, and almost warm to the touch; the latter has a blue tint and is quite smooth and cold. If the two pieces stand side by side in a good natural light, the differences are at once apparent.

There is no factory mark at all on the biscuit I am describing; the interlaced L's which are the ordinary mark on colored porcelain of the period from Vincennes and Sèvres were never used on biscuit, and if they were to be found today on a piece purporting to be Sèvres soft paste they would prove it a forgery. Frequently, however, we do find the mark of the *répareur*—a worker who did no mending but was responsible for putting together the various parts of a group when they came from their individual molds. *Répareurs* were artists of some

distinction, and some (notably one Fernex) are known to have worked both as *répareur* and as designer. The commonest of these marks are a printed F (probably for Fernex) and a cursive B (probably for Bono); others found occasionally are L. R. (for Le Riche), a pair of compasses, an arrow, and a star. Marks of *répareurs* occur on about two-thirds of the biscuit pieces and are always incised, almost invariably on the base.

Most of the soft-paste biscuit figures are in exquisite taste. This is due partly to the general high level of taste which prevailed in Court circles and spread down to the New Rich, and partly to the influence of the Pompadour —who probably did as much good to the art of France as she did harm to its political and financial position. She took a keen personal interest in the factory, and it was partly through her influence that many of the groups were based on drawings by the great Boucher, and that Falconet himself was head modeler from 1757 to 1766.

The true hard-paste porcelain which could be made after the discovery of the china-clay deposits around 1770 was easier to work, and allowed the production of the enormous pieces which appealed to the degenerating taste of that period; and by 1775 soft paste was no longer used. Before the close of the eighteenth century the factory was producing hard-paste biscuit portraits of Voltaire, the great Condé, Henry IV, and other heroes— faithful likenesses with little to commend them beyond their technical excellence. However, Sèvres has never ceased production of hard-paste copies of the charmingly idealized figures and groups shown here.

The Fox and the Bird, by Blondeau after a painting by Jean Baptiste Oudry (1686-1755); 1752. A remarkable rendition of seventeenth-century violence produced in the gentler eighteenth century. The factory was able to create such intricate groups as this within an astoundingly short time after production began.

89

Cupid, by Etienne-Maurice Falconet (1716-1791); 1758. This is one of the best-known works of the sculptor, who was head modeler at Sèvres from 1757 to 1766, when he went to Russia. The lines by Voltaire on the base may be translated *Whoever you are, here is your master,/He is, or he was, or will be hereafter.*

The Attendants of Bacchus Holding the Infant God, by an unknown artist after a drawing by Boucher; 1768. Mythological or classical subjects are among the best known although not the most numerous. The student of the history of artistic taste may be surprised to find these early indications of neo-classical influence during a period generally regarded as rococo.

Psyche, by Falconet; 1761. A companion piece to *Cupid*—Psyche has stolen his bow.

Boy with Wine Bottle, by Falconet; 1757. One of a series of "Falconet Children"—simple, small individual figures representing, more or less faithfully, working-class characters in the streets of Paris.

The Seated Venus, by Jean Baptiste Pigalle (1714-1785); 1770. The sculptor gave his name to the well-known Place Pigalle in Paris.

The Link Boy (torch-bearer), by Jesse-François-Joseph Le Riche (born 1739), from a drawing by Boucher; 1767. Le Riche was a pupil of Falconet.

The Cream Seller, by Suzanne after a drawing by Boucher; 1755. The paste of this piece is of exceptional quality.

The Seated Shepherdess, by Jean-Baptiste de Fernex (c. 1729-1783), from a drawing by Boucher; 1754. This is taken from a scene in a popular play and represents Mme. Favart, a leading comedienne. The Rue Favart beside the Comédie Française is named after her playwright husband.

The Beloved Lamb, by Fernex from a drawing by Boucher; 1754. This and *The Seated Shepherdess* were made for the Pompadour's dairy at Crécy—a predecessor of the more famous one associated with Marie Antoinette.

The Other Side of the Leaf, by Falconet; 1760. Groups of this type used symbols easily recognized by contemporaries; here the girl is clearly being tempted.

The Broken Shoe, by Falconet; 1760. This sequel to *The Other Side of the Leaf* shows the girl mourning her downfall.

Louis XV, by an unknown artist; c. 1760. Representations of the monarch are extremely rare: this one is previously unrecorded.

Tasting Grapes, by an unknown artist, after a painting by Boucher entitled *Pense-t-il aux raisins?* 1752. A very important early group.

Nursing, by Louis-Simon Boizot (1743-1809); 1774. Boizot was chief modeler at Sèvres from 1774 until 1802. This group shows the influence of Rousseau's advocacy of maternal care for children.

The Schoolmistress, by Falconet; 1762.

The useful wares of Vincennes and Sèvres

BY PHILIPPE VERDIER, Curator of medieval and subsequent decorative arts at the Walters Art Gallery

THE IDEA that Sèvres porcelain is a rather ponderous ware, usually on the monumental side, stems from the way large Sèvres vases are all too frequently displayed in serried ranks in showcases or on breakfronts. The more casual presentation accorded the small useful wares of the same factory has led to their being much less well known, though statistically they were a far from insignificant part of the factory's production.

Few of these modest artifacts have survived the daily use for which they were designed, but their varied forms

One of a pair of double liquor coolers; light blue ground with dotted decoration in white, and reserved panels of *putti*. Decorated by Dutanda; hard paste, Sèvres, 1791.
Except as noted, illustrations are from the Walters Art Gallery.

are recorded in the fragmentary accounts of the Vincennes factory from 1741 to 1753 and, for the period 1748-1758, in the important *Livre-Journal* (register) of Lazare Duvaux, Parisian dealer who was goldsmith to Louis XV (published in a scholarly two-volume edition in 1873 by Louis Courajod). The factory records are quoted in Chavagnac and Grollier: *Histoire des manufactures françaises de porcelaine* (Paris, 1906); in the excellent survey by P. Verlet, S. Grandjean, and M. Brunet: *Sèvres* (1953); and in subsequent articles written in English by Verlet. Another source of information is the inventories of the Duchesse du Barry, published by Davillier in 1870.

The ware which kept the primacy among European porcelains from the sixth decade of the eighteenth century until the French Revolution closely reflects the famous *douceur de vivre* of the French aristocracy during the most spectacular period of the *ancien régime*. For the last years of Vincennes and the first of Sèvres the production falls into three categories: vases, flowers, utensils. The vases, created by the ingenuity of Duplessis, were in the minority as far as numbers and sales were concerned. Vincennes specialized early in the production of bouquets of flowers in porcelain; these delightful blossoms account for a third of the registered porcelain in the accounts of Duvaux. But nothing suggests the many facets of a vanished civilization and style of life better than the multitude of utensils in porcelain produced at

Chocolate pot; gilt on green ground, polychrome swags on white. Decorated by Taillandier (1753-1790); no date mark; soft paste, probably Sèvres.

Breakfast set (*solitaire*),
soft paste, with
roses painted in blue.
Decorated by E. Evans;
Sèvres, 1758.

Vincennes and Sèvres. Cooking, dressing, writing, sewing, eating and drinking, hunting, smoking, the decoration of furniture, hygiene—for all of these, small porcelain objects were designed in a lighthearted spirit which transformed a material necessity into a device for intimate and extravagant display.

The emphasis in tableware was on equipment for the first course and the dessert (dishes for soups and broths, custard and ice cream cups, jam dishes, covered pots), but many items were used throughout the meal: plates, salad bowls with their oil and vinegar cruets, boats for gravy and sauces, pots for meat essence and spices, salt cellars. Ice pails had porcelain covers and metal liners. Glasses were cooled in individual or collective coolers, the latter resembling the English silver monteith and called *seaux crénelés*, or *verrières*. White wines and liquors were cooled in pails for bottles and decanters, half bottles, pints (*fillettes, topettes*). The liquor cooler is an oblong jardinière divided across its width by a pierced screen; examples make such convenient flower holders that they are often catalogued as such today, and have been in fact so used since the early eighteenth century.

Breakfast sets, which have survived in relatively large quantity, were either *solitaires* for one person or *tête à tête* for a (supposedly loving) couple. No Sèvres was designed for children, the royal family at Versailles excepted. The cream pitcher accompanying the tea served at breakfast is usually pear-shape, with three legs (called a *geigneux*). Milk was sometimes used as a substitute for the morning tea, for the nightcap, or when royalty and nobility played at the bucolic life. Milk pitchers and their bowls are difficult to distinguish from water or rosewater sets, but apparently a round bowl was used for the first and a shallow, oval bowl for the others.

Milk pitcher and bowl in blue on white;
decorated by Vieillard; soft paste, Vincennes, 1753.

Early chocolate pots are rare; they were not produced in the first years of soft paste at Sèvres. Coffeepots were made in quantity here only after the introduction of hard paste (1769-1770).

The *pot à oille*, used with the oval tureen in the first course, is round. With the punch bowl, these were the most costly of the useful items. With them were used

Unmarked strawberry dish with its *plateau*. Polychrome panel and blue zigzag decoration on white pierced hard paste; Sèvres.

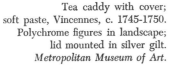

Polychrome tulip vase with figures in landscape; soft paste, Vincennes, c. 1745-1750. *Metropolitan Museum of Art.*

Tea caddy with cover; soft paste, Vincennes, c. 1745-1750. Polychrome figures in landscape; lid mounted in silver gilt. *Metropolitan Museum of Art.*

individual *écuelles* for soups and broths, each comprising a covered bowl and its stand. Saucepans and frying pans —of which, incredibly, a few examples are known even in soft paste—were not intended for use in the kitchen; with silver chafing dishes and *réchauds*, they were used in the intimacy of a private dining room.

Table sets or combinations of table sets and decorative vases were among the wares of Sèvres sent abroad by Talleyrand as what he termed *douceurs* in furtherance of his diplomacy. However important they may have been in the total production of the royal factory, such strictly private items as spittoons and chamber pots are not included in these gifts or bribes; objects pertaining to the delicate techniques of eating and tippling, however, loom large.

Other types of *ces mille riens* pertaining to the transient aspects of daily life are shown in the illustrations: a powder flask, a sponge container, a candlestick, a bulb pot (in contrast with the large ornamental vases). Fantastic as it may sound, even individual holy-water stoups

Ecuelle and tray with cockleshell motif in gold and colors. Decorated by Thévenet père; soft paste, Sèvres, 1761.

Sponge dish, probably from a shaving set; polychrome decoration on white. Hard paste, Sèvres, 1772.

were produced in Sèvres porcelain. After the secret passage between the apartment of Mme. de Pompadour and that of the king had been walled up, she bought one of these decorated with cherubs in a glory of sunbeams—a cleverly humble gesture. The same day—it was January 30, 1756—she acquired a *solitaire* breakfast set.

Today we cannot help being fascinated by what is rare in surviving eighteenth-century Sèvres. Only one complete toilet set exists (dated 1763-1764, it is in the Wallace Collection); only a few eyecups, etuis (sometimes egg-shape), and opera glasses. And what has become of the mirror frames, the watch cases, the snuffboxes of Vincennes, the lanterns, such paraphernalia for smokers as the "pot for cleansing the pipe" recorded by Lazare Duvaux? Or the coffee, mustard, and ice-cream spoons, the oyster and lemon trays?

Powder flask made for Marie Josèphe, mother of Louis XVI, when she was dauphine; soft paste, Vincennes, c. 1753. Hunting scene on turquoise ground. *Metropolitan Museum of Art.*

Below. *Left,* small sugar bowl with petal pattern in red on white. Double L mark in red; soft paste, Sèvres, no date mark. Small covered bowls very similar in shape were used for jam, pomade, and many other purposes. *Right.* Candlestick with blue roses on white; soft paste, Sèvres, 1757.

Some important Sèvres porcelain and its painters

BY CARL CHRISTIAN DAUTERMAN,
Associate curator of post-Renaissance Art,
Metropolitan Museum of Art

Fig. 1. Design for a coffer on stand, French, c. 1770-1785. Pencil, ink, and water-color working drawing for a piece of "porcelain furniture" closely related to the coffer of Figure 4 by Martin Carlin; 14¼ by 9⅜ inches. *All pieces illustrated are from the gift of the Samuel H. Kress Foundation, Metropolitan Museum of Art.*

THE ROYAL MANUFACTORY OF FRENCH PORCELAIN resulted from the reorganization in 1753 of an insolvent establishment at Vincennes. Today its courtly product is referred to as "Sèvres," after the community on the edge of Paris to which the factory was removed in 1756, on land presented by Madame de Pompadour. Here for four decades the king and his court fostered, by franchise, subsidy, and purchase, the production of porcelains expressing original departures in design and decoration, and offering new embodiments of luxury. Under these auspices, Sèvres immediately leapt to first place artistically in porcelain-hungry Europe, leaving its stamp upon the styling of furniture as upon ceramic wares during the remaining years of the monarchy.

In this article, two interrelated classes of Sèvres products are considered: flowered furniture plaques and presentation vases in the recent Kress Foundation gift to the Metropolitan Museum of Art (formerly in the renowned collection of the Lords Hillingdon).

Among porcelains, Sèvres holds the almost unique position of serving as a decorative material for the embellishment of furniture. The Chinese somewhat earlier inserted porcelain panels into their folding screens, but the French in the 1750's were the first to combine this semiprecious medium with two other luxury materials: rare wood veneers and gilt-bronze mounts. The Paris art dealer Simon-Philippe Poirier emerges as a pioneer in this development. He and a few other high-ranking dealers commissioned plaques from the Sèvres manufactory and distributed them to the cabinetmakers who worked for them, and with whom they presumably collaborated in working out designs for such furniture (Fig. 1).

Although always flat, the porcelain panels are fashioned with varying contours to suit the lines of the furniture. They are set into depressions in the wood carcass, and held in place by especially designed fire-gilt mounts of bronze. Each unit is bordered with colored glaze, usually apple-green, and has a white center upon which is painted a brillant miniature. The furniture ypes include occasional tables, ladies' desks, marriage coffers, cabinets, upright secretaries, and a writing table. Together with two related clocks and a barometer, they comprise seventeen examples in all. Obviously, such furniture never became a popular type. It was formidably expensive to produce. Therefore it was to be found only in the intimate apartments of the wealthy and the powerful.

The nature of the three-dimensional porcelains in this collection is no less exclusive. Great vases and centerpieces suitable for royal presents account for most of the fifty-five examples. Their colored grounds include the rare *rose Pompadour,* a variety of greens, and two shades of blue. Sèvres is renowned for these colors as well as for one other feature which the vessels share with the furniture plaques: the exquisite paintings of flowers, figures, birds, and trophies executed as sparking miniatures upon white medallions reserved in the colored porcelain.

One other characteristic of Sèvres is the sporadic but sometimes very illuminating information imparted by its marks. Turn over a piece of Sèvres in your hand. The chances are that you will find inscriptions including the factory mark (a pair of crossed L's), a date letter, and, more exceptionally, one or two other meaningful ciphers or symbols. Herein lies the possibility of learning the year of manufacture, the names of one or more painters, and possibly the gilder. What other ceramic ware can supply such complete documentation? It seems the collector's dream come true. But the subject is full of pitfalls, as this collection shows.

Taken jointly, the 140 furniture plaques and the numerous miniatures on the vases amount to about 260 compositions—a veritable picture gallery in miniature. A follower of Euclid might sum up the situation in this way: Given: a collection of Sèvres porcelains with 260 miniature paintings; to prove: the date and authorship of each unit. The solution of such a problem might, in the abstract, seem easy enough: merely "decode" the

Fig. 2. *Bonheur du jour* (lady's desk), French, Louis XV period. Tulipwood mounted with gilt bronze and Sèvres plaques, some dated 1768. By Martin Carlin (M. E. 1766-d. 1785). Height 32 inches.

Fig. 3. Apple-green jardinieres; 1760; decoration by Vieillard *père.*

date marks. But alas, the problems of art are rarely as simple as that.

True, a straightforward approach can be made to yield some direct results. For example, the *bonheur du jour* of Figure 2 provides a considerable number of plaques signed *Levé* (for Denis Levé) and bearing the date letters for 1768 and 1770. It is rewarding to establish by this evidence that a matching desk in the collection, with the mark of Jean-Jacques Pierre *jeune* and the date 1774, had resisted the shift of style that char-

acterized this period of transition. Similarly a group of three green fan-shape flower vases (Fig. 3) is self-documented as dating from 1760, while Vieillard *père* is identified by his mark as the author of the Teniers-like drinking scenes. A sizable number of decorators' names can be determined by this direct process of reading the marks. This applies more to the furniture plaques than to the vases, however.

There remain other and far more numerous instances in which painters' marks or any marks are either incomplete or absent. Even here, however, identification of painters is often possible by stylistic analogy. A pair of marriage coffers provides an illustration. On one (Fig. 4), the plaques are entirely unmarked. By itself, this coffer might have been regarded as dating from about 1770, in terms of its design as an article of furniture. But by good fortune the collection contains a second example, bearing the mark of Pierre *jeune* and the date letters for 1768 and 1770. One panel of the latter coffer, however, is signed by Commelin and datemarked for 1775. Doubtless it was substituted for a broken plaque.

The significance of this single differing plaque is that in the clockwise rotation of its floral motifs, as in its softness of definition, it agrees closely with the panels on the first (illustrated) coffer; so closely, indeed, as to support an attribution of those plaques to the hand of Commelin. Since the coffer bearing dated plaques is without question a 1770 production except for the one later plaque, and since the matching piece has an entire complement of plaques in the painter's style of that later panel, it may well be that the companion coffer was

Fig. 4. Coffer on stand; French, c. 1775.
By Martin Carlin.
Tulipwood veneer; marquetry of
tulipwood and harewood; height 37¼ inches.
Unmarked Sèvres plaques attributed to Commelin.

Fig. 5. Great panel c. 1790, set into the fall front of an
upright secretary; 19 by 13½ inches.

made about 1775. Apparently Commelin supplied a replacement for a plaque on the older coffer while painting all the plaques for the new one.

The three-dimensional porcelain objects lend themselves equally readily to this process of direct comparison. Certain signed examples give an immediate clue to the identity of artists responsible for unsigned pieces. The Dodin vases in Figure 6 represent an instance. Here the character of the figure painting and the foliage makes it eminently safe to assign several other miniatures to Dodin, using these signed vases as the "control."

When, by the combined evidence of marks and of idiosyncracies of style, the whole collection is classified, it becomes apparent that we are dealing with the work of more than twenty artists. Let us dispose of the statistical aspect at once. The twenty-odd artists failed to apply their marks to about one half of the miniatures, and in other instances the marks are cryptic or incomplete. This is another way of saying that between the furniture plaques and the vases, approximately 130 compositions remain anonymous after such inspection. Only a portion of these can be identified by matching piece against piece within the collection. Attribution of the balance requires something beyond our immediate resources. It calls for access to primary sources, such as the archives of the factory at Sèvres, and the opportunity to make direct stylistic comparisons between our unascribed pieces and fully marked ones in other collections.

The factory archives are huge registers covered in faded blue vellum. In the expected eighteenth-century manner, they are ruled in pencil and inscribed in ink "in a fine hand." They make rather laconic but fascinating reading, since they record not only the types and prices of objects, but also the names of purchasers, from the king on down, along with the precise date on which each sale was made. The reader has to set himself into an eighteenth-century frame of reference to use these books with profit. He must be familiar with the now-forgotten names for the colors and shapes of the things he is tracing. He must cope with abbreviations, synonyms, and lacunae. Among the scores of names for vessels referring to specific shapes alternative names frequently occur.

Sometimes the record of a single day's transactions conjures up a coterie of great personalities. For example, under *28 X^{bre} 1759* one finds purchases made by Madame Victoire (daughter of Louis XV), the Duc de Choiseul, Madame la Duchesse de Gramont, and "to the account of Versailles" for the king, the Duc d'Orléans, and Madame de Pompadour. Sometimes a side light on the king's regard for his contemporaries is provided by his purchases, as when in 1760 he is billed 720 livres for a pair of *vases hollandais nouveaux,* as a present to the controller general, in contrast to an earlier entry: *1 Buste du Roy, defectueux* intended for *Sr Falconnes.* An insight into the housekeeping at the Palace of Versailles is given by the careful separation in the books between *porcelaines d'augmentation* and *porcelaines de remplacement,* with the latter much more frequently mentioned. This is an early instance of an open-stock system in operation.

By patient plodding, one may also learn from the

Fig. 6. Pair of apple-green covered vases *à flaçon;* 1772; figure decoration by Dodin.

Fig. 7. Turquoise-green potpourri vase *en gondole;*
about 1757-1759;
figure decoration attributed to Dodin.

Fig. 8. Myrtle-green dolphin vase, c. 1765;
figure decoration attributed to Dodin.

same source of a great many quaint and curious objects not usually associated with the repertoire of Sèvres: a night lamp; plaques for wine bottles; a snuffbox; a chamber pot (in lapis blue and gold, 60 livres; undecorated, 12); a barber's basin sold to Madame du Barry in 1758; two little eggs; and, most mysteriously, *1 mélancolie.*

Entries concerning furniture plaques are relatively few, and it makes the investigator's heart beat faster to encounter dated listings that coincide with the marks and other associated evidence of known plaques. This

is the case with a great panel, nineteen by thirteen and one-half inches (Fig. 5), set into the fall front of an upright secretary in the company of Wedgwood medallions from the Lady Templeton series. Although the porcelain is not dated, an attribution of about 1790 is defensible. Our only guide to the decorator is a Y— for Bouillat *fils,* according to the published handbooks. His records, however, show that plaques were not his line; but among his father's accounts we find the following:

1790 *Aout 2 plaques quarré long bouquet*
1791 *Février 2 plaques quarré long fleurs*

The final recourse in ferreting out artists is to compare fully documented pieces in other collections with the problem pieces at hand. For instance, the painter of a pair of cupids on one of the rarest forms of vessels, a gondola-shape potpourri vase (Fig. 7), is convincingly revealed as Dodin after close scrutiny of similar figures occurring on signed porcelains in collections at home and abroad. Thus the marks and the definable personal styles of painting, taken together, can identify the painters of pastorals, Flemish peasants, harbor roustabouts, and other eighteenth-century conceits.

The visitor to the Metropolitan will find that, as a result of exploring these various avenues, the authorship of more than ninety per cent of the porcelain miniatures in the Kress collection has been established. The discoveries and attributions are announced unobtrusively on labels. The marks themselves are absorbed in the glitter of a simulated eighteenth-century art gallery, where spectacular articles of Sèvres-inlaid furniture line the walls, and impressive vases, *flambeaux,* and services fill the windows of a period shop front that once looked out on the Quai Bourbon.

French soft-paste snuffboxes at Limoges

BY HENRY-PIERRE FOUREST, *Curator, Sèvres Ceramics Museum*

IN EIGHTEENTH-CENTURY FRANCE, from about the middle of the century to the end, such small accessories as charms (*breloques*), patch boxes, sewing cases (*étuis*), and lorgnettes were very much in fashion. Perhaps the most popular of all such *bibelots* was the snuffbox (*tabatière*). These, which are sometimes difficult to distinguish from patch boxes and other small containers, were made of many different materials, and snuffboxes made of precious metal, tortoise shell, or lacquer (*vernis Martin*) have received more study than have ceramic examples.

While porcelain was probably used for this purpose somewhat less frequently than other materials—it is certainly less practical for objects designed, as most of these were, to be carried in the pocket or in a fold of the belt—it is still true that the little soft-paste caskets, with their infinite variety in form and decoration, deserve more study than they have received. The Paul Gasnault collection at the Musée Adrien-Dubouché in Limoges comprises a group of these small masterpieces second in size only to the Schlichting collection at the Musée des Arts Décoratifs in Paris, and of comparable quality. The examples shown here are drawn from this group.

Snuffboxes were popular long before they were made of porcelain: Henry Nocq and Carle Dreyfus, who prepared the catalogue of the Schlichting collection, have pointed out that the shop of Claude Bertin was listed in 1700 as "at the sign of the *Tabatière*." Then, too, covered boxes for various purposes had been produced earlier in faïence—notably the powder and holy-wafer boxes made at Moustiers. Spice boxes also exist—but all of these are without attached covers, and none were intended to be used as accessories of dress. Pierre Verlet suggests that Lazare Duvaux seems to have been the first to realize the advantage offered by porcelain for the decoration of these boxes, and certainly it is true that the well-known *Journal de Lazare Duvaux* mentions many porcelain snuffboxes given away by the king. Often the mounts are described as of gold; however, all the boxes at the Musée Adrien-Dubouché and most of those in other known collections are mounted in silver. It is probable that very few of the gold mounts survived the beginning of the nineteenth century.

M. Verlet has also pointed out that the dealers of the St. Honoré section and of the Place Dauphine strove constantly to devise novelties to catch clients' fancies. One such was the box jewelers made by mounting porcelain plaques, supplied by the manufacturers, in a metal framework (*à cage*). However, most of the little caskets were molded completely of porcelain, with the goldsmith contributing only a hinged mount to act as

Fig. 1. White snuffboxes in "rice-grain" relief, with stylized chrysanthemums in center of lids; Mennecy. Note unusual heart shape on left. *All illustrations are from the Gasnault collection in the Adrien-Dubouché Museum, Limoges.*

Fig. 2. Marked Mennecy box in basketwork relief; mark, DV in black, inside. Decoration of naturalistic flowers.

the top edge of the box and the setting for its cover. All the pieces in the Musée Adrien-Dubouché are of this type.

It is possible to divide soft-paste snuffboxes into a few main groups. Within these, dimensions vary from about three centimeters to eight, nine, or even ten; edges may be contoured, corners clipped, walls curved.

The simplest boxes—which are not necessarily the oldest —are rectangular, round, or oval. Rectangular and round boxes are fairly numerous in the Gasnault collection; many of them are of Mennecy porcelain. Models of clearly Oriental inspiration, with a "rice-grain" motif in relief and a chrysanthemum in the center of the cover, occur fairly frequently (Fig. 1). Another from this group (Fig. 2), done in basketwork relief, is more European. Sometimes the decoration consists of flowers painted in natural colors, repeated on the inside of the lid. One of the outstanding pieces of the collection is the Vincennes example in Figure 3 (left), decorated *en camaïeu*.

A second category consists of boxes in the form of fantastic creatures. These, following the mid-century taste for the unexpected, are probably the most original of all; here the potter gave his imagination free rein. Some have a slightly ivory-tinted paste, with Imari decoration applied without regard to the form of the piece. *Magots* in the Japanese manner (Fig. 4, center) are found in this group, as well as—notably—a sphinx (Fig. 5). Some of these boxes are decorated inside the lid with *japonaiseries* in gilt. An attribution to St. Cloud or Chantilly is suggested for this series.

A third group includes subjects—animal and human—treated realistically. In this category are the charming recumbent horse of Figure 3 (right), with its suggestion of the Oriental; a spaniel suckling her young at the left in Figure 6; a somewhat heraldic lion couchant; a swan (Fig. 6, right); a brindle bulldog (Fig. 7); and an astonishing monkey's head, with manganese purple "fur."

People are also represented, in contemporary costume. All of these pieces have flowers of Mennecy type on the underside of the lid. The subjects are almost always shown lying in poses designed to eliminate the projecting parts so difficult to execute in soft paste, which would also make the box too fragile to be carried in the pocket (note the position of the head of the swan in Fig. 6, right).

Two fairly large snuffboxes in the Gasnault collection representing shepherds lying on mounds (Fig. 9) remind us that the same model may have been executed at more than one factory. One of these has Imari decoration, the other is treated in the floral manner of Mennecy; and there are noticeable differences between the two in delicacy of modeling and quality of mount.

One way of dating these nearly contemporary pieces is to study the marks on the silver mounts, and a number of scholars have gone into this subject. Unfortunately, these date marks are often illegible or completely obliterated, since they were usually placed where they would be rubbed by the edge of the cover. Of the mounts whose marks are decipherable one of the earliest seems to be that of the reclining shepherd in Figure 9 (right). It bears the fox-head discharge mark used in the years 1738-1744. On several boxes of different types what appears to be the hen's-head mark of 1750-1756 can be made out. Three of the boxes attributed to Mennecy, including the recumbent horse of Figure 3 (right), show a mark which resembles the shell used from 1756 to 1762. One of the clearest sets of marks is on the rabbit with Imari decoration (Fig. 4, right); this shows the discharge mark for 1744-1750. However, Duvaux's journal makes it clear that sometimes a box was repaired—so the mounts may in some instances be later than the piece itself.

In many ways, then, it is still difficult to assign many of these soft-paste porcelain snuffboxes to particular places or dates of origin. Fortunately, the Paul Gasnault collection brings together for purposes of study a fairly large group. Perhaps insignificant in themselves, these little objects are nevertheless important as delightful examples of the small frivolities that played so large a part in the decorative art of their own day.

Translated and condensed from an article in *Cahiers de la céramique et des arts du feu*, No. 13.

Fig. 3. *Left:* Large Vincennes box, mounted in silver and decorated *en camaïeu* (monochrome) *rose;* a great rarity. On outside of lid, a landscape with a woman in Louis XV costume asleep in the shade of a tree, with three cupids hovering above; one of the cupids holds a clock with the hands at noon. The form of this box, with its shaped corners and conforming lid, is as unusual as its size. *Right:* Mennecy reclining-horse snuffbox. Silver mounts show discharge mark in form of shell—the mark for 1756-1762.

Fig. 4. Boxes attributed to St. Cloud or Chantilly: sheep, *magot* (grotesque Chinese figure), rabbit. The Imari decoration on the animals completely ignores the forms; the discharge mark of 1744-1750 on the silver mount of the rabbit dates this example.

Fig. 5. Sphinx, attributed to St. Cloud or Chantilly. Inside of lid decorated in delicate *japonaiseries* with gilding. Form and decoration reminiscent of the *style Bérain*.

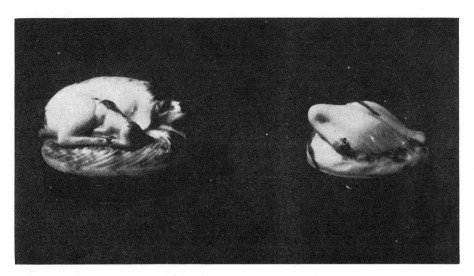

Fig. 6. Mennecy boxes which attempt naturalistic portrayals. *Left:* Spaniel suckling its young, polychrome; the collection also includes an all-white version. *Right:* Swan.

Fig. 7. Mennecy box in bulldog form. Another attempt at realism: the spots are intended to represent the brindle markings of the animal's coat.

Fig. 8. Mennecy box in the form of a monkey's head, one of the stars of the collection. Lid also simulates fur, in manganese purple.

Fig. 9. Reclining shepherds: examples of widely varying treatments of the same subject. *Left:* A certain clumsiness here is more suggestive of pottery than of porcelain. Mennecy-type flowers on the lid support an attribution to this factory. *Right:* Attributed to Chantilly because of Imari-type decoration and palette. The face is modeled with some delicacy. Mount, highly finished, is one of the earliest found on these boxes: it bears the fox-head discharge mark used on small pieces of silver between 1738 and 1744.

Chantilly porcelain in the last half of the eighteenth century

BY NICOLE BALLU-LOUREIRO

MY ARTICLE IN ANTIQUES for December 1959 told how Cicaire Cirou established a factory under the patronage of the Duke of Bourbon with a patent to make porcelain in imitation of the Japanese. For thirty years or so the directors of the factory confined themselves to producing wares nearly indistinguishable from their Oriental models. The essential difference was in the materials employed. Germany was the only European country that had learned the secret of true, hard-paste (kaolinic) porcelain; the Chantilly product was still a soft-paste, or artificial, porcelain, but its opaque white tin glaze, together with its clearly drawn decorations and the special tonality of its reds, gave many pieces of the earliest period a striking resemblance to Japanese porcelain in the called Kakiemon style.

Possibly as early as 1745 and certainly by 1752, a Cicaire Cirou had been succeeded as director by Bu de Montvallier, a new style had begun to appear Chantilly that was to form a transition between Oriental wares of the earliest period and the purely Ex pean decoration of the last. During the first ten ye that this new style was being developed neither continuity of the management nor in fact the very e ence of the factory was assured. Yet technical acc plishment was at its height; the craftsmen were not masters of their material but felt free to give rein

Plate with shaped rim and polychrome decoration in the transitional style. *Musée Condé, Chantilly.*

Ewer in transitional style with polychrome decoration and engraved silver mount; mark, a brown hunting horn. *Musée des Arts Décoratifs, Paris.*

106

January, 1

Sugar bowl and tray in transitional style with polychrome decoration of pansies and floral sprigs. *Musée National de Céramique, Sèvres.*

their own inspiration. There was a great demand for novelty, and Montvallier did not hesitate to recruit defecting artists from other porcelain centers or even to obtain, more or less legally, his rivals' secrets—frequent procedures at the time, as the records of several lawsuits show.

Only during this period does Chantilly seem to have taken up, briefly, the prevailing rococo style—influenced no doubt by Meissen, which was then enjoying its greatest success, and by the new French royal factory at Vincennes (shortly afterwards moved to Sèvres). An unusual large shell in the Sèvres museum probably dates from these years, as well as certain ewers in the form of tree trunks with accompanying basins shaped like leaves.

Instead of the flat colors of the first period, invariably outlined in black, we now find tinting, shading, and the mingling of colors by means of small brush strokes. Figures are painted somewhat theatrically, in the style of Watteau. Floral decoration shows a new tendency towards naturalism. Chrysanthemums become rarer but lose their stiffness and have natural-looking stems painted in brown instead of the angular blue stems of the earlier period. An insect arbitrarily called a beetle often animates this decorative scheme, which was soon to be supplanted by a new motif consisting of apple branches, sometimes with birds. Various kinds of flowers, still somewhat schematic but now more graceful, enliven all these compositions; the European pansy and convolvulus accompany the carnation and the rose. The last, carefully delineated, has a spiny stem with mottled green and yellow leaves. Some rare landscapes are attributed to the fan painter Dubuisson, a runaway from Vincennes who executed such decorations at Chantilly for three months in 1753.

In the latest, or "French," style, current at Chantilly from about 1757 to 1800, these trends were fully developed, while the last traces of Oriental and *rocaille* influence disappeared. The reorganization of the factory by Pierre Peyrard in 1757 had put operations on a practical

Plate with "wicker" rim and polychrome decoration in reserves, 1750-1760. *Musée National de Céramique, Sèvres.*

basis, but the mass-production methods introduced resulted, especially toward the end of the century, in a falling off of quality. Table services and utilitarian objects were turned out in quantity to reduce costs, and the making of decorative pieces in limited numbers was given up. Until the final closing of the factory Chantilly wares hardly varied in style.

Plates—so rare in Saint Cloud and Mennecy porcelain—have survived in some quantity from Chantilly. Those with rims molded to simulate basketwork enclosing re-

Plate with molded swirled ribs and decoration in monotone violet; mark, a hunting horn and *D* in rose; 1745-1760. *Musée des Arts Décoratifs.*

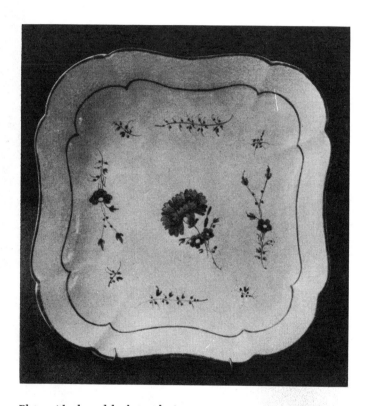

Plate with shaped basketwork rim and monochrome blue decoration consisting of a large pink (*œillet*) surrounded by sprigs; third quarter of the eighteenth century. *Musée des Arts Décoratifs.*

serves with painted flowers or landscapes are probably among the earliest products of this last period. A related series has a sketchy landscape, a fountain, and a trellis in monotone. In both these types the heaviness of the body and the numerous defects, such as black spots on the surface, especially in the basketwork and on the backs of the plates, suggest technical difficulties not yet overcome.

Basketwork rims had appeared early at Chantilly but were still in use in 1779, according to documentary evidence. There were two versions, of which the heavier was called "wicker." Chantilly copied from Tournai, probably around 1760, the German shapes with rims ornamented by swirled ribs. On plates with plain rims the edges were shaped or scalloped. Toward the end of the Old Regime there appeared a new style of plate with plain rim and decoration of floral garlands.

The decorations most frequently used were based on realistic representations of European flowers. Some of these, featuring a radiating central motif or bouquets alternating with insects and scattered flowers, are beautifully rendered. On services produced in quantity, however, the painting is mediocre, and as the century progresses the slight thickening of the enamels as well as the repetition of themes foreshadows decadence.

The typical underglaze blue decorations executed in quantity at Chantilly, where they originated, and copied at many other factories, consist of pinks (*œillets*) and sketchy sprigs. The pink had already appeared in the mixed bouquets of the transitional period. It is used alone or surrounded by scattered flowers, especially lillies of the valley, and insects. A late pattern features the pink alone framed by an undulating garland.

The "Chantilly sprig" pattern—known in French as *à la brindille*—may have developed from an early and rather rare motif of wild roses. It became more and more stylized, especially after the Revolution, and, possibly because it served so conveniently to mask small imperfections in the porcelain, enjoyed an even greater

Plate with monochrome blue "sprigged" decoration
(à la brindille) within a floral border;
mark, a blue hunting horn and C.
Musée des Arts Décoratifs.

access with Chantilly's rivals well into the nineteenth
century.

Probably most of the distinctive Chantilly wares with
"mosaic" grounds—diapered with small quatrefoils within squares—and birds, fruit, flowers, fable groups, and
hunting scenes in polychrome or, rarely, monotone
blue, were furnished by Peyrard and his successor Anthé-
ume de Surval for the various residences of the Prince
de Condé, son of the founder of the factory. A sugar
bowl decorated with a hunting scene in colors and gold,
bearing the arms of this prince, is dated 1786. An unusual pattern called the Menagerie represents a building
in the park at Chantilly, though not made for use in this
building. A service ordered by the Duke of Orléans for
the château of Villers-Cotterets is festooned with roses.

Oriental influence appears for the last time in two
decorative schemes executed in monochrome blue. One
features a willow tree on a rock with scattered flowers
and insects. The other, created later, has a bird on an
asymmetrical terrace framed by fine garlands in the
Louis XVI style.

The white porcelains of Chantilly are very rare, for
several reasons. The Chantilly paste was heavy, irregu-
lar, and reddish in color, necessitating up to the end of
the factory's existence the use of the aforementioned
glaze made opaque and white by tin oxide. (The use
of such a glaze on porcelain is peculiar to Chantilly,
which also used at the same period a transparent lead
glaze.) Even fine pieces may have defects, usually concealed by painted decoration. Only perfect examples
could do without such camouflage, which explains the
small number of plain white pieces in existence today
and the splendid quality of these wares, still too little
appreciated by collectors. Many that survived into the
nineteenth century were decorated at that time. Finally,
numerous white pieces must remain unidentified. The
molders rarely marked the bodies; it was the decorator
who "signed" a piece, and a work without decoration
was most likely to remain anonymous.

Plate with "mosaic" ground and polychrome decoration
in reserves, representing the style ordered by the
Prince of Condé, 1760-1770. *Musée Condé.*

Plate with monochrome blue decoration: chinoiserie bird
and scroll in center, border of garlands in Louis XVI style;
late eighteenth century. *Musée des Arts Décoratifs.*

Fig. 1 — BISCUIT PORCELAIN JUGS

Outwardly unglazed. The Bacchic piece retains traces of gilding. Both pieces are imitations of English Staffordshire designs — perhaps originally created by Spode. If attempts to emulate the fabric of English parian ware, they will date in the 1840's. Otherwise they could be somewhat earlier.

Except as otherwise noted, illustrations from the author's collection

Jacob Petit, Maker of Porcelain

Where and When He Worked

By EDITH MCCOY

THE gaily colored early nineteenth-century French porcelains that pass in the trade under the generic name of *Vieux Paris* are seldom to be identified by any maker's mark. One takes them or leaves them on such merits as they reveal. Yet here and there the turning over of a plate, a vase, or an exotic figurine that plays a double part as statuette and perfume bottle or perhaps squats on guard beside an inkwell will expose the two boldly executed initials J.P. These initials, invariably painted freehand in blue under the glaze, are pretty generally accepted as standing for the French potter Jacob Petit. But who Jacob Petit was or where he worked few persons know. Even the authorities on European porcelain who mention his name are singularly vague regarding his history and the nature of his product.

Thus William Burton in his *General History of Porcelain* (London, 1921) remarks: "A factory which made some ambitious hard porcelain pieces was established in Fontainebleau in 1795 by Benjamin Jacob and Aaron Smoll. . . . In its early years the wares do not appear to have been marked with any special mark belonging to this factory, but Jacob Petit, a well-known potter, appears to have owned or managed the place from about 1815, and his initials

Fig. 2 — GILDED AND ENAMELED PERFUME BOTTLE (*obverse and reverse*)

Obverse: Naturally colored flowers on a black ground. *Reverse:* A conversation. Colors of the ornamental parts include royal blue, rose Pompadour, and brilliant green. Not improbably of the 1830's

appear at that time on some of the pieces. Shortly afterwards Petit removed the enterprise to Paris, where it was still carried on in 1886, though little seems to be known of his productions." The only known marks shown by Burton are the hastily traced initials shown as *a* in Figure 4.

In his *Pottery and Porcelain* (New York, 1925) Frederick Litchfield has this to say on the subject: "A manufactory was established at Belleville in 1790 by Jacob Petit. . . . The present manufactory [1925] is in the Rue Paradis Poissonnière, Paris." This would seem to imply that Jacob Petit's successors were still going some thirty-nine years beyond the 1886 date given by Burton. Litchfield's portrayal of the factory mark is quite different from that shown by his predecessor. (See *Fig. 4 c*.)

Again, Burton and Hobson's *Handbook of Marks on Pottery & Porcelain* (London, 1928) credits two slightly varying marks to Jacob Petit, with the comment that they occur in blue "1790 onwards" on the porcelain of Belleville. These marks I am reproducing (*Fig. 4 d*). A third, very similar, mark is listed "at Belleville, 1770 — ." All three resemble that given by Litchfield, but are not identical, and depart in some respects from the mark that I have traced from an actual piece in my own collection (*Fig. 4 b*).

All this is a trifle confusing. The situation is not improved when we encounter in the Official Catalogue of the Crystal Palace exhibition in London (1851) the following entry: "Jacob, Petit, *32 Rue de Bondy, Paris* — Manufacturer. A fountain in ornamental porcelain. Porcelain biscuits, designs for patterns." From this it is evident that the English compiler of the catalogue read the potter's name as Petit Jacob rather than the other way about. In this he may have been mistaken. Unfortunately he is now beyond questioning.

Under the circumstances perhaps we would best rely on the authority of the late Marquis de Grollier's notable collection of porcelain, whose *Manuel de l'Amateur de Porcelaines Manufactures Française* was published in 1922 by August Picard of Paris. From this I quote the following regarding the pottery at Fontainebleau: "Founded in 1795 in the dependence of the Hotel de Pompadour, by Benjamin Jacob and Aaron Smoll, the pottery was . . . transferred or sold in 1810 to Jacob Petit, already owner of a pottery at Belleville."

Associated with the studies of the Marquis de Grollier, was Monsieur A. Popoff, who is still living in Paris and to whom I am indebted for not a little information. M. Popoff believes that Jacob Petit lost prestige when, as would appear, he deserted Fontainebleau for Paris, where he was in competition with hundreds of other potters, among whom were Bondy, Charonne, Popincourt, and Thiroux.

Just why Paris became the mecca of so many ceramists I cannot say. To be sure, from the 1760's until the period of the Revolution it was something of a fad for members of the French aristocracy to sponsor potteries in the capital. Most of these enterprises succumbed during the great upheaval. Of the considerable list cited by Hannover in his *Pottery and Porcelain* seemingly not more than one or two survived into the 1800's. However, we know that the upsurge of Liberty,

Fig. 3 — FIGURINE PERFUME BOTTLE
Coral beads and coral stopper. Delicate blue veil. Black and gold overdress; apricot skirt. Cream and gold complete the costume. Evidently one of a pair, though the damsel's consort has long since disappeared. Probably prior to 1850

Fraternity, and Equality was accompanied by a vast smashing of crockery. The ensuing necessity for replacing broken domestic wares may well have overstimulated production, for a time at least.

But to return to Jacob Petit. Piecing together our patchwork of small data, we find the name as early as 1770 associated with a pottery in Belleville. In 1810–1815 it reappears in connection with the pottery at Fontainebleau. Somewhat later, we know not precisely when, it bobs up in Paris. Probably, though not certainly, the "Jacob, Petit," appearing in the British Exposition catalogue of 1851 should read "Petit, Jacob." Several writers concur in the statement that the firm of Jacob Petit was still going as late as the 1880's. Obviously, if the pattern of this chronology is to hold together at all we must reconcile its seeming contradictions. The Jacob Petit who owned a factory in Belleville in 1770 and scrawled on some of his wares the signature recorded by Burton must have been long dead and buried by the 1880's. Indeed, if he was thirty years of age when he became an independent potter he would have been either deceased or incapacitated at the time of the London exposition. Hence we are driven to accept one of two alternatives: either there were two, or even three, successive Jacob Petits active during the 1770–1880 period; or the original Jacob's name was employed as a corporate title by the inheritors of the business that was established by the early potter.

The latter of these alternatives is to be preferred. Originally Jacob Petit was a significant potter, designer, and modeler: ultimately he became a ghostly figure the initials of whose name variously rendered occur on sundry articles of hard-paste French porcelain whose stylistic implications suggest a wide range of dates.

The accompanying illustrations, all portraying marked pieces, will afford some idea of the diversity of products turned out by the firm of Jacob Petit. All are in hard paste, which in the early

a. J.P JP

b. J.P.

Fig. 4 — MARKS
a. From Burton's *General History of Porcelain. b.* From a vase by Jacob Petit in the author's collection

Fig. 5 — JACOB PETIT PLATE
Printed and painted apparently in imitation of English imitations of Japanese design. Apparently before 1850.
From the Museum of Fine Arts, Boston

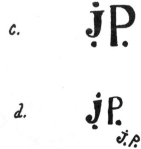

c. JP.

d. JP. JP

Fig. 4 — MARKS
c. From Litchfield's *Pottery and Porcelain. d.* From Burton and Hobson's *Marks on Pottery & Porcelain*

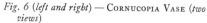
Fig. 6 (left and right) — CORNUCOPIA VASE (*two views*)
The horn is blue with delicately shaded flowers in natural tints. Base, apricot and gold. The mark may be seen on the bottom of the vase

Fig. 7 (below) — VASE WITH FLORAL ENRICHMENTS
From the A. Popoff collection

1780's quite completely supplanted the old-time soft-paste porcelain throughout the potteries of France. While my own collection includes two Jacob Petit items in unglazed biscuit, the factory, like most others of the period, favored vivid colors such as *bleu de roi* (cobalt), *jonquille* (yellow), *vert-pomme* (apple-green), *vert anglais* (grass-green). Some carmines and purples supplanted the delicate rose tints of eighteenth-century Sèvres. Profuse gilding added its quota of enrichment.

As to whether Jacob Petit porcelains are intrinsically better than other Paris wares of what in France corresponds to the English Victorian period, one opinion is probably as good as another. At any rate, the fact that many of them are marked has given them a somewhat adventitious popularity and has, it is said, prompted much imitating of the genuine signature. Pieces which carry the marks here illustrated may probably be trusted. These marks should all be painted freehand in blue *under* the glaze and should exhibit an arrangement of three dots — one crowning the *J*; one following the *P*; and the other either under the *J* or between that initial and its neighbor. The dotless mark given by Burton we may largely disregard. Avoid J. P. marks *over* the glaze.

Little is to be gained by attempting to fix the dates of individual Jacob Petit items, though here and there a guess may be permissible. I am offering a few guesses in the captions of the accompanying illustrations.

Fig. 8 — MANTEL GARNITURE
Seemingly of late period, perhaps of the 1860's or after.
From the A. Popoff collection

IV Other European Porcelain

The articles in this final section have been selected to show how porcelain spread throughout Europe during the 18th century, and how, as the techniques passed from country to country, so too did the decorative styles and traditions.

The first porcelain factory to be established after Meissen was that founded by Du Paquier at Vienna. Although many of these pieces followed the general enthusiasm for oriental styles, others showed a more individualistic debt to the decorative details of the late Renaissance. These pieces reveal a dependence both upon Italian earthenwares, and, more interestingly, upon German glass of the same period. The second article on Vienna serves as a reminder of the close relationship at the time between porcelain and enamel. Not only in Austria, but also in France and England, were enamelers and porcelain makers working side by side.

Italy was one of the first countries to succeed in making porcelain. Early experiments at Doccia, Venice, and elsewhere laid the foundation for the great flowering of the technique that occurred during the 18th century. Although obviously influenced by the universal styles of the period, Italian factories at Naples and Capodimonte managed to produce some quite individual work. As in France and Germany, these factories enjoyed royal patronage and so were able to survive without the extreme commercial pressures that affected the few independent factories. The general nature of porcelain style is underlined by the relationship between Capodimonte and its sister factory at Buen Retiro, near Madrid. Although physically far apart, these two factories were established together to produce a fairly standardized type of porcelain.

The other articles describe porcelain factories in Belgium, Switzerland, Sweden, Russia, and Portugal. In all these countries the manufacture of porcelain followed the pattern already established by Germany and France. Many were founded by potters or decorators who had broken away from established factories in other countries, and they all experienced similar financial and technical problems, the former affected directly by the level of patronage involved. Inevitably these factories were entirely dependent stylistically upon Germany and France. Their products were generally closely imitative and rarely showed any great originality. This was the inevitable result of the interchange of staff from country to country and the almost identical demands of the market which was quite unaffected by national or regional differences. This continuity of style was not simply a feature of the 18th century, but occurred also in the 19th, as shown by the description of the Portuguese and Imperial Russian factories. It is interesting that these largely derivative factories still appeal to collectors and historians when there were many other producing work of great originality, particularly during the 19th century. It is hard to believe that there is not more to 19th century porcelain than the continuity of established 18th century styles and traditions, but the more adventurous and dynamic factories still await the researcher and historian.

Early Vienna porcelain *BY YVONNE HACKENBROCH*

"For this is no ordinary craft, but a secret and most excellent art." *Patent granted to Du Paquier by Charles VI.*

EARLY VIENNA PORCELAIN owes its existence to Claudius Innocentius du Paquier, a commoner whose knowledge of chemistry was combined with considerable commercial enterprise and who in 1718 established the second European factory to produce hard-paste or true porcelain. Meissen and almost all succeeding Continental factories enjoyed royal or princely patronage, but Du Paquier had the courage to start out unsponsored. With the expiration, after twenty-five years, of the special privileges extended by Emperor Charles VI to private business profitable to his realm, Du Paquier was forced to sell his factory to the state and retire; and this brief span accounts for the rarity of Du Paquier's highly valued, most original creations.

In preparation for his venture Du Paquier had visited the Meissen factory during the previous year, intent upon acquiring the secret of porcelain making from some unscrupulous workman, and he had succeeded in attracting the enameler and goldworker Christoph Konrad Hunger to Vienna. Adding bribes to promises he also secured the services of Samuel Stölzel, "arcanist" (a workman in possession of the secret of porcelain making). Both men stayed only long enough to launch production at Vienna and to imprint their style of decoration upon some of the products; Hunger left for Venice in 1719 and Stölzel left a year later, not to be traced. After the expiration of imperial protection in 1744, the factory became state property and introduced the Vienna mark, a shield (*Bindenschild*) incised, impressed, or, more frequently, painted under the glaze of all productions.

The collection of R. Thornton Wilson, presented to the Metropolitan Museum in memory of Florence Ellsworth Wilson, offers an almost unrivaled display of early Viennese porcelain, including signed pieces which help to establish the style of individual painters. Some of these artists were attached to the factory; others, known as *Hausmaler*, worked independently. At Meissen the management, fearful of outside competition, forbade the sale of undecorated porcelain, but no such restrictions were imposed at Vienna. Thus Bohemian and Silesian *Hausmaler* enjoyed a steady supply of Du Paquier's ware, and they added diversity and color to the character of early

Vienna porcelain. They brought to their task the experience and dexterity of faïence and glass decorators, to which porcelain added a new challenge and a rapidly expanding market. Local tradition and individual talent combined to create a new style of ceramic decoration in which, following the prevailing fashion, eastern and western elements were mingled.

The earliest Vienna porcelain in the collection, and probably the earliest in existence, is a tall covered cup (Fig. 1) usually referred to as the Emperor Cup (*Kaiserbecher*). The name is derived from the standing figures of three Hapsburg emperors in full armor, wearing crowns studded with tiny rubies. These figures, with the names of Ferdinand II, Ferdinand III, and Leopold in large

Fig. 1. Beaker with portraits of three Hapsburg emperors; c. 1720. Decorated by Christoph Konrad Hunger; gilded, enameled in rose, gray, and green, and set with stones. Height 11 1/16 inches.

Fig. 2. Small handleless cup with saucer, decorated in *Schwarzlot* (black monochrome) with touches of gold; c. 1720 or 1725. The scene on the saucer is copied from the engraving by Cornelius Galle shown below. Cup, 1½ inches in height; saucer, 4½ inches in diameter.

Fig. 3. Engraving by Cornelius Galle after Johannes Stradanus of Bruges (1523-1605), No. 26 in *Venationes Ferarium Auium, Piscium;* Antwerp, 1578. *New York Public Library.*

capitals, are rendered in thin sheets of stamped and tooled gold, partly covered by translucent enamel in three colors. The figures are separated by arcades and encircled by friezes of raised and gilded strapwork below, and of raised floral scrolls in gold and colors above. The stippled line drawing with which the ground is filled is reminiscent of glass or crystal decoration, as is the rigid character of the inscription. Straight, inflexible lines seem to indicate the burin of the gold or glass engraver rather than the paintbrush of the porcelain decorator, and therein also lies a certain archaism.

The basic shape of the beaker is derived from glass or metal, though modified under the influence, if not by the hand, of Hunger. Unlike any other porcelain vessel in character, this appears to be an early trial piece made before the specific propensities of porcelain had been fully recognized at Vienna. However, the raised and enameled gold decoration is typical of Hunger's work; he may have learned this technique at St. Cloud, before joining Böttger at Vienna. There is a Vienna porcelain bowl with similar gold decoration, and Hunger's signature, in the Austrian Museum at Vienna, which suggests the same authorship for both pieces. Moreover, it appears that after Hunger's departure for Venice in 1720 no similar raised gold decoration was done at Vienna, but it was continued at the Vezzi factory in Venice, which he helped to set up.

The handleless cup and saucer (Fig. 2) are, by contrast, of traditional Chinese shape. The decoration, however, is characteristically western; it is done in *Schwarzlot* (black monochrome) heightened with touches of gold. The curious scene on the saucer, a fight between armored knights and bears with the unequal opponents facing one another in an open landscape, is copied from an engraving by Cornelius Galle (Fig. 3).

It is interesting that the Bohemian *Hausmaler* should adopt a Dutch engraving for his *Schwarzlot* design, since the use of this technique on porcelain is thought to have been introduced into Bohemia by a Dutch glass painter, Daniel Preissler, who settled at Friedrichswalde, near the Bohemian border. There he and his son Ignaz founded a school of glass, pottery, and porcelain decoration, working in black or red monochrome and occasionally in colors. Some of their designs are not unlike the earlier productions of such Nuremberg faïence and glass painters as Johann Schaper and Johann Ludwig Faber.

To Ignaz Preissler, whose work, in the absence of signed pieces, is identified by means of contemporary records and descriptions, may be attributed two slender vases with lion-mask handles, *Schwarzlot* decoration, and touches of gilding (Fig. 4). These vases, of purely European ceramic conception, demonstrate the astounding development of porcelain design during the brief period of about ten years which divides them from the Emperor Cup. The black monochrome arabesques, inspired by designs by Berain, admirably emphasize the brilliance and purity of the white glaze. Preissler's work on porcelain is by no means confined to Vienna; it also includes Meissen and Chinese export ware. There is a pair of Chinese vases in the collection with decoration in under-

Fig. 4. Pair of vases, decorated in black monochrome with touches of gilding by Ignaz Preissler; c. 1730. Height 6⅝ inches.

117

Fig. 5. Coffeepot ascribed to Ignaz Bottengruber; sepia with yellow and blue; c. 1725-1730. Height 8¾ inches. Formerly in the Darmstädter collection.

Fig. 6. Covered cup decorated by Johann Karl Wendelin Anreiter von Zirnfeld (1702-1747); decorated in polychrome with gilding; c. 1735. Height 3 7/16 inches, width 4 11/16. Stand not shown. These signed pieces bear the artist's cipher and family crest.

1730. Perhaps this indicates factory employment: signatures of individual artists were rarely tolerated by the management.

There is a saucer in the collection signed and dated *Bottengruber* at *Breslau 1726*, decorated with a battle scene in purple monochrome surrounded by baroque scrolls and trophies in vivid colors. A coffeepot ascribed to Bottengruber depicts scenes from the story of Apollo amid strap- and scrollwork in sepia, heightened with pale yellow and blue (Fig. 5). Mythological and battle scenes are characteristic of this master, as are crowded compositions and the combination on one piece of monochrome and strong color.

The landscape painter Johann Karl Wendelin Anreiter von Zirnfeld (1702-1747) was an aristocratic artist whose close contact with Du Paquier led to temporary employment at the factory about 1725. He left to assist at the founding of the Ginori factory at Doccia. A covered cup (Fig. 6) with stand bears not only the artist's signature but also his cipher and family crest. The cup, which must have been made for a member of the painter's family, displays a pair of fashionably attired lovers in a landscape.

All these painters helped to form a new style of decoration on porcelain, but it is at the factory, under Du Paquier's own supervision, that a final synthesis was achieved. A flower vase (Fig. 7) decorated in mauve monochrome with gilding depicts Du Paquier seated at a table where he examines porcelain models—cups and saucers, candlesticks, bowls, and a bottle—of types produced at the factory. The scene does not lack in actuality or humor, and the surrounding inscription reveals a certain pride of accomplishment: *China tuas ultra ignotas ne dixeris Artes/En Europaô vinceris ingeniô . . . Viennœ* (China, do not claim that thy arts are unknown beyond thy boundaries: Behold, thou shalt be conquered by European ingenuity—at Vienna).

glaze red and gold, to which Preissler or one of his followers added chinoiserie figures in *Schwarzlot*.

Another *Hausmaler* whose style reveals great individuality, and whose work occasional signatures help to identify, is Ignaz Bottengruber, active at Breslau and Vienna between 1720 and 1740. His early work is executed on Chinese and Meissen porcelain. After 1730, however, when the Meissen decree forbidding the sale of white porcelain to *Hausmaler* took effect, Bottengruber concentrated on Du Paquier porcelain. He settled at Vienna, but no signed or dated work from his hand is known after

Fig. 7. Vase decorated in mauve monochrome
with touches of gilding;
c. 1725. Height 6⅜ inches.
The seated figure is thought
to represent Du Paquier.

Fig. 8. Covered cup decorated with black and gold chinoiseries after Elias Baeck of Augsburg; c. 1725. Height
to rim 4½ inches; over-all, 6¼ inches. Stand not shown.

Fig. 9. Dish in strapwork and trellis pattern, decorated in
polychrome with touches of gilding; c. 1730. Depth
1 7/16th inches, length 9⅜, width 7.

Factory decoration of this early period includes exotic
flowers in vivid colors—prunus sprigs, chrysanthemums,
and peonies—fantastic birds, and pavilions built upon
strange rock formations, inspired by Japanese lacquer-
work and color prints. A tea caddy and several plaques
from the Dubsky porcelain room, originally installed at
Bruenn, illustrate this style, which prevailed until shortly
before 1730. Thereafter Du Paquier's factory painters
favored the black monochrome of Bohemian *Hausmaler*.
European designs, frequently featuring Chinese figure
subjects, gained popularity; an example is the covered
cup (Fig. 8) and stand painted with black and gold
chinoiseries after Elias Baeck of Augsburg. Also about
this time *Deutsche Blumen* (German flowers) replaced
the exotic specimens of the earlier period. A pilgrim bottle
with relief portraits of Emperor Charles VI and his consort (illustrated in ANTIQUES, June 1951, page 453) is
characteristic of this change. Anticipating, and also differing from, a similar fashion at Meissen, Du Paquier's
flowers are of natural colors and generous size, spreading
boldly over the entire surface of the piece.

The motif which distinguishes Du Paquier's finest productions of the thirties is the strapwork and trellis pattern, often interspersed with flowers and fruits, painted in
iron red and other colors. Originally conceived as a border
ornament, it complemented floral or figural representations. In its mature form, however, strapwork emerges as
an entirely independent motif, and perfect harmony is
achieved between basic ceramic shape and applied decoration, each enhancing the other (Fig. 9).

Financial difficulties, never quite absent, resulted in
the sale of Du Paquier's establishment to the state in 1744.
Thereafter economic recovery became the immediate
concern of the new management, and aesthetic considerations and the hitherto unfailing devotion to detail
were occasionally sacrificed.

Christoph and Johann von Jünger, enamel manufacturers in Vienna

BY R. J. CHARLESTON, *Department of ceramics and glass, Victoria and Albert Museum*

THERE IS IN THE VICTORIA AND ALBERT MUSEUM, London, a cup and saucer of painted enamel on copper which was for a long time favored with no better attribution than "Austrian (? Vienna); middle of 18th century" (Fig. 1). Although the form of the cup is unsatisfactory, and both cup and saucer suffer from the ills of chipping and cracking to which time subjects most painted enamels, the flower painting which decorates them is of the highest possible quality, and the gilt rococo scrollwork borders are both free and delicate. This last feature might itself have suggested the attribution to Vienna, for it is very reminiscent of the gilt scrolls which decorate the bases of Vienna porcelain figures of the third quarter of the eighteenth century. The final clue to the identification of these pieces, however, lay in an album of photographs preserved in the department of ceramics at the Victoria and Albert Museum. One of these photo-

graphs showed an enamel *cachepot*, which at the time of taking was in the possession of a dealer in London, and an accompanying note stated that the piece was signed *Ch: v. Junger*. I rediscovered this *cachepot* and the companion to it in the Henry Francis du Pont Winterthur Museum in the winter of 1957-1958 (Figs. 2 and 3). A tray with closely similar flower painting, and with gilt scrolls resembling those on the cup and saucer, is in the Museum für Kunst und Gewerbe, Hamburg (Fig. 4).

Christoph von Jünger appears to have escaped the notice of writers of the standard works on enamels, but fortunately not that of G. E. Pazaurek (*Deutsche Fayence—und Porzellanmaler*, Breslau, 1929, Vol. II, p. 404) or of Leo Grünstein, author of the relevant article in Thieme-Becker's *Künsterlexikon*. Of the pieces by or attributable to the Von Jüngers which are men-

Fig. 1. Cup and saucer, painted in colors and gilt on a white ground. Height of cup, 2½ inches. *Victoria and Albert Museum; crown copyright.*

Fig. 2. *Cachepot,* painted in colors and gilt on a white ground; signed *Ch: v. Junger.*
Henry Francis du Pont
Winterthur Museum.

Fig. 3. Signature on the *cachepot* in Fig. 2.

tioned in these articles, however, it has been possible to trace only a few.

From these authorities we learn that Christoph von Jünger, enamel painter, engraver, and *Ziseleur,* was born in Vienna, the son of an engraver named Clemens Jünger. In 1762, having given proofs of his skill, he was granted a decree of protection (presumably from the terms of the monopoly of the imperial porcelain factory) to work on his own account and with journeymen. In 1764 he applied to the government for a grant, and in the proceedings was referred to as "enameler with protected status" *(Schutzverwandter Emailleur).* By 1766 his undertaking appears to have prospered, for in that year he designated himself "director of the Oriental enamel-factory," employing fifty workmen. His petition for an exclusive privilege was turned down in the following year on the strength of adverse evidence given by an ex-employee. In the *Wienerische Mercantil-Schema* of 1768 he is referred to as "Christoph Jung," living in the Alstergasse near the little Church of the Holy Trinity.

In 1772 Christoph von Jünger fell into trouble with the authorities. He had established a kiln in the "Gräflich Batthyanischem Garten," and began, with the assistance of Claudius Mayer, a thrower from the imperial Vienna porcelain factory, actually to manufacture porcelain. This infringement of the imperial prerogative was not allowed to go unchecked. Von Jünger was surprised by night, arrested, and his kiln suppressed. He himself was imprisoned for not repaying his debt to the state (presumably the grant of 1764) and for making porcelain on his own account. In these proceedings he was referred to as "Court enamel-manufacturer" *(Hofbefreyte Emaillefabrikant).* His status, however, was not perma-

Fig. 4. Tray, painted in colors and gilt on a white ground.
Diameter approximately 11¾ inches.
Museum für Kunst und Gewerbe, Hamburg.

nently jeopardized, for at the time of his death, on July 21, 1777, he is referred to as director of the imperial Nadelburg (k. k. priv. Nadelburger) enamel manufacture, in Josefstadt, a suburb of Vienna.

Johann (von) Jünger, enamel painter and *Ziseleur*, the younger brother of Christoph, was already in partnership with him by 1767, and continued the work until 1780. The Osterreichisches Museum für Angewandte Kunst in Vienna possesses a pair of wine coolers (Fig. 5) signed and dated *J:Junger 1778*. These appear to be the pieces referred to by E. W. Braun in *Kunst und Kunsthandwerk*, 1905 (p. 390).

The work produced at the Von Jüngers' factory was by no means unambitious. Far from limiting themselves to the boxes and trinkets which were the stock in trade of the average eighteenth-century enamel manufacturer, they produced vessels of considerable size and complexity of form. Their *cachepots* (Figs. 2 and 3) and covered bowls (Figs. 6 and 7) give evidence of that emulation of porcelain which was eventually to lead them into trouble with the authorities. Not content with the magnificent "German flowers" of their (presumably) earlier products (Figs. 1, 2, 4), they soon aspired to copy the ground colors and the ground designs popularized by the Sèvres porcelain factory in the third quarter of the eighteenth century—*bleu de roi* (Figs. 5, 6), *bleu céleste* (Fig. 7), *fond caillouté* (Fig. 5), and the rest. The ormolu on some of these pieces (Figs. 5, 6) lends point to the brothers' designation as *Ziseleurs*.

The splendid flower painting on these pieces seems to be all in one style, if not by one hand. If the bouquet on the wine cooler signed by J. Jünger (Fig. 5) is perhaps somewhat tighter than those on the earlier pieces, the difference is very slight and may be due to the discrepancy in date. In all probability, the signatures on these pieces are to be taken as factory-marks, and the work as that of a single painter working successively for both brothers. The covered bowl in Figure 6 gives an unmistakable clue to the place of manufacture of the pieces in Figure 8, and the bowl on the right in that illustration shows a middle stage between the fine flower painting already seen and the very summary work on the other pieces pictured.

The final degeneration of the factory's work may be observed in the tray and small cup illustrated in Figure 9. Both were considered to be of English make when they were acquired by the Victoria and Albert Museum in 1868 and 1869 respectively. Their affinity with the pieces illustrated in Figure 8 now makes their attribution certain. The barbaric character of such pieces and the appearance of small cups in this material suggest that they may have been made for the Oriental market; they recall the small coffee cups (*Türkencöpgen*) which were a specialty also of the imperial Vienna porcelain factory. Their debased character causes one to wonder whether perhaps the enamel factory did not continue to produce for the Oriental market after Johann von Jünger's death in 1780.

Fig. 5. Wine cooler, painted in colors and gilt on a blue ground: signed *J:Junger 1778*. Height approximately 7⅛ inches. *Osterreichisches Museum für Angewandte Kunst, Vienna.*

Fig. 6. Covered bowl and stand, painted in colors and gilt on a blue ground; signed *Christoph v Junger* on the bowl, and *Christoph v Junger* on the stand. Diameter of bowl approximately 8¼ inches. *Osterreichisches Museum für Angewandte Kunst, Vienna.*

Fig. 7. Covered bowl, painted in colors and gilt, on a turquoise ground; signed *Christo v: Junger*. Height with cover, approximately 5½ inches. *Osterreichisches Museum für Angewandte Kunst, Vienna.*

Fig. 8. Covered bowls, painted in colors and gilt on pink and blue grounds. Height of center bowl, 7⅞ inches. *Glynn Vivian Art Gallery, Swansea; photograph by Colquhoun, Ltd.*

Fig. 9. Tray and cup, painted in colors and gilt on a pink ground. Diameter of tray, 10¼ inches. *Victoria and Albert Museum.*

123

The porcelain of Naples

BY NICOLETTA AVOGADRO DAL POZZO

THE NAME CAPODIMONTE has often been misused, today as well as in the nineteenth century, and applied to all sorts of porcelains produced in Naples and elsewhere. In fact, Capodimonte is one of the most debated porcelains in the world. (See ANTIQUES, May 1946, p. 300.) It may be helpful to review briefly the history of the two Bourbon porcelain factories that flourished in the city of Naples during the eighteenth century and into the nineteenth: the Royal Manufactory of Porcelain at the palace of Capodimonte, which between 1743 and 1759 made the older and finer porcelains that are correctly called Capodimonte; and the Royal Manufactory of Naples, which was in operation from 1771 to 1806. Later Neapolitan porcelains, made during the post-royal period between 1807 and 1834, when the factory closed down, are generally referred to as "Naples, nineteenth century."

The Royal Manufactory of Porcelain was founded by Charles of Bourbon, King of Naples and Sicily, and son of Philip V of Spain. In 1738 Charles had married Maria Amelia, daughter of Frederick Augustus II ("the Strong"), King of Poland, Elector of Saxony, and founder of the Meissen factory. The bride's dowry included seventeen cases of gold-tooled red leather, each containing a superb table service of her father's hard-paste porcelain. Naples claimed an old tradition in ceramic production that had flourished largely in the sixteenth and seventeenth centuries, but by the eighteenth century there were only a few manufacturers still in business, producing rough, unrefined earthenware. Charles wanted to restore this once-strong industry for economic reasons, but also, like other European sovereigns at that time, he wanted to duplicate the great advances being made in the manufacture of porcelain at Augustus' factory in Saxony.

The first attempts in Naples to compete with Meissen took place in a building on the grounds of the royal palace of Capodimonte when, in 1743, Charles inaugurated the Royal Manufactory of Porcelain. Livio Ottavio Schepers, a chemist, was in charge of the paste, which was then made of a fine powder from Verruccola and, later, from Fuscaldo. This powder, while similar to kaolin, was not the same and the resulting porcelain was a grayish and very brittle soft paste, not a white hard paste like that made at Meissen. Giovanni Caselli was appointed head painter of the new factory and Giuseppe Grossi supervised the ovens and lathes.

In 1744 Schepers' son Gaetano replaced his father and

Three characters of the Italian Comedy. Royal Manufactory of Porcelain, Capodimonte, 1743-1759. Mark: fleur-de-lis impressed in a circle. Height 7 1/16 inches. *Except as noted, all illustrations are from the Museo Teatrale alla Scala, Milan.*

made an important discovery: a new paste based on powder found near Cosenza. This formula gave a much better product than the powder from either Verruccola or Fuscaldo. It was still a soft paste, but the finished porcelain was a beautiful white, sometimes with a tinge of green, yellow, or pink, and was highly translucent and plastic.

Other important appointments included, in 1745, that of the Tuscan chemist Giovanni Remici as director of coloring and gilding and Giuseppe Gricci as chief modeler. It was Remici who created the famous Capodimonte shades of green, brown, purple-pink, and orange-red. And it was Gricci who modeled many of the factory's masterpieces, such as the admirable *Madonna della Pietà* and, unquestionably his most distinctive work, made between 1757 and 1759, the Parlor of the Queen (also known as the *Sala di Porcellana*, or the Porcelain Room) in the royal villa at Portici. This room was moved in part in 1865 to the palace of Capodimonte where it remains today. The walls of the Portici porcelain room, which measures eighteen by fourteen feet and is fourteen feet high, are covered with porcelain plaques, interrupted only by five large mirrors and one door. Fixed to the plaques with screws are *chinoiserie* porcelain figures in high relief, vases and flowers, ribbons, garlands, and frames—all colored by Giovanni Sigismond Fischer and Luigi Restile, two of the factory's best painters. (A detail of one wall is illustrated in Arthur Lane's *Italian Porcelain*, New York, 1955, Pl. 81.) Among others who decorated Capodimonte porcelains with exquisite delicacy were Maria Caselli (niece of Giovanni Caselli), who specialized in floral painting; Giuseppe della Torre, known for his monochrome blue, purple, and violet sea- and landscapes on tea services; and the miniaturist Jean Morghen.

By 1755, the manufactory was at the height of its activity, with fifty-six artists and specialized artisans producing the lovely, much sought-after porcelains. But four years later Charles inherited the Spanish crown from his half-brother and became Charles III of Spain, leaving the throne of the Kingdom of Naples and Sicily to his third son, Ferdinand IV, then a child of eight. Charles did not want to abandon his hobby, however, so the Royal Manufactory at Capodimonte was transported to Spain, where it became the well-known Royal Manufactory of Buen Retiro. On October 7, 1759, the Capodimonte factory was closed and the tools, molds, finished ware, prepared paste, and even many of the workers were sent to Madrid, where production continued at the works near the Buen Retiro palace from 1760 to 1808.

In 1771 Ferdinand IV decided to restore his father's Neapolitan porcelain plant and established, in the villa of Portici, the Royal Manufactory of Porcelain (which was moved two years later to the royal palace at Naples and was henceforward called the Royal Manufactory of Naples), under the direction first of the Marchese Ricci, then, on his death six months later, of Tomasso Perez. A search was made for former workers at Capodimonte who had not gone to Spain and, when possible, these experienced hands were engaged. Supervisor of the kiln and director of paste composition was Gaetano Tucci; turners included Carlo Tucci and Nicola Bottini; chief modeler until 1781 was the sculptor Francesco Celebrano; head painter was Saverio Maria Grue, and other painters were Francesco Pascale and Antonio Cioffi.

Captain Spacca, an Italian Comedy figure.
Capodimonte. Unmarked.
Height 12 9/16 inches.

At first, the quality of the paste in Ferdinand's factory was not extraordinary, but it improved gradually. The manufactory grew from seven painters and six modelers in 1777 to eleven painters and sixteen modelers in 1780. When Perez died in 1781, Domenico Venuti succeeded him as director of the plant and contributed much to its success. The noted sculptor Filippo Tagliolini was called from the Imperial Factory in Vienna to become chief modeler, and he particularly excelled in composing white glazed or biscuit groups of classical inspiration. In accord with the neoclassical taste, white biscuit was often used for reproducing the sculptures found in the excavations nearby at Herculaneum (begun by Ferdinand's father in 1738) and Pompeii, as well as for busts of the royal family and other important personages. A particularly fine modeler who specialized in this type of work was Giuseppe Giordano, better known as Peppe, who was active until the end of the century; his pieces are often recognizable by their lack of a base.

Finally, in 1784, kaolin, that precious clay whose discovery in Saxony had given Meissen its head start in the making of hard-paste porcelain, was discovered at Caprarola (near Viterbo); and the coveted formula for hard paste was developed in Naples shortly after that.

However, the Royal Manufactory of Naples was threatened by the Napoleonic invasions, and in 1806 it was taken over by the French government and almost immediately sold to a French joint stock company directed by Jean Poulard Prad. Ferdinand IV was restored to the throne in 1815 (as Ferdinand I), but had lost interest in porcelain by then. Prad sold half the factory in 1818 to Claude Guillard and Giovanni Tourné, and the next year the rest was bought by Francesco Paolo del Re. Ferdinand II, grandson of Ferdinand IV, or I, tried to reestablish the prestige of the Royal Manufactory, but the effort failed. In 1834 the entire factory complex was sold to the Parthenopean Society. Yet before the society could begin any regular production, all its premises were requisitioned by the government, which needed emergency hospital space because of a cholera epidemic in Naples. From that day on, the factory was closed and any Neapolitan production of ceramics was left in the hands of private artisans and limited mainly to earthenware and majolica. For all practical purposes, however, it can be said that the activity of the Royal Manufactory of Naples was officially ended in 1806, when Bourbon patronage ceased.

This brief history of the two Bourbon factories of Naples is presented to underline the problems facing the collector seeking true Capodimonte porcelain. The chief difficulty is how to distinguish the porcelains of the various periods and factories from each other. First it is necessary to identify the mark correctly, then to note carefully the quality and type of paste, and finally to study the style of the piece and its decoration. But even these steps may not lead to easy answers.

Most Capodimonte porcelains bear the Bourbon fleur-de-lis enclosed in a circle, impressed in the paste on figures and painted in underglaze blue on other wares. However, it must be noted that the very earliest products of Capodimonte often bore no marks at all. (All the marks are reproduced in W. B. Honey, *European Ceramic Art*, London, 1952, p. 441.)

The crowned monograms F R F, F R, or R F in blue, red, crimson, purple, or black enamel appear on the porcelains of the Royal Manufactory of Naples. Toward the end of the eighteenth century the famous mark of the crowned N came into use, either impressed in the paste or painted in underglaze blue. This mark has created much confusion, because in the middle of the nineteenth century many firms, including the Florentine factory of Doccia, began to imitate it. But although the wares of Doccia are easily recognized by the expert eye, it is very difficult to distinguish the porcelains of Capodimonte from those of Buen Retiro, since the latter was a continuation of the former, under the same patron, and using the fleur-de-lis mark (in blue or, more rarely, in gold), often the same paste, and even many of the same workmen.

As has been said, occasionally early Capodimonte is unmarked, and sometimes a mark is used fraudulently. Therefore, a careful study of the paste is important. Capodimonte porcelain, made while Charles was in Naples, is made of a soft paste that, especially in the pieces made after 1749, is of a warm white, with a tinge of light yellow, green, or pink. The paste is very plastic and highly

Plate decorated with a view of the San Carlo Theater of Naples. Royal Manufactory of Naples, 1814. Mark: N under a closed crown, with the inscription *Napoli 1814* under a closed crown. Diameter 9⅝ inches.

Two caricatures, *Right:* The abbot Ferdinand Galliani, a Neapolitan scholar and statesman. Unmarked. Height 5¾ inches. *Left:* The Marchese Bernardo Tanucci, a statesman and minister of Charles, King of Naples and Sicily, and Ferdinand IV, his son. Unmarked. Height 5⅛ inches. These two figures differ in both modeling and quality of glaze, and the plastic qualities of the Galliani figure are superior to those of the Tanucci. A close examination of the glaze and of the flesh colors confirms Elena Romano's attribution of the Galliani figure to the Royal Manufactory of Naples (Ferdinand IV period, 1771-1806) and the Tanucci figure to the Tuscan manufactory of Doccia, c. 1773.

Group representing a miser counting his money. Capodimonte. Unmarked.

translucent, and the glaze, while it may be of varying thickness, has a smooth, never too shiny, luster. The undersides are usually not glazed. The paste used in the Royal Manufactory of Naples, especially in the early years, was similar but not equal to that of Capodimonte. Ferdinand's product is a very translucent glassy white or cream-color soft paste, often with a yellow tinge during the early years of the manufactory. To hide this defect, an opaque white tin glaze was used; later, when the color of the paste was improved, the glaze was translucent.

The next clue in identifying Neapolitan porcelain is the pictorial decoration. In Capodimonte, the colors were usually stippled on; this technique is similar to that used in miniature painting and is easily recognizable. Flesh tones and flowers, however, were done with very minute and fine brush strokes. Designs drawn in outline were painted in muted colors. The first painted decorations were in monochrome violet, blue, black, and crimson. Colored designs are recorded as early as 1745 and the most characteristic colors of Capodimonte are pale orange, crimson, brown, red, grayish green, and olive green, A well-known peculiarity worth looking for is a violet shading that can often be found on clouds and in the flesh tones.

The most common subjects for the Capodimonte artisans were *chinoiseries*, land- and seascapes, battles and other historic events, gallant figures, flowers, and fruits. Both the subject matter and the shapes of some pieces show the German baroque influence of Meissen, but in the later years of Capodimonte production the rococo style was also used (the Portici porcelain room is an excellent example of this type of decoration). Among the Capodimonte products were many pieces for everyday use: plates, coffee cups, tea services, snuffboxes, cane heads—with gold and silver mounts which, after 1750, were frequently worked by the French artist Pierre Chevalier—openwork baskets, tureens, table sets, and portrait lockets. The figures, which today are considered among the most valuable in the world, portray typical popular characters of their day, such as fishermen, servants,

lovers, beggars, as well as characters of the Italian Comedy.

In its early days, the Royal Manufactory of Naples tried to imitate Capodimonte porcelains not only in paste composition but also in coloring, shape, and decoration. But under Venuti's direction a few years later, production acquired more originality and passed from the rococo style (with baroque tendencies) to a pronounced neoclassicism. Among the famous products of this period is the "Etruscan" table service. Other productions of this later period include interesting neoclassical white biscuit and glazed figures and delightfully humorous Neapolitan folk figures. Among the pictorial subjects painted on the tablewares are Neapolitan landscapes, characters in local costumes, hunting scenes, warships, fish, birds, and flowers.

Two-handled cup and cover, with polychrome and gold decoration. Royal Manufactory of Naples (Ferdinand IV period). Mark: R F under a crown painted in red enamel. Height 4 5/16 inches. *Privately owned.*

Figure of a gentleman. Royal Manufactory of Naples (Ferdinand IV period). Mark: crowned N painted in black enamel. *Privately owned.*

Very characteristic is the decoration in two tones of gold, which gives a beautiful effect but is extremely delicate.

Many forgeries of the nineteenth-century porcelains turn up in the market today. Somewhat paradoxically, the older forgeries are more readily recognizable than the newer, as the latter benefit from improved techniques. A few tips that may be useful to the collector in separating the true from the false are: 1) The imitations are usually heavier than the originals. In this connection, it is interesting to note that a well-known porcelain expert in Milan discovered recently that a figure of Captain

Spacca, a famous character of the Italian Comedy, was a fake. The piece had been bought in Switzerland by a collector as original Capodimonte, but the purchaser was sadly disillusioned when the expert noted, first, that the mark, the traditional fleur-de-lis, was impressed but not enclosed in a circle; and, second, that the piece was heavier than a similar piece—unquestionably authentic—which is in the Museo Teatrale alla Scala in Milan. The finishing touch was the discovery that there were some scratches under the glaze; that is, they had been incised in the paste before firing to make the piece look old and slightly damaged.

2) The mark of the crowned N used by the Royal Manufactory of Naples after 1771 is very unreliable as a criterion of authenticity. This mark has been used fraudulently not only in Italy but also in France and other countries. In the first decades of this century, for example, certain manufacturers in Dresden used to send their representatives to Italy with albums of photographs of their porcelains (mostly figures), and their Italian customers were asked to specify what mark they wished on each order. Many would choose the crowned N, which could be taken by a prospective buyer as representing either Naples or Doccia porcelains.

3) Forgeries can often be spotted by a study of the style. These fakes are usually figures of romantic ladies in crinolines, laces, or tulle, and of gentlemen dressed in the fashions of the eighteenth century. They are often in white glazed porcelain and their bases are of nineteenth-century rococo style. The glaze is usually very glassy and the paste is often a bluish white, quite different from that used in genuine pieces. Moreover, these forgeries are elaborate and lack the naïveté that is one of the main charms of true Neapolitan porcelains of the eighteenth century. The modelers and painters of the Bourbon factories at Naples were often excellent artists who demonstrated their exceptional talents in the modeling and decoration of such small pieces. Because of these qualities, the eighteenth-century porcelains of Naples—and particularly those of the Royal Manufactory at Capodimonte—rank high among the very best contemporary work of European factories.

CAPODIMONTE
AND BUEN RETIRO PORCELAIN

By JOAN PRENTICE

FEW EIGHTEENTH-CENTURY PRODUCTS offer so many pitfalls to the unwary as Capodimonte porcelain. Almost the entire surviving body of material remains in Italy, and only about a hundred pieces, it is estimated, have found their way to other parts of Europe and to America. For this reason few fellow-European and almost no American authors have attempted to outline the chronology, composition, or distinguishing features of the ware. Those that have are divided in their opinions, accounts conflict, and so far we have not been able to obtain in this country a catalogue of the important exhibition held in Naples in 1877 which would undoubtedly be the source of much valuable information. Even more discouraging is the fact that Europe and America are flooded with reproductions of the white porcelain decorated with mythological scenes in colored relief (*Figs. 5 and 7*) which is particularly associated with this factory. Not only has the Ginori factory made quantities of comparable pieces from the original molds, but other factories in Germany, France, and Italy have copied and adapted the same. About 1860 the making of these Capodimonte-style pieces reached great perfection. Well-known factories sometimes used their own marks, but like many of the originals, the imitations will usually be found with a crowned *N* for Naples in underglaze blue.

The most that can be attempted here is to show a few pieces of unquestionable authenticity, and a few reproductions with which to compare them. A careful analysis of the qualities of each should reveal some standards by which to judge.

A search for real examples within a reasonable distance went virtually unrewarded. Fifteen of the leading museums and private collections in the east and middle west were consulted, and hardly a piece turned up. A few early figure groups of colored porcelain in the collection of Judge Irwin Untermyer,

including a remarkable pair of dwarfs after etchings by Jacques Callot, and the pieces illustrated in Figures 1, 5, and 7 are therefore the only important ones we know of in America which can be attributed to Capodimonte with considerable certainty. At the same time a surprising number of Buen Retiro figures, vases, and other objects came to light. As this factory was an offshoot of the one at Naples, so closely bound to it at first that the products are almost indistinguishable, it seems advisable to discuss the two together. A brief outline and history of the two factories follow.

CAPODIMONTE—ITALY

Date	Location	Rule	Mark
1st Period 1743-1759	Capodimonte (near Naples)	Charles III	Bourbon fleur-de-lis
2nd Period 1771-1773	Portici	Ferdinand IV	R.F. F.R.F.
1773-1807	Naples	until 1806	N crowned
1807	Naples	Purchased by a Commercial Company	
1806-1814	Naples	French Government	
1821	Naples	Return of Ferdinand IV Compelled to close Models sold	

FIG. 1 (*left*) — PAIR OF CANDLESTICKS. Capodimonte, before 1759. Figures in Near-Eastern dress. *Courtesy of the Philadelphia Museum of Art.*

FIG. 2 (*right*) — PAIR OF FIGURINES by Vicente Rocco. Buen Retiro, 1770-1780. One signed. *Courtesy of Judge Irwin Untermyer.*

FIG. 3 (*left*) — VASE with purple monochrome painting. Buen Retiro, *c.* 1780. Double *C* mark. *Courtesy of the Hispanic Society of America.*

FIG. 4 (*right*) — PAIR OF VASES decorated with classical medallion on a black ground. Landscapes in sepia on the back. Buen Retiro, *c.* 1805. *Courtesy of the Metropolitan Museum of Art.*

Charles III, a Bourbon, King of Naples and Sicily from 1735, married Maria-Amelia, daughter of Frederick Augustus II of Saxony, who brought with her to Italy quantities of the fine white Meissen porcelain then unique in Europe. Inspired by these models the King resolved to start a factory at the palace. Appointing Giovanni Caselli director, he engaged Livio Ottavio Schepers, a chemist of Belgian origin, as chief technician. The exact composition of the true porcelain being made at Meissen was a closely guarded secret, but it was believed that the formula could be duplicated. Experiments with Italian clays began. Soon the space at the palace proved inadequate and the King decided to transform the Royal Villa of Capodimonte near-by into suitable quarters. Plans were approved, and the factory commenced operations in 1743. Not, however, until 1785, according to some authorities, was the long-sought formula for hard-paste porcelain secured. In the intervening years at least four totally different kinds of mixed pastes were employed: one greenish grey, one yellow, and two white but still imperfect.

The products of the first period were of soft-paste porcelain, the majority small in size. Oriental, French rococo, and Meissen influences were all apparent, in addition to a predominant native taste for rocks and sea-forms. Jugs and goblets, coffee and chocolate services, snuffboxes, and cane handles were made, and some statuettes. Figures in contemporary costume, and a variety of actors in scenes from the Italian comedies (*compare Fig. 2*), are among the most original and delightful contributions of this factory. Objects were for sale as early as 1745. In 1758 the celebrated Sala de Porcelana, the ceiling and walls of which were decorated with porcelain, was begun and finished the following year. By this time mirror frames and

clock cases were being made, and ornamental vases (*compare Fig. 3*). At the height of achievement Charles III inherited the throne of Spain. Resigning the Kingdom of the Two Sicilies to his third son, Ferdinand IV, he moved to Madrid. He took with him, to start another factory, molds, materials, and the majority of the ablest workmen, who demolished furnaces and destroyed much that could not be transported in order that their reputations should remain unimpaired.

In 1771 King Ferdinand, then twenty years old, decided to revive the royal factory which had languished in the meantime but had not entirely died. Under the auspices of the Marchese Ricci it was transferred to Portici, but after his death the following year the factory was moved again, this time to Naples. The productive years of the second period brought glory to the nation. Profoundly affected by the treasures unearthed at Herculaneum and Pompeii under Charles III and later, the baroque style was soon overwhelmed by a classic revival which penetrated to the farthest corners of Europe. Best known, though largely because of the many reproductions, are the pieces decorated with mythological scenes in relief (*Figs. 5 and 7*). This style was never copied at Buen Retiro which would seem to indicate that it originated after the departure of Charles III for Spain. Services were decorated with flowers more sophisticated than those of the first period, seashells, local views, and peasant scenes, but classical motifs were chiefly in demand. Portrait busts, and a whole Olympus in biscuit soon appeared. Vases ornamented with black and gold, and plain surfaces with medallions from the antique (*compare Fig. 4*) were fashionable. The peak of perfection was reached during the 1780's when Ferdinand presented a full dinner service to his father, and ordered another in the Etruscan style for the King of England. Success lasted to within a few years of the invasion of Naples by the armies of Napoleon. About 1807 the manufacture of colored and decorated porcelain ceased, and only a broken and curtailed production of biscuit continued until the factories' final and complete collapse a few years later. In 1821 molds and models were sold, the majority passing into the hands of the Ginori factory of Doccia.

Fig. 5—Bowl with scenes representing Ariadne and the flood of Deucaleon, Capodimonte, 1771-1780. Crowned *N* impressed. *Courtesy of Miss Henrietta G. Ricketts.*

Fig. 6—Sugar Bowl, with mythological scenes from a Capodimonte mold. Ginori, twentieth century. Crowned *N* in underglaze blue. *Courtesy of Miss Henrietta G. Ricketts.*

Buen Retiro — Spain

Date	Location	Rule	Mark
1st Period 1760-1804	Madrid	Charles III (King 1759-1788)	Bourbon fleur-de-lis and Double C (toward end of reign)
		Charles IV (King 1788-1808)	The same
2nd Period 1804-1808	Madrid	Charles IV	Md crowned or not
1808-1814	Madrid	Ferdinand VII French Invasion-British Entry Return of Ferdinand VII	
1817	Madrid	End	

The history of the Buen Retiro factory differs only slightly from that of the parent organization. A site was selected at no great distance from the Royal Palace at Madrid, and there the leading Capodimonte artisans, with Giuseppe Gricci, chief modeler, at their head, continued operations almost as if there had been no interruption. The Neapolitan influence, with but slight Spanish infiltrations, was predominant until the last descendants of the Gricci and Schepers families died at the end of the century. So close were the products of the first period to those of Capodimonte that in many cases the ware was indistinguishable. The same processes were employed, the same workmanship, even the same pastes, and when marked at all, the fleur-de-lis was generally used. Presents were exchanged between the courts, and some of the pieces, it is said, were begun in Naples and finished at Buen Retiro. Almost at once two extravagant porcelain rooms were designed at Aranjuez and the Royal Palace at Madrid. Continual experiments with clay were carried on here as at Naples, for the soft paste in use at first was excellent for sculpture groups, but very defective for services. An improved paste was authorized about 1785, but true hard paste lingered until the turn of the century. Intense rivalry and discord prevailed between the Gricci and Schepers families and disputes arose between Italian and Spanish workmen. Money was spent recklessly on the enterprise to keep it going, for objects were produced exclusively for the ornamentation of the palaces. Without the stimulus of trade, and with little contact with the outside world, vitality ebbed. In an effort to secure funds some porcelain was placed on sale in Madrid in 1788, but the results did not come up to the King's expectations.

Products of the long first period were very like those of Capodimonte. Glazed and colored groups were made in the early days, with a freshness and vivacity about the figures that are exceptionally attractive (*Fig. 2*). Lively postures, natural charm, and unusual coloring characterized many of the compositions until gradually the neo-classic style, creeping like a glacier across the frontiers, touched all the artists with its icy fingers. Of vases and other large decorative pieces there was an abundant and varied production. The Mirror Room at the Royal Palace contains magnificent specimens. Many pieces were decorated in the Chinese manner, others were in imitation of Wedgwood, or with garlands of flowers and wide bands of black, red, blue, or gold. The large vase with country scenes in monochrome (*Fig. 3*) shows a typical kind of blurred painting done with the end of the brush, which is very effective when applied to landscape. Biscuit and representations of the antique gradually gained the ascendancy.

In a brief second period the factory underwent a complete change. Charles IV, on his accession to the throne, resolved to introduce new methods. Presently D. Bartolomé Sureda, an energetic, progressive, and intelligent man, was sent to Paris to study the processes in use at Sèvres. Familiarizing himself with both the French and English manufacturing systems, he returned to Spain with knowledge of the composition of true porcelain, and two skilled French workmen. Having been appointed director of the factory, he immediately set about obtaining a new paste. So resourceful were his efforts that he succeeded in creating an original formula. Ingredients capable of substituting for kaolin were found which gave a particular brilliance and beauty to the products of this period. The paste could be subjected to the highest temperatures without harm, and the biscuit was said to be superior to that of Sèvres. Dinner services on a grand scale, and a variety of useful objects were produced, and it was hoped that the factory would soon be able to compete in the foreign market. The neo-classic style prevailed, and French influence was very marked (*Fig. 4*). The active years of the Sureda régime were only too short-lived. The calamity of the French invasion dealt the factory its death blow. Detachments of French troops converted its buildings into a fortress, and the looting of the foreign soldiers was followed by an uprising of Spanish patriots who in their fury destroyed everything they could lay their hands on. In 1817 the remaining equipment was moved to Moncloa.

Reproductions

Foremost in the minds of all connoisseurs, collectors, and museums is the ever-present problem of reproductions. The clear line of demarcation between original creative works of art and the long series of adaptations and modifications to which they invariably give rise becomes very faint indeed when one attempts to draw it between such so-called style-pieces and reproductions. Art vocabularies run the gamut from "copy of" or "in the style or manner of" to "reminiscent of" and "inspired by," in a laudable effort to distinguish between various degrees of indebtedness, but the reproduction proper is something else. As crime is judged on the basis of premeditation, so reproductions can best be judged on creation *with intent to deceive*. How can such be recognized?

In the case of Capodimonte and Buen Retiro porcelain little reliance can be placed upon the marks. Quantities of real pieces from both factories have no marks of any kind, and many, if not most, Capodimonte reproductions have a crowned *N* in underglaze blue. To complicate the matter further, both factories used the Bourbon fleur-de-lis, usually in blue, but sometimes in red, gold, the predominant color of the decoration, or impressed. Other factories, particularly in France, also used the fleur-de-lis. A star has been ascribed by some authors to early Capodimonte pieces, but illustrations show it to be very similar to one used by Doccia. In like manner, unmarked Buen Retiro can easily be mistaken for kindred Alcora porcelain. Attribution, therefore, must depend on other characteristics: size, shape, weight, coloring, and modeling; the quality and composition of the paste; analysis of the style; a considered general impression of the whole. Far from being discouraged by these facts, experience teaches that hope springs eternal in the collector's breast. The Rembrandt, the Chippendale, the Ming, or the Capodimonte are either already in one's possession, or just around the corner. Let him speak who, having once begun, ever lost heart.

Fortunately we know of no reproductions of Buen Retiro porcelain, and few, if any, dangerous ones of Capodimonte, other than those in the colored relief style, with the possible exception of figure groups, which may or may not have been intended reproductions. Let us then carefully consider Figures 5-8. The pieces shown in Figures 5 and 7 we confidently believe are authentic. An interesting comparison can be made between the bowl of Figure 5 and the sugar bowl (*Fig. 6*), as the same scene occurs on both, although a different side of the bowl has been chosen for illustration. The sugar bowl, which has handles in the form of coral, is a modern Ginori piece made, or at least adapted, from a Capodimonte mold. Close examination reveals these differences:

General Impression

Old: Black color rarely used.
   Shading and outlines principally in grays, browns, and purples, which blend in with other colors.
   Bright but delicate coloring. Hair and flesh tints very pale.
   Blank areas above, below, and within the design.
New: Black freely employed.
   Land, rocks and water streaked with black, outlines of the same.
   Harsh and garish coloring.
   Space overfilled. Few, if any, blank areas. Design continuous from the bottom. Clouds in color at the top.

Figures

Old: Red outlines rarely used, and only faintly perceptible.
   Stippling hardly apparent. It must be examined at close range to be seen.
New: Crudely outlined with solid red line.
   Stippling dark and pronounced. Unreal, spotted appearance.

Comparing the coffeepot (*Fig. 7*) with quite a number of doubtful pieces, including those of Figure 8, corroborates the above except that some reproductions make no use of black, and clouds are not always present. Additional observations are:

Coloring

Old: When two or more colors are used on a single object or area, one is put on *over* the other. Colors do not shade from one *into* the other.
   The painting is done with considerable irregularity, variety, and charm.
New: A single object or expanse will often shade from brown *into* green *into* yellow, for example, so that the coloring lies in bands.
   The painting is either finicking and streaked, or slapdash. Monotonous regularity in both cases.

Gold

Old: The coffeepot has red underpainting beneath the gold. Scrollwork *not* outlined or shaded with black.
New: Many of the reproductions show no red underpainting beneath the gold. Scrollwork *often* outlined or shaded with black. (See bases of outer pair of ewers, Figure 8).

The utmost caution should be used in the presence of large, showy, or brilliantly colored pieces. The crude fake is far more easily detectable than the gorgeous one. And let it constantly be kept in mind that real Capodimonte, of the kind we are discussing, is extremely rare outside of Italy. It must have an eighteenth-century look. A thick, soapy, or off-white body; firing cracks and small imperfections in the glaze; small size, delicate coloring, and faithful workmanship are favorable indications. A pure white body, harsh coloring, overcrowding and overelaboration of detail, a preponderance of black or gold, gold outlined with black, the use of a gold rose to fill a blank space on the inside of a cup or saucer, or beneath a handle, are unfavorable indications. If one hard and fast rule could be laid down it would be this — let all who have to do with Capodimonte porcelain be slow, be doubtful, and beware.

FIG. 7 (*left*) — COFFEEPOT, showing the Judgment of Paris. Capodimonte, 1771-1780. *Courtesy of the Philadelphia Museum of Art.*

FIG. 8 (*right*) — EWERS in the Capodimonte style. Crowned *N* in underglaze blue on all. *Courtesy of Mrs. G. L. Hitchcock.*

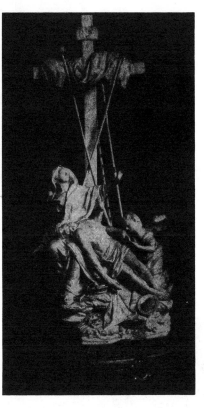

Left, biscuit group depicting the Descent from the Cross, by Gauron or Lecreux, with ormolu base (c. 1765-1770). Height 28 inches. Right, similar subject from Chelsea, by Gauron or Willems. Height 10 inches. *Collection of J. J. Tufnell.*

The porcelain of Tournai *BY KITTY RUEFF*

THOUGH IT IS NOT FRENCH, Tournai porcelain is very close to French soft-paste, possessing the same charm and elegance. Since 1830 Belgian, the town of Tournai, on the banks of the Scheldt, belonged to the southern part of the Low Countries at the time when they were under Austrian rule. Prior to the establishment of a porcelain factory there, Tournai was known chiefly for its tapestries, its goldsmiths' art, and its cathedral.

Early in 1750 François Carpentier started a pottery factory in Tournai with the financial help of the town. Less than a year later, he felt obliged to sell his establishment to François-Joseph Peterinck, who was born in Lille in 1719 and had been a merchant at Ath (Hainaut) until he became interested in making soft-paste porcelain.

Peterinck had as his partners for a period of two and a half years the brothers Dubois. They had worked at St. Cloud and Chantilly and later started the famous factory of Vincennes, and their advice proved of immense value in the development of the Tournai factory. Peterinck appealed to Maria Theresa, Empress of Austria, to be allowed to call his establishment Manufacture Imperiale et Royale, and to have exclusive use of the tower and crossed swords with stars in the angles as his porcelain marks. The factory was permitted to sell to all countries under Austrian rule, and many pieces slipped into France, since Tournai was near the frontier.

From the beginning Peterinck employed skilled labor and the most accomplished decorators, and turned out fine ornamental work, including busts, groups, figures in biscuit or enameled in white or polychrome, perfume burners, vases, plaques, small boxes, polychrome table services, and so on. In the earlier days of the factory a most elaborate chandelier was produced.

Economic considerations, however, forced Peterinck to manufacture also utilitarian tableware in blue and white such as was produced at Chantilly and St. Cloud. This was sold in great quantities and contributed towards financing the elaborate polychrome pieces, which were often ruined during the successive firings. Today in many Belgian families complete services, monochrome and polychrome, are still found in frequent use. Rival factories at St. Amand-les-Eaux and Arras tried to copy Tournai's blue-and-white services, but without great success.

Peterinck was constantly in financial difficulties, though he was always helped by the magistrates of Tournai and the governors of the Low Countries. His enterprise developed rapidly, and he was soon employing over a hundred workmen. By the time of the factory's peak, in the 1770's and 1780's, the number had increased to four hundred.

Several of Peterinck's artists had worked at Chelsea before coming to Tournai, and others migrated to England after leaving his employ, so that there is a close link between the two factories. Henri-Joseph Duvivier, who was born in Tournai, was employed for many years at Chelsea and acquired there much of O'Neale's technique. He later did outstanding work at Tournai, executing

Oblong polychrome plaque, originally framed in black wood and inlaid in a bureau, representing a harbor scene probably inspired by Italian paintings, with a temple at left and a statue of Neptune inscribed *Tableau de porcelaine fait a la fabrique de Tournay le janvier 1787 par J. J. Mayer, eleve de la fabrique.* Size 19 by 12 inches.

Left and right, pair of white enamel-glazed covered perfume burners, ornamented with garlands of flowers and Cupids and swans, with applied flowers on the base (c. 1770). Height 6 inches. Center, figure group of a boy leaning against a tree conversing a girl who sits at his feet, inspired by Chelsea (c. 1765). Height 9½ inches. *Collection of P. Delplace.*

Pair of polychrome statuettes of a fruit vendor and flower girl, showing strong Chelsea influence (c. 1770). The same models exist in white. Height 6½ inches.

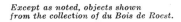

Except as noted, objects shown from the collection of du Bois de Roest.

Examples reflecting the work of Duvivier (c. 1775). Left, covered sucrier decorated with a peacock and exotic birds, painted in bold colors, with the acorn finial frequently used at Tournai. Height 4 inches. Center, plate in *camaieu rose*, with a fable subject from La Fontaine, reeded rim found on many Tournai plates, and fine gold border. Diameter 4 inches. Right, covered milk jug with fable subject in brown and green with touches of gold. Height 6 inches.

Three typical oval Tournai boxes, with silver and silver-gilt mounts. Left, landscape with figures and river scene in polychrome on bleu de Roi ground with gold, painted by Mayer (c. 1775). Height 1½ inches. Center, rural scene with figures on outside of box and wedding scene inside lid, in polychrome on bleu de Roi ground, enhanced with gold. Length 4½ inches. Right, fruit and birds in rural settings. Length 3½ inches.

Two chinoiserie plates from one of Tournai's finest services, called *camaieu vert*, in soft olive, with gold line around the edge (c. 1775). Probably by Duvivier, the decoration shows resemblances to O'Neale's technique. *Collection Delattre.*

Three covered custard pots decorated with polychrome flowers (c. 1765). Left and right, showing Mennecy influence, the left one reeded the other plain, both with a fruit finial. Center, reserve panels framed by a diaper pattern in rust, with twisted finial. *Collection P. Delplace.*

Jardiniere with dolphin handles, decorated with exotic birds in strong colors, the border touched with gold (c. 1775). Length 12 inches. *Privately owned.*

Left, knifegrinder group, composed of two cupids, the boy with quiver at his side grinding an arrow, the little girl handing him another (c. 1775). Vividly colored, the same model exists also in white enamel. Height 8 inches. Right, one of Tournai's figure masterpieces, showing a young boy with a magic lantern on his back playing a hurdy-gurdy (c. 1775). In various tones of red, rust, brown, and white, the same model exists in biscuit and white enamel. Height 7 inches.

fables, birds, and classical landscapes with figures, and in 1765 became Directeur de l'Academie de Tournai. Other artists who worked at Tournai after having been at Chelsea were the Paris-born Nicholas-Joseph Gauron, a master modeler, who made busts, groups, and statuettes, and Joseph Willems, a native of Brussels and a skilled sculptor, who made groups and figures.

Tournai never attempted hard-paste porcelain. The clay used was of an off-white color and finely grained. Clay from the same region near Tournai was used also by Delft, as well as by the faience factories of Lille, St. Amand-les-Eaux, and St. Omer. The paste in the beginning had a slightly gray appearance but was soon perfected to the finest quality, with a brilliant glaze. Like most eighteenth-century factories, Tournai reflected the influence of Chinese designs and the work of the great factories—Meissen, Chelsea, Mennecy, Vincennes, and Sèvres. Beautiful designs of birds and fruit and the outstanding *camaieu rose* characterize the productions of Tournai at its zenith, around 1775-1790.

Peterinck died in 1799, and was succeeded by Bettignies, his son-in-law. The Tournai factory remained in operation into the nineteenth century, but the output began to show signs of decadence. Tournai at this time was under Dutch rule. A considerable quantity of undecorated porcelain was sent to The Hague and decorated there, such wares bearing the mark of a stork.

Today France is the only country outside Belgium where collections of Tournai may be found. This is most unfortunate, in view of the beautiful pieces that were turned out by the factory in the eighteenth century. At the time of the coronation of Queen Elizabeth II, Londoners were given an opportunity to see Tournai porcelain in an exhibition held at the Belgian Institute. Examples were selected from museums and private collections, and the showing aroused wide interest, since porcelain from Belgium had not been previously exhibited in England. Several examples of Chelsea were also on view, enabling visitors to compare the work of the two factories.

Plate and pair of cache pots of the famous service, *aux oiseaux de Buffon*, by Joseph Mayer, one of the factory's finest artists, inspired by Buffon's natural history (c. 1780-1785). Large bands of bleu de Roi, enhanced with innumerable kinds of gold ornament, and polychrome reserve panels decorated with birds, all of them different, as well as butterflies and grisaille heads. The names of the birds are marked in black on the reverse. The service was ordered by Philippe Duke of Orleans. *Collection P. Delplace.*

Four small polychrome statuettes representing hunting subjects, with a strong resemblance to Chelsea red-anchor figures, delicately modeled and partially painted in pale colors (c. 1765). Height 3½ inches.

Plate with design of Chinese type, made up of peonies, a butterfly, and small flowers in the center, a diaper border with flower reserves, an outer border containing Chinese utensils, and a rim finished in a Greek fret motif (c. 1770).

Very early cup and saucer, similar to Vincennes examples, decorated with yellow and red tulips and flowers in blue, red, and puce, with green leaves (c. 1755). *Collection P. Delplace.*

Deep plate with a central landscape surrounded by a wide border of polychrome flowers and golden trellis work on a puce ground. *Collection of D. Goldblatt.*

White enameled group of fishers and gardeners, with four figures around a tree on a rocky terrace, a fishing net hung on the tree, and shells, grass, and flowers in relief on the base (c. 1765). Height 11 inches. *Privately owned.*

Fig. 1 — Covered Chocolate Cup (*Nyon, c. 1795*)
Louis XVI in form and general decoration; but the silhouette portraits and the rather tight handling of the
garlands are strongly reminiscent of German practice.
From descendants of Augustin Alexandre Bonnard

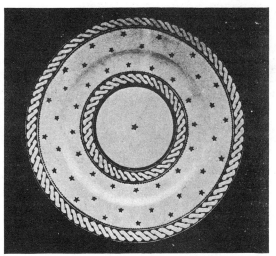

Fig. 2 — Plate (*Nyon, second period*)
An example of the finer grade of Nyon. White with border
and star design in gold. Ferdinand Müller's most important
contribution to the Nyon works was concerned with his
ability to fire gold. *By permission of Orell Füssli, Zürich*

Porcelaine de Nyon

An Imitative Swiss Pottery of the Eighteenth Century

By Frances M. Dear

Writers on Continental porcelain are inclined to dismiss the wares of Nyon as of no great moment. The factory that produced them was, indeed, short-lived and its work imitative rather than dominantly influential. Nevertheless, among the souvenirs of Nyon's more successful days are many delicately potted and charmingly decorated pieces well deserving of the attention of collectors. The author of the following article has been fortunate in obtaining photographs of some of the best of these — items that, in general, have hitherto escaped publication. For her historical data she has relied, very largely, upon A. de Molin's *Histoire Documentaire de la Manufacture de Porcelaine de Nyon*, published at Lausanne in 1904. Personal investigation in Switzerland supplemented her study. Hence she is able to correct various misstatements concerning Nyon, current in many works on Continental porcelain. — *The Editor.*

IN THE little village of Nyon, on the shore of Lake Geneva, was established, in 1781, by two potters, Ferdinand Müller of Frankenthal, and his son-in-law, Jacques Dortu of Berlin, a porcelain factory whose products are known as *porcelaine de Nyon*. This village is situated in the Canton of Vaud, which, until 1798, was under the domination of Bern; and it was from the Bernese government that Müller finally obtained his patent.

The factory was continued under the direction of Müller and Dortu until 1786, when the two separated, Dortu returning to Berlin. Müller then carried on alone; but in the following year began to transport certain materials to Geneva, perhaps with the idea of starting a branch of the business in that more populous centre.

The inhabitants of Nyon, however, had no wish to lose an industry almost miraculously arrived in their midst, and their chief source of revenue. The vice-bailiff of the village complained to Bern, and Müller was forthwith compelled to abandon both his Geneva project and the community of Nyon. Thus ended the first period in the brief history of the factory. To this time are attributed the few surviving examples of china that give evidence of Louis XV and early Louis XVI influence.

Fig. 3 — Four Cups (*Nyon, c. 1790*)
Decorated with silhouettes of the Bonnard family, symmetrically arranged to present a balance, right and left, on the china shelves.
From descendants of Jean André Bonnard, third son of Moïse

Fig. 4 — Variants of the Cornflower Pattern

The first three items are from Nyon; the fourth is the French ware of Clignancourt. Number one is of faïence, which was to some extent made in the early days of Nyon. Number two is of coarse porcelain, perhaps of the second period. Note the difference in thickness in the rims of one and two. Number three, while similar in form to the cups of Figure 3, has a deeper saucer, and may be later. Its resemblance to the French example beside it is obvious. At right is illustrated the Nyon mark — a fish in underglaze blue. This mark, however, cannot be depended upon as a means of identification.

From the Musée Historique Vaudois, Lausanne

A half year of inactivity followed. Then Zinkernagle, once Müller's foreman, took over the operation of the factory. But the task was beyond his powers. Dortu was thereupon recalled, and the firm continued as Dortu, Zinkernagle & Co. This name soon disappeared, and, in 1789, we find Société Bonnard, Veret & Cie., or Dortu & Co., an organization in which Henri Veret and Moïse Bonnard, a woolen merchant of Nyon, were partners. Figure 3 pictures four cups decorated with the silhouettes of Moïse Bonnard, his two eldest sons, François (*right*) and Augustin Alexandre, and their mother, Françoise Goncerut. Above the medallion of Moïse Bonnard, in addition to the pink rosebuds common to all four designs, are mercantile symbols — two bolts of cloth, an open book, and an anchor, together with the initials *M B*, and the number *218*. The gilt Louis XVI border is the finest that occurs on this porcelain. Around the base of each cup runs a golden vine, a favorite and charming design of the Nyon decorators. Scattered over cup and saucer are tiny golden twigs, forget-me-nots, and pansies. Pleasing restraint is shown in their use; the artist took care not to overload the piece. On the back of each cup appears a monogram in pink rosebuds and laurel leaves interlaced. Says A. de Molin, "This was an easy and economical way of having one's portrait, and it is quite natural that the potters of Nyon were asked to reproduce on their cups the silhouettes of the persons to whom it was desired to present them."

The second period, which endured for another decade (*1789-1799*), was the most productive era of the factory. While one cannot arbitrarily draw a dividing line between the two styles, the decoration of the numerous pieces attributed to this second period is distinctly in the Louis XVI taste, which was favored in Switzerland until about 1800. Trouble again arose in 1798, when Vaud revolted against Bern, and affairs went badly at the porcelain works until 1809 when the firm was incorporated, with Veret, Bonnard, and Duvillard-L'Etang among the stockholders. Figure 1 shows a two-handled chocolate cup, or *trembleuse*, ornamented with the silhouettes of Monsieur and Madame Duvillard-L'Etang, framed in garlands of ribbon and roses, surmounted by a crown with five blue pearls, and richly deco-

Fig. 5 — Fruit Basket with Pierced Rim (*Nyon, second period*)
Decorated with floral sprays in plum color.
From the Landesmuseum, Zürich

rated with gold. This covered cup, sunk in a deep well in the saucer, is one of the rarest and most interesting forms of Nyon porcelain. The portraits are well drawn; their background is faintly rose in tone. The rest of the decoration is exquisitely handled.

Sales, however, did not augment, and, in a last effort to please the public, Dortu produced a few imitations of Etruscan pottery and faïence in the manner of Wedgwood, but this measure was insufficient to save the business. Liquidation took place in 1813. The two main reasons for the Nyon failure were the high cost of importing the necessary kaolin from Saxony, and competition with English earthenware, which, toward the end of the eighteenth century, was flooding Europe. All that we have of "vieux Nyon" was produced within the short space of thirty-two years. Most surviving

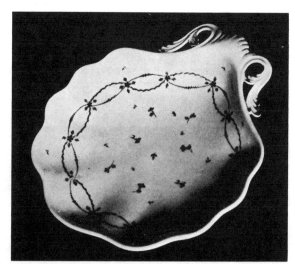

Fig. 6 — Porcelain Dish (*Nyon*)
One of a pair. Heavy, imperfect paste. Cornflowers in border of rose and plum-colored festoons; in centre, rose and plum color, alternating. Twigs and handle coloring in reddish purple.
From the descendants of Jean André Bonnard

Fig. 7 — CUSTARD OR WHIPPED-CREAM CUPS AND MINIATURE URNS (*Nyon*)
    All showing Sèvres influence. The urns in Sèvres blue and gold with floral sprigs in full color.
    From the Edmond Chenevière collection

specimens of the ware are in private collections or museums. Their rarity makes for value; and the few tea sets which find their way from someone's estate into antique shops bring very high prices.

Dortu's ancestors were French refugees; and after his experience at Berlin, the young man worked with French artists at Marieberg, Sweden, where he was initiator of the true porcelain. He rather than Müller is to be accepted as the creator of the industry at Nyon. Several pieces in the Stockholm Museum are attributed directly to him. So, although both Müller and Dortu were Germans, it is the French influence that is most strongly felt in their porcelain, which has been described as "a manufacture of Germanic articles for current use, and French articles de luxe." Dortu was an artist, not a business man. Temperamentally, too, he was of the eighteenth century, and could not accustom himself to the tastes of the post-revolutionary era. Perhaps further he lacked any really fresh creative gifts: under his guidance Nyon imitated everything, not only the porcelain of Saxony and Berlin, but of Sèvres, Clignancourt, Rue Thiroux. The ware's chief claim to originality lies in the skill with which it combined the ideas gathered from a variety of other sources. Müller's foremost contribution seems to have been an expert knowledge of firing gold.

The porcelain of Nyon is white, sometimes approaching a bluish tinge. Its thickness is variable. In services for current use, the paste is rather heavy; in those of first choice, it is very fine and translucent. The imperfections resulting from the baking, indistinguishable in the finer pieces, above all in those or-

namented only with gold (*Fig. 2*), are not uncommon in average wares. Here, however, they are cleverly disguised beneath quantities of small, painted flowers scattered over the surface. This design, popularly known as the cornflower pattern, originated at Meissen and spread to France, notably to Clignancourt, and was especially favored by Marie Antoinette. So we find many pieces of second-choice Nyon covered with this design.

The artists of Nyon succeeded in individualizing it. Their flowers are never overconventionalized: they are real yet artistic, and are placed with a well-controlled appearance of abandon, which results in a charming naïveté that has made this popular motive the one by which Nyon porcelain is best known. The principal variations are cornflowers in blue, in pink, and in plum color, interspersed with golden twigs. Then there are combinations of these. On occasion one finds what may be mistaken for cornflowers, though, in reality, the flowers are of wild chicory. Other arrangements show a scattering of roses, moss roses, pansies, forget-me-nots, and more rarely violets; and sometimes, in addition, tiny wild flowers of a vivid orange color (*Fig. 8, sugar bowl, centre*).

This last design may be said to be entirely original with Nyon. Variations show the cornflowers placed in regular horizontal zones, and, more rarely, in spirals.

The potters borrowed their mark from the arms of the village. It is a fish, of the perch family, summarily drawn in underglaze blue. But presence or absence of this mark is not an infallible guide in identification. Sometimes the fish was placed on four or five pieces out of a whole service. Again, it has been copied by

Fig. 8 — NYON PORCELAIN
    The varied floral design of the sugar bowl (*centre*) is said to be original with Nyon. The decoration at the right seems reminiscent of Meissen.
    From the Landesmuseum, Zürich

later potteries in Thuringia. An authentic fish of Nyon is shown in Figure 4.

It is impossible to say that any one form of Nyon cup is characteristic of a specific period; but, in general, the *timbale* shape without a handle is early. In the large tureens and plates of the last period of manufacture — the period of decadence — forms become heavy and thick, and the painting is clumsy, while the gold is treated in a rudimentary fashion. Figure 6 shows a Louis XV shell-shaped dish that is one of a pair.

The ribbon and garland pattern is the most delicate of those produced by the potters of Nyon. Here the influence is altogether French. Figure 8 (*left*) shows a cup and saucer ornamented in gold, encircled with a broad band of yellow, which forms the background for a garland of pink roses interlaced with a white ribbon. In one particularly lovely variation of this design the artist harmonizes violet flowers and a pale-green ribbon on a yellow background. The cup and saucer in Figure 9 have a montgolfier as a motive. Green and gold chains of laurel leaves cross in a geometric design. The golden border is scalloped.

Fig. 9 — Cup and Saucer (*Nyon, late eighteenth century*)
Balloon motives with gilt border and gold and green interlacing swags. A rare design.
By permission of Orell Füssli, Zürich

Fig. 10 — Armorial Porcelain (*Nyon, late eighteenth century*)
Unidentified arms in tones of salmon pink. Gold border. *From the Musée Historique Vaudois, Lausanne*

Pieces in this design are particularly scarce.

Very rare in Nyon is armorial porcelain. The Lausanne Museum possesses a cup bearing an unidentified coat of arms executed in tones of salmon pink. The scalloped border is gold and salmon pink (*Fig. 10*). Figure 11 shows a cup and a hot-water jug bearing a coat of arms.

During the latter half of the eighteenth century and the beginning of the nineteenth, Geneva was the centre of a school of landscape painters, among them Johann Huber and Adam Toepffer, whose landscapes animated with figures influenced, as is often the case, their contemporaries in the ceramic art. The decoration of the *trembleuse* and of the two cups in Figure 12 well illustrates the influence of this school.

An attractive product of the factory is a teapot (*Fig. 13*) decorated with a view of Nyon, surrounded by graceful arabesques in gold. It is thought to represent the old factory building of Müller's time, and is a reproduction of a colored engraving now lost. The other side presents a view of Madame de Staël's château at Coppet. "These are very probably the youthful works of the landscape painter P. L. de la Rive (*1753–1817*), who in 1782 and 1783 lived very near there in the parish of Celigny," says Daniel Baud Bovy in his *Peintres Génevois*.

On the outer side of the tray may be seen the fish. The landscape on the hot-water jug represents the Port of Nyon, and when compared with that on the teapot seems to be from the same source. At the extreme right is the factory; in the background are the French Alps. The

Fig. 11 — Armorial Porcelain (*Nyon, late eighteenth century*)
A familiar gold border. The arms display the Nyon silver perch and a star-surmounted vessel against a blue ground.
From the Landesmuseum, Zürich

Fig. 12 — Landscape Decoration (*Nyon, late eighteenth century*)
Under the influence of the Geneva landscape school, Nyon porcelain of the late eighteenth and early nineteenth centuries portrays figures of burghers, peasants, peddlers, and the like, against carefully painted landscape backgrounds.
From the Landesmuseum, Zürich

boat is of the type seen today only on the Nile and on Lake Geneva. During the eighteenth century, when there was much commerce on the lake, such boats were used for the transportation of vegetables, but the few that remain today are dedicated to conveying stone. These two pieces are interesting not only as porcelain but as documents in the history of the factory.

Under the Empire, Nyon attempted the classic style, and its landscapes are replaced by mythological subjects. The three Graces on the sugar bowl in Figure 14 dance over a few rocks and sparse bushes, all in sepia. The handles and the border are in gold. But this is the period of decadence, and soon great twists of foliage invade the whiteness of the porcelain in a most irritating manner. Figure 14 shows also a small soup tureen on which are pale blue medallions, in the manner of Wedgwood. The figures are badly drawn. Thick, golden foliage is superabundant. On the cover are the torch and quiver of love; below is a family crest.

It is impossible to detail here the immense variety of decoration that characterizes Nyon porcelain. It suffices to mention, in addition to

those already described, some remaining designs of the early period, which are little more than copies of Meissen. Some have an all-over pattern of blue and white; others, bouquets of flowers

Fig. 13 — Landscape Decoration (*Nyon, late eighteenth century*)
Jug with scene of the Port of Nyon; teapot with architectural view.
From the collection of Doctor Monastier

in divers colors, or in *camaïeu* rose (*Fig. 8, right*), and, very rare in Nyon, *camaïeu* green. A sugar bowl, pitcher, and cup, belonging to Doctor Monastier, and ranking with the most valuable pieces, attain a lovely effect with their bunches of roses in a soft but intense green against the pure white porcelain. Faïence and porcelain were often decorated with simple garlands of flowers. On some services are displayed the symbols of the amorous sentimentality of the later eighteenth century; the attributes of music, and of gardening — cupids, doves, and torches with a few roses and forget-me-nots thrown in. On others multicolored butterflies and other insects are displayed with amazing fidelity to nature.

There are at least one hundred and fifty variants of the patterns cited in this article. They are all imitative rather than original. Their individuality lies, as has been stated, in a happy adaptation of the designs of other factories.

Fig. 14 — The Classic Influence (*Nyon, late period*)
Sugar bowl depicting the three Graces, in sepia; small tureen with elaborate scrolls supporting rather badly drawn figure medallions in pale blue.
From the Musée Ariana, Geneva

THE MARIEBERG PORCELAIN FACTORY

By CARL HERNMARCK

Translated from the Swedish by Holger Lundbergh

Carl Hernmarck, first curator of the National Museum, Stockholm, received his doctorate in philosophy at Uppsala in 1934. He has published many books, among them one on Marieberg ware (1946), and the guide to the decorative art collections of the National Museum. He also contributed to a four-volume work on Swedish silversmiths.

Holger Lundbergh, who translated Doctor Hernmarck's article, has long been associated with the American-Swedish News Exchange in this country. A member of the Poetry Society of America, he has contributed much prose as well as verse to American magazines.

SWEDEN'S OLDEST ceramic factory, the Rörstrand works, was founded in 1726. It produced faience, usually decorated with blue color, achieved at an extremely high temperature of firing. As was the case everywhere in Europe at this time, the dream was to produce porcelain of Chinese type, such as Meissen had succeeded in making. With the aid of Christopher Conrad Hunger, from the Meissen factory, Rörstrand tried to turn out porcelain, but without success. The plant therefore continued to manufacture faience, and the most important innovation in this line was use of the so-called muffle colors with which the faience was painted from the year 1758. Yet all this time Rörstrand claimed to be *the* factory for the making of porcelain, and even succeeded

FIG. 1 — MARIEBERG faience potpourri jar with freely designed flower sprigs (*c. 1765*).

in preventing other works from receiving manufacturing rights.

In the summer of 1758, however, there appeared a royal court dentist, Johann Ludwig Eberhard Ehrenreich, who declared that he could make porcelain. With the help of samples imported from abroad, and aided by influential persons, he founded a company which purchased the estate of Marieberg, near Stockholm. Here a factory was built, and the making of porcelain began according to a process which Ehrenreich declared had earlier turned out very well. Immediately after the first test, the building caught fire and burned to the ground. Thanks to renewed energetic attempts, Ehrenreich succeeded in collecting enough money to build a second plant. This was ready for use in January 1760, and manufacture started immediately. What was made here, however, was not the coveted porcelain, but ordinary faience.

Obviously, Ehrenreich failed in making porcelain simply because he did not know its ingredients. It may seem extraordinary that a dentist should venture so far afield, but the explanation must be that he had been experimenting with porcelain for dental work.

During Ehrenreich's whole life, the secret of porcelain remained for him unsolved. There exists only one single bowl of unfinished so-called soft paste which bears Ehrenreich's signature, well known from his faience pieces. It is regarded as the one remaining sample of the first fatal test. However, the manufacture of porcelain was one condition on which the factory had received its privilege. In 1765 Ehrenreich was therefore forced to accept this stern fact and call in a porcelain expert, Pierre Berthevin. Only a year later this enterprising gentleman had managed to unseat Ehrenreich as head of the factory and make himself director.

But Ehrenreich's career cannot be called a failure. His faience speedily developed into the most important in Scandinavia. Only a year after the fire, the number of workers at Marieberg was greater than that at the competing Rörstrand plant. The quality of the faience was very high — even according to international standards. The glaze was cream colored and very even, the pieces were designed by the foremost artists available in the country at the time. The patterns follow the mobile trend of the rococo, which particularly emphasized the reproduction of flowers and animals (*Figs. 1, 2*). The color, to begin with, played no important part, but as early as 1763 Ehrenreich had reached such skill in firing muffle colors that Rörstrand gave up the competition and devoted itself entirely to high-temperature colors. The number of workers increased speedily and Ehrenreich had great plans for expanding the factory, when the owners demanded that the manufacture show some profit. It was then discovered that the plant had been operating at a great loss and was close to bankruptcy. In this predicament, Ehrenreich's resignation was accepted, and Berthevin was made his successor. There was never any doubt as to Ehrenreich's honesty. He left Sweden to open a faience works in Stralsund, in Germany, and carried with him the warm praise and the genuine esteem of the highest authorities in Sweden.

Ehrenreich's contribution was, above all, his ability to spur and stimulate, to find sufficient capital with which to realize his lofty plans. His technical knowledge was obviously limited, and the manufacture of porcelain, the basis of the plant's rights, remained during his life an unfulfilled promise. Not even in the making of faience was he an important force. He succeeded in hiring from

FIG. 2 — MARIEBERG faience tureen (*c. 1765*). French model, with a dolphin on the lid.

FIG. 3 — MARIEBERG faience tureen from a table service made for the French ambassador, Louis Auguste Le Tonnelier de Bréteuil (*1768*).

Rörstrand the skillful and well-known ceramic worker, Johann Buchwald. It was through Buchwald that many deft and imaginative workers were brought in from Denmark — always a step ahead of Sweden in ceramic development. Especially fortunate was the acquisition of a family of faience painters known as Frantzen. They came from the remarkable, but little known, Kastrup plant near Copenhagen, where Joseph Adam Hannong worked in 1754. Thus the line of development runs clear from Strasburg. For it was Strasburg which, toward the middle of the eighteenth century,

had become the ideal that most of the faience factories in Europe tried to emulate as closely as possible. Marieberg succeeded very well in this respect, but Strasburg's specialty, the red color, was something that could not be copied until Berthevin arrived on the scene.

Before muffle painting was perfected there was a period when modeling played a greater part. Ehrenreich succeeded in finding several prominent persons as designers, among them Pierre Hubert L'Archevêque, royal court sculptor. In addition to many models

FIG. 4 — FAIENCE group from Marieberg (*1760's*), by P. H. L'Archevêque.

FIG. 5 — "PEASANT GIRL" (*1766–1769*). Marieberg soft-paste porcelain.

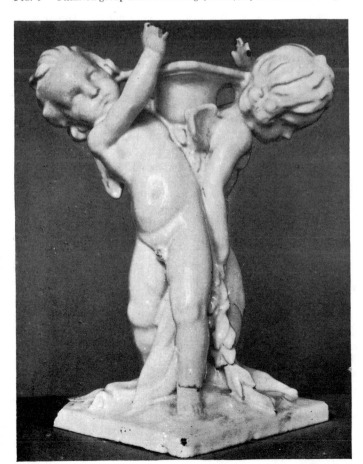

FIG. 6 — MARIEBERG hard-paste porcelain teapot in classic design (*c. 1780*).

FIG. 7 — MARIEBERG semi-porcelain urn with blue background (*c. 1780*).

for utility pieces, figurines in faience were also fashioned (*Fig. 4*), such as, for instance, the *Four Elements* and characters from the Italian comedy. These were meant as substitutes for porcelain.

By combining a rich form with — especially after 1764 — a bright color scale, Ehrenreich's faiences gave an impression of verve and joy. In this respect, no other faience made in Scandinavia at the time was superior to his.

From the time that Berthevin took over as head in 1766, the factory output underwent considerable changes. So far as the designs were concerned they plainly revealed a budding classicism. Urns with foot or base adorned with sober bayleaf garlands now began to take the place of potpourri jars with their flower sprigs. The decoration received a valuable addition in a bright red color, but the manner of painting changed to a more minute and careful one, blended with simple motifs in gold. The fact that Berthevin had received his training and education at the porcelain works of Mennecy-Villeroy is quite clearly shown.

Berthevin was the first person to make porcelain in Sweden. It was, however, the so-called soft paste which was made in France, at Mennecy-Villeroy and other places. The output at Marieberg was of very modest size. It consisted mostly of cream jars or pitchers, small vases, and ungraceful figurines. The material was unclean and greenish (*Fig. 5*).

The making of faience played a much greater role at the factory. A novelty in the faience line was introduction of the transfer-printing technique. This method had been discovered in England about 1749, and in 1768 it was spoken of at Marieberg as a new development. It is disputable whether it was Berthevin or a man named Anders Stenman who introduced the method into Sweden. It was frequently used both at Marieberg and Rörstrand.

The biggest commission received by the factory during Berthevin's tenure was a service for the French Ambassador, Louis Auguste Le Tonnelier de Bréteuil. It was painted in several colors, but the Ambassador's coat of arms was printed on (*Fig. 3*).

Berthevin remained only a little more than two years. During this time the factory's finances did not improve. The output slumped far below what it had been in the days of Ehrenreich, and the porcelain manufacture did not at all come up to expectations. Berthevin was therefore discharged and supplanted by a Swede named Henrik Sten, who worked at the plant until 1782. It was then purchased by the competing Rörstrand and carried on in a minor way until 1788 when it was closed.

Sten had a rather active and successful time at Marieberg. He managed to pull the production out of the slough and introduced a couple of technical novelties of great importance: so-called *flintporslin*, a white lead-glazed earthenware or semi-porcelain, and hard-paste porcelain, containing kaolin.

Sten was primarily a technical man, and experimented a great deal with mixtures, glazes, and colors. The artistic end suffered thereby and his faiences from this time seem dry and unimaginative, as compared with the earlier ones. The dawning classicism with its soberer lines was not a happy era for the faience factories, and the increasingly popular *flintporslin* or semi-porcelain could not be compared esthetically with the faience.

The most important event of this period is doubtless the introduction of hard paste. The output remained, however, always a trifle, quantitatively, in comparison with the faience, and also with the semi-porcelain. In quality, too, it was inferior. Teapots, cream jugs, tea canisters, and so on, were rather attractively turned out, usually with little painted flower bouquets, but the figurines were quite unimportant, at best copies of models from the big porcelain factories on the Continent. Most of them were made by the factory's own artists and were very stereotyped.

The biggest piece manufactured at Marieberg was a tureen; table services were not even attempted. The reason for this was the imperfect porcelain mixture, which allowed for only small articles. The quality of the mixture was very uneven. Many experts have wondered why. The most logical explanation has been offered by Emil Hannover in his *Pottery and Porcelain.* He points out that a part of Marieberg's output was of a fine, hard mixture, faintly transparent, while most of it consisted of a chalky white, almost opaque mixture, which was hard fired and contained kaolin. Among the workers at Marieberg there was for a short time, 1777–1778, a man by the name of Jacob Dortu. He apparently knew porcelain, and from 1781 on was connected with a factory at Nyon, in Switzerland. Hannover says that Dortu brought his knowledge with him when he came, and took it when he left. It is possible that he had carried a supply of kaolin with him, and the quality declined when this was exhausted.

His importance to the factory is obvious when we see how the output increased as soon as he was employed. On the other hand, his tenure did not mean an artistic revolution. The hard, transparent paste appeared in the same forms and with the same decoration as the rest of the products, even though the types increased.

Stylistically, the porcelain belonged to a transition period between rococo and classicism. The teapots were usually cylindrical with fluted sides adorned with formal garlands in relief (*Fig. 6*). The custard cups or cream pots, the factory's most popular porcelain pieces, retained their rococo form from the days of Berthevin. Many objects showed details of both classic and rococo origin.

The figurines were mostly expressions of the rococo style, although to a great extent they were "borrowed" from the big factories abroad. Some bore witness to their Swedish origin by depicting the "Swedish costume" which was adopted by the Swedish nobility and burghers on the order of King Gustaf III.

The making of faience continued during Sten's time. The models stemmed mostly from the factory's first days, although several new ones were also created, usually sternly classic in appearance. The decoration was partly in polychrome, as it was during the early years, and partly in monochrome, according to the taste of the time — green, rose, but predominantly sepia.

Among the big orders executed during Sten's incumbency was a table service, made for the then owner of the factory, Baron Johan Liljencrantz. It is a close copy of Strasburg faience, brightly colored in red and green. Of all the factories which at that time tried to imitate Strasburg there were hardly any that managed to come as close to the original as Marieberg.

The printing method attracted great interest. It was continued mainly with transfers which had been brought in by Berthevin, but new ones were also designed. Around 1775, this decoration was discontinued. Another material moved into the spotlight.

This was the semi-porcelain, developed in England, which comparatively soon killed almost all faience manufacture in Europe. It was especially Wedgwood's "cream-colored" ware which both Rörstrand and Marieberg tried to duplicate. They began to make it in 1770, and its importance grew from year to year. Apparently Sten had something to do personally with the introduction of semi-porcelain, because in 1772 he received a government grant for his work. The pieces were mostly urns in classic form, sometimes with a colored background and usually adorned with gilded garlands in relief (*Fig. 7*).

When in 1782 Marieberg was sold to Rörstrand, Sten resigned. The new head was Philip Andreas Schirmer, a German émigré. The output gradually fell off until in 1788 the works closed.

Marieberg's faience pieces were as a rule clearly signed (*Fig. 8*). The trade mark was an *M* and a *B*, written together under three crowns, and next to this an *E* for Ehrenreich and a *B* for Berthevin. Very often there was also the date of manufacture and, for the muffle-colored pieces, the signature of the painter and the date.

The semi-porcelain has an impressed *MB* and, during Sten's time, also his name.

The porcelain from the time of Berthevin has an *MB* scratched on the bottom. That of Sten is marked in many different ways: sometimes an *MB* under three crowns, sometimes a lily under three crowns, and sometimes again only by three blue dots. On rare occasions the porcelain also carries the date, 1780 or 1781.

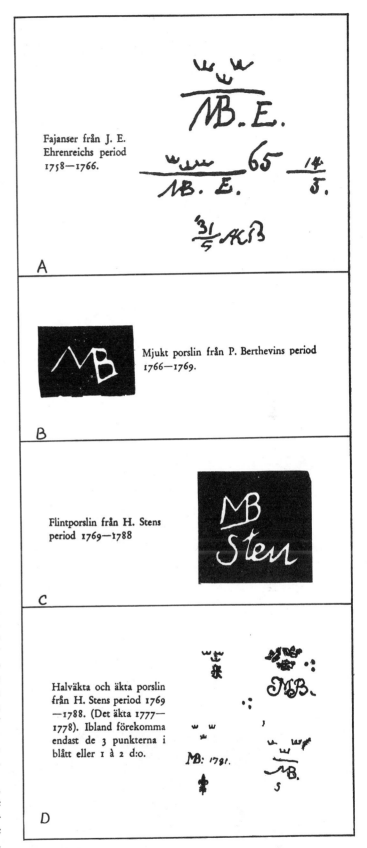

Fajanser från J. E. Ehrenreichs period 1758–1766.

A

Mjukt porslin från P. Berthevins period 1766–1769.

B

Flintporslin från H. Stens period 1769–1788

C

Halväkta och äkta porslin från H. Stens period 1769 –1788. (Det äkta 1777– 1778). Ibland förekomma endast de 3 punkterna i blått eller 1 à 2 d:o.

D

FIG. 8 — MARKS on Marieberg ware: (a) Faience from period of J. E. Ehrenreich (*1758–1766*). (b) Soft-paste porcelain from period of P. Berthevin (*1766–1769*). (c) Semi-porcelain from period of H. Sten (*1769–1788*). (d) Semi-porcelain and true porcelain from period of H. Sten (*1769–1788*). The true porcelain dates from 1777–1778. Sometimes there occur only the three dots in blue, or one or two dots.

All illustrations of Marieberg ware are from the National Museum, Stockholm.

Imperial Russian Porcelain

By Laura Lorenson

EUROPE was still puzzling over the composition of Chinese porcelain, though it had solved the problems of making fine earthenware, when Peter the Great of Russia visited England, Holland, and Germany in the closing years of the seventeenth century. He returned to his empire, with its mixture of occidental and oriental races, an admirer of western European civilization. He seems also to have succumbed to the elusive charms of porcelain and pottery and to have attempted to found a royal pottery in his new capital at St. Petersburg. The effort was not successful; but, nevertheless, a seed was sown which later bore fruit.

Once the turmoil of the succession had subsided, and Elizabeth was firmly seated on the throne of her father, Russia resumed her interrupted progress in industry and the arts. It was at the moment the correct thing for royalty to encourage the manufacture of porcelain, and the Empress began casting about for ways and means of establishing a factory.

The fame of Meissen had traveled far, and almost anyone who claimed to know its secrets was considered invaluable. Christoph Conrad Hunger, a former gilder at the Saxon factory, was living in Stockholm when the Empress Elizabeth's agent discovered him. He had gained some ideas of Böttger's methods and pretended to be a master of ceramics. One authority says that Hunger was kidnapped by the Russian government and secretly brought to St. Petersburg; but it is generally believed that he drove a hard bargain with the anxious Empress. His contract required that he build and conduct a porcelain factory in St. Petersburg. Instead, he wasted three or four years in futile experiments, blamed the witches for his failures, and was eventually discharged.

DATES TO REMEMBER

Peter the Great....	1682–1725	Alexander I.....	1801–1825
Elizabeth.........	1741–1761	Nicholas I.......	1825–1855
Peter III.........	1761–1762	Alexander II....	1855–1881
Catherine II......	1762–1796	Alexander III....	1881–1894
Paul I...........	1796–1801	Nicholas II......	1894–1917

It is to Hunger's assistant and successor, Dimitri Vinogradoff, a talented young Russian, that the Imperial Porcelain Factory owes its first measure of success. Vinogradoff superintended the building of a pottery on the site beside the River Neva occupied by the present factory. He experimented with native clays until he found the combination of materials best suited to his purpose. The techniques of coloring, glazing, and firing he gradually mastered. His porcelain was very hard and of a bluish tint. It was not Chinese, Sèvres, nor Meissen in character. It was Russian. Vinogradoff did not live to complete his experiments. Before he was forty years old he died from an affliction all too common among ceramists of the period — dissipation.

Court life under Elizabeth became luxurious. The Empress delighted in presenting her favorites with porcelain snuffboxes made at the Imperial Factory. Some were in the form of sealed envelopes bearing the names of the recipients; others were decorated with miniature paintings. A set of figurines representing negroes and other exotic folk was ordered for the Winter Palace. Monochrome and gold decoration on useful ware was supplemented by a more extended palette. A Saxon, Johann Gottfried Müller, was one of the successors of Vinogradoff, and the Meissen style was dominant during the reign of Elizabeth.

When, in 1762, Catherine II, a German princess, wrenched the Russian throne from her husband Peter III, French taste had already invaded Meissen, and the neoclassical style that was soon to cast its spell over western Europe was in the making. This amazing Empress — herself an artist and writer of no mean ability, and a collector of art and antiquities — was an ardent admirer of French culture. Nevertheless, she wished to

Fig. 1 (above) — PERIOD ELIZABETH
Sauce boat bearing initials and arms of Prince Rumiantsev. Laurel wreath, in high relief, green and gold on white ground.
This and other illustrations not otherwise credited, from the collections of L'Ermitage Galleries

Fig. 2 (below) — PERIOD CATHERINE II
The basketry borders and the character of the floral decoration betray indebtedness to the designs of Meissen. Of the two platters in the centre, that at the left is of the period Paul I, and exemplifies the Russian habit of repeating earlier designs.
From the collection of Old Russia

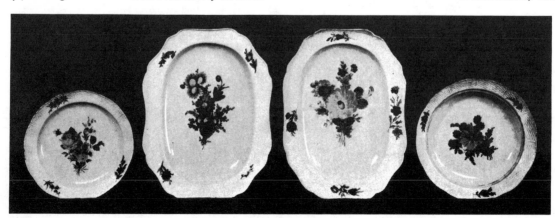

views of Italy. The few pieces from these sets that have survived to the present day have nearly all found their way into museum collections.

During the five-year reign of Paul I, the Mad Czar, imperial table services were reduced to from eight to twenty covers; but the vogue for Italian landscapes and classical motives, which had begun during the time of Catherine, continued. Alexander I,

have her porcelain express something of a truly national character. This was achieved in a series of charming colored figurines depicting the many racial types of the imperial domain. Most of the products of the Imperial Factory, however, followed

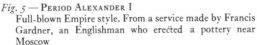

the European trend, responding, no doubt, to the influence of the magnificent Wedgwood queen's ware and the Sèvres porcelain services ordered by Catherine II. The Imperial Factory drew heavily on foreign talent while it maintained a school for young Russian apprentices. The famous service "*Les Arabesques*," for sixty covers, was completed in 1784. It was decorated with portrayals of antique cameos amid elaborate arabesques. Another service, quite similar in decoration, was known as the "Yacht Service." The "Cabinet Service" was decorated with wild flowers and

whose reign began in 1801, reorganized the factory and employed more foreign assistants. The Empire period was in full swing, and the French artist Swebach is credited with considerable influence although he was not long at the factory. Nicholas I, who succeeded his brother, Alexander I, in 1825, decided that since the Imperial

147

Factory was intended to serve as a model to the other Russian porcelain factories it should be supported by the state. From that time until the Revolution its entire output was taken by the court for its own use and for diplomatic gifts. Exhibitions were held in Moscow, St. Petersburg, and London. At the London exhibition in 1851 Russian porcelain won the gold medal. Technique had reached perfection, but taste in porcelain had declined. Famous paintings, especially military scenes, were minutely copied, and monumental vases became popular. During the reign of Alexander II, which began in 1855, the Imperial Factory continued to repeat old ideas, and there was no marked change in the style of decoration. The output, however, was tremendous.

The consort of Alexander III was a Danish princess. In her honor an attempt was made to introduce the Danish style of underglaze painting. When Nicholas II ascended the throne in 1894, imitation was a fixed habit, although the chemists and technicians had become remarkably expert. Throughout its history the Imperial Factory repeated its popular services again and again. It also replaced broken pieces from its own early services and from those of other factories. This habit makes it sometimes difficult to reconcile the marks with the apparent date of a design.

The marks of the Imperial Porcelain Factory varied with the reigns. The imperial, double-headed eagle was used in the time of Elizabeth and Peter III. Beginning with Catherine II, the cypher of the monarch was used. Alexander II indicated the year of his reign with dots; Alexander III added the year, as, for example, *81*, and Nicholas II the full date.

The Imperial Factory served as a model for a number of privately owned potteries, of which, in 1800, there were nearly twenty in operation. Among these was the interesting establishment founded by Gardner, an Englishman, in the Moscow district. The quality of Gardner's work so

Fig. 8 (above) — PERIOD ALEXANDER II
The return to naturalistic floral designs, probably somewhat late in the period.
From the collection of Mrs. Claus Spreckles, California

Fig. 9 (left) — PERIOD NICHOLAS I
Vase in turquoise and gold with portrait panel in full color. The propriety of using fine porcelain as a ground for extensive application of metal and for elaborate pictorial treatment is questioned by most critics of the ceramic art. But since such utilization called for great technical skill and obviously involved high cost, it has long enjoyed a considerable vogue

delighted the Empress Catherine II that she had him make a suitably decorated service for each of the Russian orders of knighthood. By 1861 the number of potteries had increased to about seventy. The freeing of the serfs, however, wrought a great and sudden change. Owing to increase in labor costs many factories were discontinued. Others, among which was the Gardner pottery, consolidated and put their output on a strictly commercial basis.

The porcelain of the Imperial Factory and, to a certain extent, that of the private potteries reflect the culture of western Europe rather than the native Russian taste. Few of its patterns are truly Russian in character, though the figurines of Russian racial types constitute, perhaps, a striking and original contribution to ceramic art. The idea probably originated with Catherine II; but the series produced for her by the Imperial Factory was followed by very many others.

Since the Revolution the porcelain once reserved for the use of the Russian court has been finding its way to the United States, where it has been well received by collectors. Covering, as it does, about a century and a half of production, it makes an interesting addition to the antique china here obtainable.

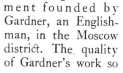

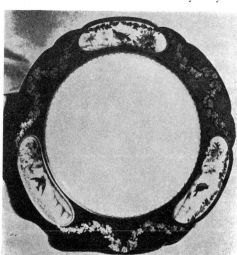

Fig. 10 — PERIOD ALEXANDER III
A Russian copy of Copenhagen porcelain with underglaze decoration, in smoky blues and greens on a white ground

Fig. 11 — PERIOD NICHOLAS II
From a favorite dinner service of the Czar. Turquoise-blue rim with medallion reserves depicting a variety of birds in natural colors. Oak garlands in heavy gold.
From the collection of J. Von Houten, New Mexico

Vista Alegre

Portuguese porcelain of the nineteenth century

BY ROBERT C. SMITH, *University of Pennsylvania and Winterthur*

IN THE SIXTEENTH century Portugal introduced Chinese porcelain to Europe, and thereby profoundly affected the cultural history of the Western world. Subsequently the Portuguese anticipated the Dutch by at least fifty years in imitating in faïence the patterns of Oriental porcelain. In spite of these achievements, however, no porcelain was made in Portugal until the 1770's, when a few sporadic experiments began to be carried out. It was not until 1824 that a factory was established at Vista Alegre which was destined to attain commercial success, technical and artistic distinction, and also continuous production. Last year the flourishing factory observed its 140th anniversary by opening a new building to serve

as a museum of its earliest wares. The resulting exhibition, enriched by notable pieces lent by descendants of the founder, cannot fail to interest readers of ANTIQUES, who will recall that the history of porcelain making in the United States, in the efforts of Bonnin and Morris and of Tucker, offers a striking chronological parallel to the history of Portuguese ware.

At the time of its founding in 1824 Vista Alegre was the only porcelain factory in Portugal. Other factories have since been organized and some have prospered but none has ever approached the achievement of the nineteenth-century porcelain makers of Vista Alegre. They attained a very respectable technique and attractive style

Fig. 1. Statuette of the founder, José Ferreira Pinto Basto; height, approximately 10 inches. Modeled in soft paste by Anselmo Ferreira before 1839 in imitation of Staffordshire figures, this statuette has a marbleized base bearing the initials of the factory in a design derived from the first mark used there. *Except as noted, all illustrations from the Vista Alegre Museum. Photographs by the author.*

Fig. 2. Porcelain portrait plaque of the founder; 14½ by 10 inches. Signed by Duarte José de Magalhães and dated 1880, the black and white plaque is a handsome portrait of the great merchant and industrialist whose fortune, based on the tobacco trade, enabled him to establish soda and soap factories in addition to the one at Vista Alegre, which also produced, in its early days, pressed and cut glass.

Fig. 3. Cream pitchers and sugar bowl, c. 1830. Typical of the early creamware products are these pieces inspired by English silver of the early nineteenth century, which was widely imitated by the silversmiths of Oporto; reminiscent too of Wedgwood and other English creamware. Plates, sometimes octagonal, and other pieces with raised floral borders were also made in this style.

Fig. 4. Pompey plate, earthenware, dated 1828; diameter 8¾ inches. Painted, probably by Manuel Ramos, in imitation of an antique cameo portrait and perhaps inspired by a similar Sèvres plate of 1810. One of a series showing Roman figures, this plate suggests the taste of the English artist John Flaxman. The borders are rose, coffee, and white.

of decoration, without, however, producing any masterpieces. The chief interest of their work lies in the variety of its forms and the diversity of its sources of inspiration. In this respect Vista Alegre porcelain is characteristic of Portuguese art, which has constantly been influenced by that of other countries. The opening of the new museum at Vista Alegre therefore offers to students of the decorative arts of the nineteenth century a unique opportunity to study, in handsome surroundings, a hitherto little-known aspect of the influence abroad of a wide range of English and French porcelain models.

The factory of Vista Alegre was established in an old country house at Ilhavo near the port of Aveiro by José Ferreira Pinto Basto (1774-1839), an extremely successful merchant of Lisbon, whose ships, like those of some of his New England contemporaries, traded di-

Fig. 5. Peacock vase, c. 1836-1851; height 8¾ inches. An outstanding product of the regime of Victor Rousseau, this small parcel-gilt porcelain vase with ram's-head handles is derived from French Empire models. The lavender flowers of the mimosalike tree suggest the Brazilian *jacarandá*, a form of rosewood, planted for decorative purposes in Portugal. *Collection of D. Vera Ferreira Pinto Ribeiro da Cunha.*

Fig. 6. Porcelain Cameos plate, dated 1835; diameter 8½ inches. Probably one of the first works of Rousseau at Vista Alegre, the plate honors the great sixteenth-century epic poet, Luís de Camoes. In addition to symbolic laurel and oak wreaths, it displays a neo-Gothic border of the sort associated with the style of Charles X and the Duchess of Berri in France. The colors are coffee and black. *Collection of Alberto Brandly Ferreira Pinto.*

Fig. 7. Porcelain inkwell in the form of a ship, c. 1836-1851; length 10¼ inches. One of a number of elegant pieces showing the influence of the porcelains of Sèvres in the use of blue and gold in combination with miniature roses. The decoration represents the revival of early Sèvres patterns while the nautical form reflects an eighteenth-century Portuguese fondness for ship models in wood carving and silver.

Fig. 8. Armorial sample plate, porcelain, c. 1860-1880; diameter 9½ inches. A sample plate from which clients could choose numbered monograms and coronets. In the center appear the royal arms of Portugal.

rectly with China and Brazil and docked at wharves adjacent to the owner's offices. Pinto Basto, who is represented in two important pieces of Vista Alegre workmanship (Figs. 1, 2), had no less than fifteen children, including ten sons, one of whom managed the factory after his father's death. He in turn was succeeded by his son, who was eventually replaced by a cousin. This man's connection with Vista Alegre continued until 1909.

The site near Aveiro, which was purchased in 1817, was chosen because of the quality of the clay of the nearby Vouga River, which had been used in some of the late eighteenth-century experiments in porcelain making. In 1832 kaolin was found there in such quantity as to guarantee the supply of the struggling young factory. Until then most of the products of Vista Alegre had been of soft paste or earthenware and were based on English models (Figs. 1, 3, 4) popular in Portugal in the years following the Peninsular Wars, when Great Britain intervened to wrest control of the country from the invading armies of Napoleon. Much of the work was undecorated cream-color ware, but there are some pieces painted by João Maria Fabre before his death in 1829 and Manuel de Morais da Silva Ramos (1806-1872), both of whom worked with the modeler Anselmo Ferreira, author of Figure 1. All three were orphan boys brought to Vista Alegre by the practical-minded founder, who among many other offices held that of president of the Lisbon orphanage. He also imported from Saxony an experienced German porcelain maker, Joseph Scorder, who in the first years of its history did much to develop the factory. It was in this period that the mark VA was established and this mark in blue has been maintained, although the blue laurel wreath and crown, the latter symbolizing a royal patent of 1826, which originally accompanied the letters, were subsequently abandoned.

The golden period of Vista Alegre's early history began in 1835 with the arrival at Ilhavo of the French artist Victor François Chartier Rousseau, who remained

Fig. 9. Covered dish in the form of a swan, c. 1850-1870; length 15½ inches. In Portugal, where Chinese porcelain figures have always been popular, bird and animal dishes were imitated in Lisbon faïence in the eighteenth century. This rare example in white porcelain was probably inspired by the same Oriental pieces.

Fig. 10. Porcelain water-lily plate, c. 1890-1900; diameter 14¾ inches. An extraordinary decorative plate in high relief, painted in pastel colors, reflecting formulas of *art nouveau* and Parisian *Salon* painting of the turn of the century. It was intended to be hung on a wall.

until his death in 1852 the factory's chief painter. Said to have been a descendant of the philosopher Jean Jacques Rousseau, he was discovered by a brother of José Pinto Basto in London, where he was a political exile. During Rousseau's regime the quality of the Vista Alegre porcelain was greatly improved, hard paste became the standard product, and the early English models were replaced by forms taken from the products of the French factory of Sèvres. The work of this period shows late classical influences (Fig. 5) side by side with those of the romantic Gothic taste (Fig. 6) and of the nascent nineteenth-century rococo revival (Fig. 7).

French influence continued under Rousseau's successor, Gustave Fortier, who served as artistic director at Vista Alegre from 1851 to 1856 and from 1861 to 1869. The factory prospered in this period, winning prizes at the Crystal Palace Exposition in London in 1851 and in the Universal Exposition at Paris in 1855. On May 24, 1852, King Ferdinand visited Vista Alegre and ordered a special set of fruit plates as well as several dinner and tea and coffee services. This stamp of royal approval brought the patronage of the nobility and persons of wealth throughout the country, for whom the factory prepared a number of sample plates displaying a wide choice of monograms and of coronets (Fig. 8).

But Vista Alegre, like porcelain all over Europe and America, suffered from late Victorian taste. In the period between 1870 and 1881, when the Portuguese Joaquim José de Oliveira served as first painter, the factory also underwent a financial crisis, the results of which continued under his successors Francisco da Rocha Freire (1881-1889) and Duarte José de Magalhães (1889-1921). The latter, who painted the portrait plaque of the founder (Fig. 2), was probably responsible for a number of ornamental plates whose high-relief decoration may have been influenced by experiments in the faïence of Ratinho carried out after 1872 by the sculptress Duchess of Palmela and her friend the Countess of Ficalho. Several of these Vista Alegre pieces, which are

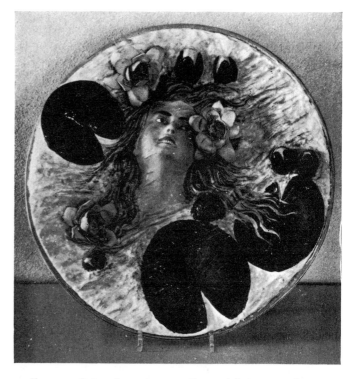

really porcelain plaques, are of special interest because of the vibrant themes taken from contemporary French *Salon* painting, with overtones from the *art nouveau* movement (Fig. 10).

In 1924, on the occasion of its first centennial anniversary, Vista Alegre was reorganized and a new program of production was undertaken. The chief concern of the factory became the perfecting of classical patterns of great elegance and distinction. This policy remains in effect, although some handsome contemporary designs have been introduced. It has been extremely successful and the factory, still controlled by the descendants of the patriarch José Ferreira Pinto Basto, now employs one thousand workmen.

Bibliography

Cushion, John P. *Continental China Collecting for Amateurs.* Alhambra, Calif., n.d.

_____. *Pocket Book of French and Italian Ceramic Marks.* London, 1965.

_____. *Pocket Book of German Ceramic Marks.* London and New York, 1961.

de Chavagnac, S. and A. de Grollier. *Histoire des manufactures françaises de porcelaine.* Paris, 1906.

de Jonge, C. H. *Delft Ceramics.* London, 1970.

Ducret, Siegfried. *German Porcelain and Faïence.* Translated by Diana Imber. New York, 1962.

_____. *Meissen Porcelain.* Translated by Marjorie Gibson Craig. New York, 1975.

Eisner, Eisenhof, Angelo, Baron von. *Le porcellane di Capo-Di-Monte.* Milan, 1925.

Giacomotti, Jeanne. *French Faïence.* Translated by Diana Imber. New York, 1963.

Hackenbroch, Yvonne. *Meissen and Other Continental Porcelain: Faïence and Enamel in the Irwin Untermyer Collection.* Cambridge, Mass.: 1956.

Haggar, Reginald G. *The Concise Encyclopedia of Continental Pottery and Porcelain.* London, 1960.

Hannover, E. *Pottery and Porcelain.* London, 1924.

Hayward, J. *Viennese Porcelain of the Du Paquier Period.* London, 1952.

Honey, William Bowyer. *European Ceramic Art: From the End of the Middle Ages to About 1815.* 2 vols. London, 1952.

_____. *French Porcelain of the Eighteenth Century.* 2nd. ed. London and New York, 1972.

_____. *German Porcelain.* London, 1947.

Lane, Arthur. *French Faïence.* 2nd. ed. London and New York, 1970.

_____. *Italian Porcelain.* London, 1954.

Liverani, Giuseppe. *Five Centuries of Italian Maiolica.* London, 1960.

Penkala, Maria. *European Porcelain.* Rutland, Vt., 1969.

_____. *European Pottery.* Rutland, Vt., 1968.

Rackham, Bernard. *Italian Maiolica.* 2nd. ed. London and New York, 1963.

Reinheckel, Gunter. *German and Austrian Ceramics.* Vol. 8, Western and Near Eastern Ceramics Series. New York, 1978.

Staehlin, Walter S. *The Book of Porcelain.* Translated by Michael Bullock. Bern, 1965.

Syz, Hans, et al. *Catalogue of the Hans Syz Collection: Meissen Porcelain and Hausmalerei.* Washington, D.C., 1976.

Terasson, J. *Les Hannong et leurs manufactures Strasbourg, Frankenthal.* Paris-Lausanne, 1971.

Tilley, Frank. *Principal Marks on Continental Porcelain of the Eighteenth Century.* Cambridge, 1955.

Walcha, O. *Meissner Porzellan.* Güterloh, 1975.

Index